Martin Alonso Pomare Howard

Clamor of the Islands
Saint Andrew and Old Providence under Colombian Rule

Juan Duchesne Winter, *editor*

Malunga Series Editor
Jerome Branche

ISBN: 978-958-49-2203-8

© Martin Alonso Pomare Howard, 2021
© Serie Malunga, 2021
INSTITUTO INTERNACIONAL DE
LITERATURA IBEROAMERICANA
Universidad de Pittsburgh
1312 Cathedral of Learning
Pittsburgh, PA 15260
(412) 624-5246 • (412) 624-0829 Fax
iili@pitt.edu • www.iilionline.org

Colaboraron en la preparación de este libro:

Edición: Juan Duchesne Winter
Composición y diseño gráfico: Erika Arredondo
Correctores: Geo Maroon y Lana Sims
Tapa imagen de Jeisson Castillo
Ensayo fotográfico *Imágenes de Providencia*
Fotografías de Constanza Ussa y Jeisson Castillo
Cuidado Editorial Manuela Mejía
Coordinación de impresión: Ofrenda Editorial

Clamor of the Islands
Saint Andrew and Old Providence under Colombian Rule

FOREWORD BY THE EDITOR 7
ACKNOWLEDGEMENTS 11
PREAMBLE 13
WHAT IS KNOWN ABOUT THE FIRST INHABITANTS OF
OLD PROVIDENCE AND SAINT ANDREW? 16
WHERE ARE SAINT ANDREW AND OLD PROVIDENCE? 25
PHYSIOGRAPHIC DESCRIPTION 25
MEANS OF COMMUNICATION 26
THE PURITANS 27
EDWARD MANSFIELD 30
HENRY MORGAN 32
TIME FOR ABOLITION 34
LOUIS-MICHEL AURY 37
RELIGION ON THE ISLANDS 51
BAPTISTS 52
ROMAN CATHOLICS AND ADVENTISTS 52
RELIGIOUS PERSECUTION 54
REPORTS OF A COMMISIONER FROM BOGOTA IN 1911 61
BIG COMMERCE 78
THE FREE PORT 78
THE DOWNFALL 80

BIG SALE	83
VESSELS OWNED BY NATIVES	85
BIG ENTERTAINMENT	94
WHAT WAS TAKING PLACE IN OLD PROVIDENCE DURING THESE DISASTERS IN SAINT ANDREW?	96
THE BOMB	99
THE LANGUAGE PROBLEM	100
BILINGUALISM IN THE ISLANDS	103
THE PRESENT SITUATION	113
THE CIVIC MOVEMENT	145
THE STRUGGLE	148
MILITARIZATION	154
PROTESTS	155
PUBLIC EMPLOYEES	159
THE TOTAL STRIKE	160
THE TURBULENT FUTURE	165
OVERPOPULATION AND THE OCCRE	168
IMBALANCED POPULATION	176
PARABLE OF THE ALLIGATORS	178
CORALINA	184
TOURISM	186
RACISM	191
VIOLENCE IN OLD PROVIDENCE	195
IS THERE REALLY ANY HOPE FOR BETTERMENT?	197
THE COLOMBIA-NICARAGUA DISPUTE AND THE DEMANDS OF THE RAIZAL PEOPLE OF THE ARCHIPELAGO	198
CUSTOMS ON THE ISLANDS	205
THE SOCIAL LEVEL	206
FARMING	206

COCONUTS ON THE ISLANDS 220
SUGAR CANE 221
CUSTOMARY FOOD 223
EDUCATION ON THE ISLANDS 224
SO-CALLED 'MODERNISM' 227
EASTER 227
FISHING 230
ENTERTAINMENT 232
THE QUEEN CONTEST 233
STORYTELLING AND RIDDLES 234
WHAT ABOUT OBEAH? 235
WOMEN'S ROLE IN THE HOME 236
THE 'STERICS' 237
THE SEASONS OF THE YEAR 238
SPORTS ON THE ISLANDS 239
BASEBALL 242
CHRISTMAS AND NEW YEAR 242

ADDENDUM
Secret Plan for San Andres and Old Providence 246

Foreword by the Editor

San Andrés and Providencia are part of an archipelago that spans hundreds of square kilometers in the western Caribbean Sea. The two islands have areas of 32 and 17 square kilometers respectively, are approximately 80 kilometers apart, and lie among many smaller islands and keys, the larger of which, Corn and Little Corn islands, are also large enough to be continuously inhabited. Santa Catalina, with an area of 1 square kilometer, is separated from Providencia by a very narrow man-made channel and is generally considered as a separate island. San Andrés, Providencia and Santa Catalina belong to Colombia although they are much closer to the Central American isthmus, off the coasts of Panama and Nicaragua. In geographical, historical and cultural terms, the archipelago is part of the English-speaking sphere of the Caribbean basin, known as the West Indies, which is largely shaped by the African diaspora and British colonization.

In that context, the department of Colombia officially named "San Andrés, Providencia and Catalina" belongs to a particular culturescape of West Indian populations that are under the sovereignty of Spanish speaking nations in the western Caribbean, where they constitute subaltern minorities. Other population centers belonging to this culturescape are Colón, Bocas del Toro (Panama), the Corn islands, Bluefield, Greytown (Nicaragua), Puerto Limón (Costa Rica), the Roatán islands (Honduras), and Livingston (Guatemala). They claim to be part of what the internationally acclaimed musician Elkin Robinson of Providencia calls a *Creole nation* in the lyrics of "Bring My People Back" and "Creole Vibration". As contemporary linguists sustain, World English includes a sundry assortment of variants that very different societies have made their own after recreating them as creole expressions with relative degrees of departure from so-called Standard English. What Elkin Robinson calls the *Creole nation* is a network of cultural, social, and historical relationships that he claims as the ancestral lifeworld connecting the natives of San Andrés and Providencia to the larger Caribbean. He sings, "We need our language/ We need our culture/ I need my Creole vibration." This demand involves language rights and much more than that, inasmuch as it comprises broader political, territorial, and ecological claims of the islanders in face of the exclusion and marginalization fostered by successive Colombian governments along many decades.

Historical and sociological studies about these insular territories of Colombia have been available. It is not difficult to come up with a reliable bibliography offering data, statistics, analyses, and presumably objective records of events. But what is largely missing from the official bibliography is the voice of the islanders, their own interpretation of their collective experience, their feelings about their whole situation. The eloquent and riveting testimony in the following pages written by Martin Pomare, a native of Providencia and long-time resident of San Andrés, provides just that. He offers us a vernacular history that rises above the cold records of academic historiography in order to bring the collective clamor of a people. The ordinary trappings of academic discourse are not relevant here because what is at play is the wealth of knowledge provided by an expression that articulates the perspective of the islanders regarding collective events and situations crucial to their lives. The accurate rendering of historical facts is important here as reference to an experience, not as a gate keeper to the expression of that experience, so in our edition of this book we have focused on the emotional and affective value of historical information that is referenced with main sources. In the incredibly challenging conditions of libraries, archives, internet connections and equipment in the islands, Martin Pomare has heroically put together factually sound accounts, with plenty quotations, references, figures, statistics and documentation.

In light of the intimate but mostly invisibilized interpenetration of the various geocultural spheres (Hispanophone, Anglophone, Francophone and others) corresponding to the colonial powers historically active in the Caribbean, we consider Martin Pomare's book to be a powerful expression relevant to Latin American Studies. It provides a concrete testimony of the intersection and mixture of those language and culture spheres; with the challenging contradictions and paradoxes they convey. It is particularly interesting that Pomare's English language text, mixed with subtle registers of the creole vernacular, surges as subaltern challenge to Spanish language hegemony in the national Colombian context involving factors of race, ethnicity, and class. Upper middle-class kids in Bogotá attend English-only private schools while Spanish is imposed on San Andres and Providencia English/Creole speakers as the exclusive medium of instruction and public communication. Moreover,

Saint Andresans and Providencians are denied bilingual education. The so-called Standard English taught in Bogotá to white criollo kids of the upper middle class is a mark of distinction, while the English/Creole spoken by mostly black islanders is aggressively unwelcome in schools and other institutions of the public and private sector. The act of publishing this book in the native English of Martin Pomare, and of Providencia and San Andrés, constitutes, thus, a statement of solidarity with the Creole vibration.

This book acquires extraordinary relevance in the aftermath of the climatic catastrophe caused by category 5 hurricane Iota, that hit Providencia days before these lines are being written, razing practically all buildings and wiping out most agriculture, as well as major portions of the flora and fauna, thus placing the entire ecosystem of the island, as well as its human lifeworld on the brink of total disarray and extinction. This Clamor of the Islands, rendered here in the voice of Martin Pomare, should serve as a collective call of solidarity and as a forewarning of attempts at repeating the kind of exclusionary and expropriative policies that have devastated Providencia, Santa Catalina and San Andrés in the past. The Iota catastrophe and its tragic consequences should be an occasion for Providencians to determine the reconstruction of their islands as world-class models of social and ecological adaptations to climatic change in response to the needs of the islanders.

Juan Duchesne Winter
University of Pittsburgh
November 2020

Acknowledgements

This book is the result of fortunate encounters propitiated in many ways by a research project that Dr. Juan Duchesne Winter conducted in Providencia Island thanks to two faculty research grants and additional research funds provided to him by the University of Pittsburgh's Center for Latin American Studies (CLAS) and the Dietrich School of Arts and Sciences. Professor Duchesne's research became part of a broader effort involving cultural activists of Providencia and San Andrés islands, codirected with Miguel Penilla and Constanza Ussa. While Juan Duchesne was staying in the island with his wife, Constanza Ussa, Miguel Penilla and Constanza helped him organize writing workshops with local adults and children. Miguel Penilla is an anthropologist who lives in the island and is engaged with cultural activism and promotion. Constanza Ussa is an anthropologist and freelance consultant in human rights with vast experience in many parts of Colombia. Yohaira Howard, director of the Providencia Library, and Aminta Robinson, director of the Bottom House school library, graciously collaborated in the organization of these workshops. Gina Ávila, Nayive Thyme, and Wendy Howard, promoters of reading at City Hall, also gave their generous collaboration. The author of this book, Martin Pomare, participated in the workshops, where he eventually brought a manuscript on which he had been working by himself for close to ten years. Aminta Robinson was key in encouraging Mr. Martin to bring his writing to the workshop. The manuscript was a fascinating historical chronicle written in a flowing, lively prose that delivered a poignant testimony of the collective experience of the islanders. Soon enough, Juan Duchesne and Mr. Martin started meeting separately to work on the manuscript. Mr. Martin would come every afternoon on weekdays to the cabin rented by Juan and Constanza in the Maroon Hill sector of the island, to review and edit the text together, until it became the book that you have in your hands. Both the author, Martin Pomare, and the editor, Juan Duchesne, want to thank all persons named above, with a special expression of gratitude to Miguel Penilla, Constanza Ussa, Aminta Robinson, Yohaira Howard, and, last but not least, Jaime Vélez, the resident island photographer and great reader and conversationist, who also helped in so many ways.

Preamble

"Islanders have always been loyal to Colombia, trusting that for its part, the Colombian Government always had their best interests at heart, even when it seemed incapable of doing anything right. However, it turns out that this trust has been just like the house built upon the sand." This is the introductory remark made by the Sons of the Soil (S.O.S.) Movement to a Colombian government document marked "Secret," a copy of which they (and this author) were able to obtain. As they say, "It is proof of the betrayal of the native people by the Colombian government [...]. It is a written record of Colombia's official decision to eliminate the 'diversity' of the native people, root out their language, religion, and culture, and break up their racial unity. It explicitly states that Protestantism and the English language of the islanders hinder 'the complete integration of the Archipelago into Colombia's Nationality'." The document also confirms that the emigration of Colombians into Saint Andrew is not accidental but is the result of the deliberate application of this colonialist policy."

The introductory remark signed by the S.O.S. Movement continues to say that even though the document carries no date, its contents allow us to infer that it was prepared between 1977 and 1978. According to them there is no doubt of its authenticity, for all major decisions regarding the islands since 1978 conform exactly to the plan. One example they mention is the increased militarization. The justification given for it is that, "it would not only ensure sovereignty before foreigners but would also serve to dissuade any separatist movement that might be attempted." Likewise, they mention that steps have been taken lately to make Saint Andrew and Old Providence into a center for spreading Colombian culture and wiping out the native culture.

The reader of this book will understand, in the pages that follow, why, as the Sons of the Soil say, "Efforts to persuade Colombian authorities only by appealing to their good faith and sense of justice toward the natives to take steps to stop the flow of immigrants and restore the English language and culture in general have always been doomed to failure." Immigration, of course, has become the agent of the islands' ruin. In spite of all the problems, Colombian mainlanders, including people from the Andean region continue to pour in. Here I make their words my own to add that the only group benefiting from this grave situation are the so-called "investors," which are the relatively small number of foreigners and Colombians who own the hotels and stores, who rake in more than the 80 percent of the total island income using and misusing the islands' resources for their own personal and economic profit. On the other hand, and as an example of the cultural ethnocide that has reduced islanders intellectually as well as in many other ways, the government has completely imposed Spanish on all television and radio stations. The truth is that, "It all takes place according to this monstrous and detestable plan."[1]

---

[1] See "Addendum: Secret Plan for San Andres and Providence" in final section of this book. Available copies of this document are extant in English translation only; translator is unknown. Other quotations of documents originally written in Spanish are rendered in English by the author, Martin Pomare. (Note of the Editor —from now on N.E.)

WHAT IS KNOWN ABOUT THE FIRST INHABITANTS OF OLD PROVIDENCE AND SAINT ANDREW?

The purpose of writing this book is to give brief information of what the islands of Old Providence and Saint Andrew were in the past and what they are today, and the environment of the people throughout the centuries. What inspires me, the author, most of all, is to express the discrimination and constant suffering of the native people of these Islands. This book does not register the complete historical events since the so-called discovery; however, it contains a summary of the islands' first inhabitants, their activities and submission to various authorities at different times, the keeping of their traditions amidst difficulties during survival, and the development of an imposed culture influenced by religion and language since 1926. Another reason is to also develop consciousness in the natives of the Archipelago of Old Providence and Saint Andrew of their background and abuses committed by the Colombian government for more than a century. Because there has never been any teaching of the islands' history in the insular schools at any time, the historical sketches of this book might be an incentive for the local government to develop a program for the teaching of the islands' history in all the schools. I deemed it convenient to organize my comments and historical sketches under separate headings such as: "First inhabitants," "Religion," "The downfall of Saint Andrew," and "The Present Situation." The general purpose is to show the vast changes in different aspects from the time of colonization to the present day, and reasons why the inhabitants of this archipelago are dissatisfied, and their greatest desire is to be a free people with self-determination and self-government. I appreciate the collaboration of friends who willingly shared information to make this text a reality and boost up my spirit in moments of discouragement.

Clamor of the Islands

Clamor of the Islands

Clamor of the Islands

WHERE ARE SAINT ANDREW AND OLD PROVIDENCE?

The Archipelago of Saint Andrew, Old Providence, and Ketlena (Santa Catalina)[2] is located in the Caribbean Sea to the northeast of the continental territory of Colombia, 180 km from the Central American coast, 400 km from Jamaica and 480 km from the Colombian coast. The Island of Saint Andrew is approximately 12.8 km long and 3.5 km wide. The total area of Old Providence and Ketlena is approximately 25 sq. km. The island of Saint Andrew, which is the principal island, is located between 12° 29' and 12°36' north latitude and 81°41' and 81°43' longitude of Greenwich; and Old Providence between 13°19' and 13°23' north latitude and 81°21' and 81°23' longitude west of Greenwich. The Archipelago is 720 kilometers from Cartagena, Colombia and 230 km from the coast of the Republic of Nicaragua and Costa Rica.

PHYSIOGRAPHIC DESCRIPTION

The two main islands are made up of different rocks: Saint Andrew is the product of recent limestone sediments and Old Providence is the result of an andesine volcano, extinguished during the Miocene period. The first of them features a small mountainous system with maximum heights of 85 meters that span the island from south to north. The cays there have small coral reefs formed from sand and very little elevation.

Old Providence has a mountainous aspect with an elevation of up to 550 meters above sea level at the top of the Peak, at the central part of the island. Ketlena Island, separated from Old Providence by a 300-meter wide channel, is

---

[2] The three islands that are at present a department of Colombia are officially called San Andrés, Providencia and Santa Catalina in Spanish. Here we will use the English names. Providence is also called Old Providence in English. Saint Catherine is named Ketlena, Ketleena and Ketlina in this book according to the West Indies English variants of this name. These are the actual names of the three inhabited islands that comprise the archipelago as a political unit. Historically, they had different names: Saint Andrew was also called Henrietta, and Providence was called Santa Catalina (Saint Catherine). Other names for Saint Andrew in colonial times were Andrea and Abacoa (Petersen 2002). The Corn islands, called Mangle, or Maíz in Spanish were historically and politically part of this archipelago. In 1822 they were part of the Cantón Islas San Andrés of the Provincia de Cartagena, República de la Gran Colombia. (N.E.)

relatively uneven, with an elevation of up to 133 meters above sea level. There are 7 cays off the coast, namely: Ketlena's cays (2), Crab Cay (1), the Three Brothers Cays (3) and an unnamed one off Bottom House. They are all formed from rocks with hills of low elevation. The climate of the entire archipelago is characterized by high temperature and is subject to the influence of trade winds from the northeast, which determines the rainy season from August to December. It has an average temperature of 29°C and 1800 mm of average yearly rainfall. At present, there is a footbridge made in its greater part of wood that connects Old Providence to Ketlena. The middle of the bridge is elevated just enough to allow launches to pass under it.

Means of Communication

Transportation between the islands and continental Colombia for passengers is only by airplane and for cargo both by sea and by cargo plane. Passengers travel between the two islands by sea and by air on small aircraft. There are jet planes with direct flights from Saint Andrew to Colombia and to Panama. However, there are no flights from Old Providence to elsewhere besides the island of Saint Andrew. Big cargo boats also go to Saint Andrew from Cartagena and Barranquilla, Colombia, likewise from Colón, Panama, and Costa Rica. Saint Andrew offers a large and secure bay for ships of different sizes for anchorage and also a dock for cargo ships. There are only small cargo boats traveling between Saint Andrew and Old Providence with no passengers; there is one boat owned by Rodolfo Howard, which goes from Old Providence to Cartagena. Old Providence also has a secured harbor with a small dock. Saint Andrew has a highway that goes around the island and other roads leading to different districts. Old Providence has a highway that goes around the island (ring road) connecting all the coastal hamlets, such as Fresh Water Bay, South West Bay, Smooth Water Bay, Manganeel Bay, Bottom House and Town (Santa Isabel).

THE PURITANS

The early records of Old Providence and Saint Andrew vary in one way or another. Peter J. Wilson (1973) affirms that Old Providence was discovered by Christopher Columbus on his fourth trip in 1502. According to his sources, in May of said year Columbus sailed into Old Providence harbor and two years later to Saint Andrew. Parsons (1964), argues that there is no record of such discovery by Christopher Columbus. Walwin Petersen (2002), historian from the island of Saint Andrew, agrees with Parson. On the other hand, apparently, there is no exact reference or evidence of who, besides the Miskito and other Amerindians of the region, really discovered the islands. Peter J. Wilson states that in 1595 the Spanish government ordered the construction of fortifications on Old Providence and Ketlena to garrison the islands. Although the island of Old Providence seemed to have been in possession of the Spanish Crown, evidence points that the Spanish did not engage in fortifying it until after they expelled the English in 1641. J.C. Robinson (1996), historian from the island of Old Providence, concludes, after doing a lot of research, collecting and analyzing a great amount of data, that the first known and recorded settlement in Old Providence Island occurred in 1631 by English Puritans who were recruited and transported there by the Providence Company, established by wealthy aristocrats and prominent members of the English gentry and the Parliament.[3] Settlers recruited by the Providence Company arrived on the island, on the sail ship the Sea Flower, by the end of May 1631. The settlers, close to 500 of them, including 50 women, resided in an area called New Westminster, at more or less what is now known as Old Town. The Company did not want many women to arrive on the island apart from those who were legally married and accompanying their husbands, because they believed that the presence of women would distract the men from living the religious faith up to a high standard. Puritans come from the "Pure" a group of English subjects who protested against the Anglican Church, which, according to their concept "was not living up to the precepts of the Bible."

---

[3] At the time of the Puritan settlement on the island the official name was "Providence Island" and the company that was organized in England to support the settlers was called "Providence Company." By 1666, given the existence of two other locations named Providence, one in the Bahamas (New Providence), the other in Rhode Island (Providence), this Caribbean island occupied by the Puritans was called Old Providence.

Their settlement on the Island was an experiment that could have had two purposes: the first, to prove that it was possible to establish and maintain a community based on the teaching of the Bible, as interpreted by the "Puritan faith" in the midst of a tropical environment; the second was to establish an English presence pointed at the heart of the Spanish Empire in the New World, especially the continental Spanish territories of Central America. Accordingly, the settlers of Old Providence were meant to expand their influence throughout the Central American area to undermine Spanish claims to that territory. The English built forts on Ketlena (Saint Catherine), the smaller island adjacent north of Old Providence. The area abounded with fish, turtles, parrots, tall trees, fig pomegranates, tropical fruits, cotton, tobacco, cedars, wild vines, oranges, lemons and whatever was cultivated for food. Lewis Morgan, an unmarried, devout scholar who was the first minister selected and sent by the Providence Company serving the Puritans, said that Old Providence could be compared with "the Eden of God" (J.C. Robinson 1996).

There were some Dutch smugglers and privateers commanded by one captain Blauvelt (also called Bluefield) operating out of Old Providence, which was then called Santa Catalina (along with the smaller island adjacent to it). They had fortified the island just before 1629.[4] There were also some Puritans in Saint Andrew (then also called Henrietta) who had plantations there but abandoned it just before 1630.[5] Because the tropical climate was not favorable to the European expeditionaries, slaves were brought from Africa as cheaper laborers who were believed to be more resistant to the heat. By such means, there was more economic profit that brought satisfaction to the sponsors. Some of the slaves arriving then were native Africans and others were creoles (of mixed ancestry and/or born in the so-called "New World"). Some historians agree that the first slaves arrived with the Puritan colonizers and planters from Jamaica within the years 1629 and 1633. As they arrived on the islands they created a vibrant culture all their own, in interaction with the dominant Anglophone population (in a situation in which most people of African descent were enslaved to individuals of European descent). Amerindian natives, mostly Miskito from the coast of what is today Nicaragua, are known to have been regular visitors

---

[4] According to Petersen (2002: 21): "Another Dutchman, Captain John Haine, established himself on the eastern side of Saint Andrew and renamed the island "Henrietta"... Captain Haine exploited the forest of Saint Andrew with a group of woodsmen..." (N.E.)

[5] Petersen (2002:24) says: "It was Cammock [one of the stakeholders of the Providence Company] who brought 30 pilgrims on his first trip to the island of Andrea (or Henrietta) on the ship Earl of Warwick in 1627 and established the new group near Haine's Bight." (N.E.)

to both islands long before the arrival of "Old World" populations. Later, Carib natives displaced by colonization of the Eastern Caribbean mixed with the Miskito, other Amerindians, and Africans. For this reason, coastal and insular territories of the western Caribbean are inhabited at present by significant communities of Afro-Carib speakers of English based creole languages.

The Puritans in Old Providence did not live up to their religious standards as it was expected. This brought discontent among them and some left the Island and went to Central America. Due to numerous problems with the settlers, and their failure to produce a return on the investments of the Providence Company in England placed in charge of the settlement, company shareholders became discouraged and discontinued their support. Moreover, the English presence was becoming a thorn in the Spaniards' side, increasing the pressure to expel the British settlers from what was considered part of the Spanish Empire.

In 1641 the Spanish general Francisco Díaz Pimienta arrived in Old Providence with several warships and approximately 1,700 men with the intention to annihilate the English presence so close to the Spanish Main. At that time several groups of the Puritans living in Old Providence had already left the island and had settled in other communities along the Central American Coast. The outstanding group surrendered to General Francisco Diaz Pimienta. Most inhabitants, with the exception of part of the Black population, were expelled and the island remained under Spanish control.[6] The English investors were totally immersed at the time in intense parliamentary struggles, which limited their interest in recovering their losses. These struggles in the English Parliament resulted in the execution of the King of England and brought the Puritan leader Oliver Cromwell to supreme power. A broader English interest in the western Caribbean developing beyond the specific limitations of the Providence Company set the stage for the occupation of Jamaica in 1665. The "Western Design" dreamed by William Cromwell, the Lord Protector of England, was to make the Caribbean a British sea and to remove the Catholic Spanish Empire from Central America and beyond. This idea was supported by the Providence Company as part of their revenge against the Spaniards for their personal losses and as an established principle of religious duty.[7]

---

[6] According to Arthur Percival Newton (1985: 248), close to 600 Black inhabitants, presumed to be slaves, were kept as war booty by the Spanish. Petersen (2002:28) says that more than 500 colonists escaped from Providence Island at the time of this attack.

[7] According to Newton the experience in Providence Island set the stage for a deeper and long standing involvement of the English in the western Caribbean and Central America after 1665. (N.E.)

Edward Mansfield

It was not until 1666 when Edward Mansfield, an English filibuster also known as Eduard Mansvelt, planned on getting a fleet together in Jamaica to raid the mainland. Upon meeting with Sir Henry Morgan, an English pirate, and seeing that he was very courageous, he invited him to join the expedition and made him vice-admiral of his fleet. They set out to sea with approximately 200 men on 5 ships and their first landing was on Old Providence on May 25, 1666. Mansfield seized Old Providence leading his squadron towards the Southwestern part of the Island through "Playa de Los Naranjos" (now known as Manganeel Bay) and arriving at "Aguada Grande" (now known as Fresh Water Bay) during the night of said date. They surprised and captured Don Esteban de Ocampo, who was a Spaniard defending Old Providence. Early the following morning, May 26, 1666, the English flag was flying.

Soon after conquering Old Providence, Mansfield had the Spanish surrender all the fortifications. He ordered to demolish some and reinforce others. The remaining artillery was taken to Ketlena. After the defenses were set up and put in good order, Mansfield burned down the houses on Old Providence, left 100 men together with all the slaves who had belonged to the Spanish, leaving one St. Simon, a Frenchman, in charge, then set out to sea taking all the Spanish prisoners with him. After arriving in Porto Belo (Porto Bello), a port near Colon, Panama, he put off the prisoners and cruised along the Costa Rican coast. With the intention to plunder all the villages, he proceeded to the town of Natá, (in the bay of Panama), but the governor of Panama heard of it and had him retreat with a strong force. By then the whole coast was on the alert.

Mansfield, realizing the situation, acknowledged that there would be little profit by raiding at the moment, and returned to Old Providence. The intention was to hold on to the island of Old Providence as it made an excellent base for the buccaneers, having a good harbor and lying near the Spanish mainland. He thought of reinforcing the garrison to fend off possible attacks by Spanish forces. With this plan in mind, he returned to Jamaica and on his arrival, he explained to the governor his ideas and asked him for support, but the governor refused. Following this disappointment, he decided to go to Tortuga (an island just off the northwest coast of Haiti, a base for buccaneers and pirates in the 17th century) to ask the governor there for help since he of himself could not achieve his objective. Unfortunately, he did not accomplish his desire being prevented by death.[8]

For the Spanish Governor of Panama at that time, Don Juan Pérez De Guzmán, knight of the order of Santiago, Governor and Captain General of the realm of Tierra Firme and the province of Veragua, the loss of Old Providence was inconceivable and he became so desperate and outraged upon learning the news that the English were in possession of the Island, that he could not wait for higher authorization, so he appointed José Sánchez Ximénez, a Spaniard who at the moment was the town major of Portobello and was considered to be a very good soldier, leader of an expedition to retake the Island. Governor Pérez De Guzman chartered a ship of the Company of Negroes, the St. Vicente, which was well provided with munitions of war, and gave Ximénez 227 men; in addition, 47 of those previously taken prisoners on Ketlena joined the expedition. There were also 34 Spaniards from the garrison, 12 Indians skillful in shooting arrows; one surgeon, 7 expert gunners, 2 pilots, and a monk to confess them.

After Pérez de Guzmán had made an encouraging speech emphasizing that they were bound to uphold the holy Catholic faith and punish the heretics for plundering the churches, Don Juan instructed the commander to go to Cartagena and request assistance from the Governor with ships and men to take the Island. Should the governor of Cartagena not instantly assist him, he was to present him a request in the name of his Majesty. On arriving in Cartagena on July 22 the commander handed over the instructions to the Governor. The governor, on seeing these bold plans decided to help him with a frigate, a galleon, and 3 barques together with 126 men consisting of 66 Spaniards and 60 mulattoes. The expedition sailed from Cartagena on the 2nd of August. On the 10th of August, they anchored in the port of Old Providence after the loss of a barque on the reef of Quitasueño in a storm. The Spanish commander sent one of his officers on shore to summon the pirates to surrender or if not they should all be put to death by the sword. However, the reply was that the island had formerly belonged to the English Crown, and they would rather die than to give it up again.

---

[8] The Europeans (many of whom were French speakers) who took refuge in Hispaniola and later were called "buccaneers," got that name because of a method they learned from surviving Carib Indians for making smoke-dried beef, which became their stock-in-trade. The meat was hung in strips over a frame of green sticks and dried above a fire fed with animal bones and hide trimmings. Both the wooden grating and the place where the curing was done were called by the Carib name of "boucan," and the hunters engaged in this work became known as "boucaniers" (French) or "buccaneers."

Governor Simon ordered his men to defend the forts: El Castillo and Cortadura in Ketlena, also Fort Santiago (or Saint Iago) in Old Providence, today known as Camp. The Spanish attacked and the English initially resisted. But on the 13th of August 1666, three Negroes deserted from the pirates, went on board the admiral's ship and stated that the pirates were only seventy-two strong and full of fear on seeing such a powerful invading force.[9] With such assurance, the island was attacked fearlessly with heavy cannonade and firing muskets. On the 17th the Spanish landed ashore and, well prepared with men and munitions, attacked the forts simultaneously with such fury and without retreat so that six of the English men were killed. The English, seeing that they could not win the battle, surrendered to Major Don José Sánchez Ximénez. He ordered that three of them be taken to Panama and the others to Portobello to work on the fort of St. Jerome. Old Providence was once more under the control of the Spanish. Alexander O. Exquemelin, a Frenchman accompanying the English, presumes that notwithstanding the might of the Spaniards, if the buccaneers had really wished to hold the island, they could easily have driven them off.

HENRY MORGAN

Henry Morgan, the privateer dedicated to the sacking of Spanish ships on high seas with authorization of the English monarch, who had already joined Mansfield, decided to recapture the island. On the 24th of December 1670, he arrived in Old Providence with 38 warships and 1,000 men, landing them at Aguada Grande, now known as Fresh Water Bay. The Spaniards had formerly mounted a battery of four cannons in that section. Morgan with his troops had no local guides but those of their own company who had been there with the Mansfield invasion. They marched through the woods and reached to where the governor's residence was in those days (near the battery already mentioned of St. Iago, more or less what is known today as Camp), but no one was found there. The Spaniards had already moved to Ketlena (Sta. Catalina) for an easier

---

[9] The Spanish, who had permission from the Pope to conquer the territories of the West Indies (while the English took it for granted that marauding along the coast and capturing the Spanish ships was their right), considered the English as pirates. Her Majesty the Queen knighted some of these pirates.

defense. On that same night, the pirates could not attack because of a heavy rainfall from midnight until daylight.

Marching toward Ketlena, the rain began worse than before, while the Spaniards renewed their bombardment to demonstrate that their powder was still dry. The English dared not to attack the fortress in the rain, but rather look for houses where they could protect their weapons from the heavy rain. Morgan's men became desperately hungry and would prefer to return to the ship. They found an old horse with sores abandoned by the Spaniards that they shot and made a meal from roasting it.

Morgan was firm in taking the island. He sent messengers across in a canoe with a white flag about midday summoning the Spaniards to give up the island, adding that he would give no quarter with them if they would not surrender without delay. The Spaniards sent a canoe with the flag of armistice and two persons to arrange the capitulation. However, before landing they requested two hostages from Morgan before having a talk with him. This agreement was carried out, the matter was discussed, and the Spaniards agreed to surrender because their forces, they said, could not fight against Morgan's for a victory. However, they asked Morgan to let them save their reputation by putting up a mock-battle in order to report to the superiors that the Spanish captain had put up a fight. Morgan agreed on such proposal, on the condition that none of his men should suffer injury or death; otherwise, he would give no quarter.

The mock battle was performed and the Spaniards released the island. After counting the people on the island, there were about 450 altogether. The Spaniards were disarmed; the men were allowed to get food from the plantations, while the ladies were kept locked up in the church. All fortifications were inspected. Morgan ordered that all the military supplies be taken on board his ships, the guns were spiked, the batteries, and one of the forts (St. José), were abandoned. Later, after deciding he would not have enough men to garrison the island, he destroyed the fortifications reconstructed by the Spaniards, preserving only one of the forts from complete destruction. Morgan was knighted in 1675; in 1677 he was appointed Deputy Governor of Jamaica with a salary of £600. He was recalled to England during the reign of James II on account of his intrigues and his assisting in the depravations committed by the English pirates on the fleets and subjects of Spain.

Morgan did not return to Old Providence. The older folks in Old Providence speculate that Morgan left a lot of treasures on the island and that gold was found there on different occasions. Historians do not agree much with such hypotheses. However, it is confirmed by C. F. Collette, that if time did not permit the pirates to lavish their booty away in their usual debaucheries, they used to hide it in the desert cays which they frequented and where much valuable treasure was supposed to be concealed. It is reasonable to suppose that if Henry Morgan himself had left such valuable treasures, he would have returned to the island to rescue them. Down through the ages, people in Old Providence have speculated that when the pirates were hiding their treasures they would ask someone to guard them and whoever accepted would be shot dead and buried with such treasure.

People still believe these stories and on different occasions have been seen searching for gold with special machines. Even though Morgan's stay on Old Providence was not possibly more than three months, his fame and legend have loomed highly in the folklore of the island. On the Southwest end of Ketlena Island, there is a very remarkable rock formation in the likeness of a man's head, which has come to be known as Morgan's Head, named after the privateer. It rises approximately 40 ft. from sea level and it is not easily distinguished until closely approached. In spite of conflicts between the Spanish and the British over the Island of Old Providence and the different attacks upon it, and major events taking place around the entire Caribbean Sea, life in Old Providence remained relatively peaceful from 1670 to the first two decades of the 19th century (Robinson 1996).[10]

TIME FOR ABOLITION

Why was Saint Andrew more at ease and hardly mentioned during the various attacks of different conquerors in those days? During the dispute for

---

[10] To sum up: Mansfield invaded Providence in 1666; the Spanish recaptured it in 1667; Morgan invaded it in 1670 and left within two months. Thereafter followed a century and a half without major attacks or violent armed occupations. According to Parsons (1964:31), a Spanish reconnoitring expedition in 1688 declared to have found no inhabitants or evidence thereof on either Providence or Saint Andrews. It can be presupposed, nevertheless, that there must have been a continuing human inhabitation in both islands. Petersen (2002:31) describes in detail how residents of Saint Andrew at the time took elaborate measures in order to go unnoticed by unwanted visitors to the island. Most probably, residents of Providence must have taken similar precautions during those years. Díez Bermúdez (2014:77) says that by 1730, planters from Jamaica and other Caribbean territories settled by English subjects were drifting little by little to the archipelago, bringing their African slaves with them. (N.E.)

Old Providence, Saint Andrew was left alone without giving such importance to the pirates. This was due to the geographical configuration and position of the island of Old Providence itself. It was easier for the buccaneers to view the ships from afar thanks to the high hills. The harbor of itself offered a better service to suit their demands.

In a treaty signed between Spain and England in 1786 (the Treaty of Versailles), England agreed to relocate all British loyalists, this meant English speakers and non-Catholics, from the Central American coast and adjacent islands including Old Providence, to a single area to be called British Honduras, which is now the Republic of Belize. It was a difficult case for the English to relocate the settlers back to England. Although the English wanted to gather the people of the coast of Costa Rica, Honduras, and Nicaragua to have them to settle in British Honduras, many of them refused, including those on Old Providence and St. Andrew. Little mention is made of Old Providence till 1795 when a few families from Bluefields, on the Mosquito Coast, settled there with permission from the Spaniards. From that time till 1817 the island remained quite tranquil until Aury's arrival (more on him below.)

After all the conflicts between the Spaniards and the English, there was relief and quietness. This shows that these islands and maybe others in the Caribbean did not meet the perspectives of the Spaniards to colonize and maintain them; neither did the English fight to keep them forever. As a matter of fact, these islands were only used as ports of call for the fleets. Whenever the pirates were bold enough to make attacks against the interests of the Spaniards (ports of call or fleets) the Spanish Crown would show or try to show imperial sovereignty. With this behavior, the islands were going from one power/possession to another. When the English retreated for one reason or another, they left their belongings to their slaves supposedly to irritate the Spaniards. The English administrated their properties by delegation and some never returned. The succeeding governor of Spain also distributed lands to their personnel and clients reserving some properties for themselves and their families. This operation caused administrators and laborers to be promoted to ownership. Sadly, the Colombian state has never recognized the native born islanders' such condition as first owners of the islands.

According to historian Parsons (1964), after the treaty between England and Spain (1786) there were only 220 residents in St. Andrew who required permission from the Spanish Crown to remain on their beloved island, offering to become loyal subjects to the king of Spain, to accept the Catholic religion and to cease trading with Jamaica. The population had increased to 1,220 in St. Andrew by 1806. Many of these were Negro slaves, evacuated from Bluefields and Corn Island. Surprisingly, the islanders on Saint Andrew continued their commercial and cultural ties with Kingston rather than with Cartagena. The Governor of Saint Andrew, Thomas O'Neill, wrote about the Saint Andrewans in 1803 that its inhabitants still spoke the English language without any knowledge of the Spanish language. "Several youths of both sexes, he said, have been permitted to travel to England and the United States... of the Catholic religion they have no idea... of Christianity, they know nothing but baptism."

In 1787 Captain Francis Archbold, a British subject in possession of a land grant awarded by the Crown of Spain, arrived in Old Providence from Jamaica with several settlers and some black slaves. He was captain of one of those slave-trading ships taking wood used as ballast to Jamaica and England in those days. He settled in Bottom House (on the southern tip) with good fertile land. Even when it was said that his stay on the island was to strengthen the Spanish presence in a strategic location, J. C. Robinson states that in 1805 Captain Archbold appealed to Sir George Nugent, the British Governor of Jamaica for protection, confessing that although the island was claimed by Spain, he was, in reality, a British subject and had always considered himself as such. This leads us to assume that he only pretended to be a Catholic when swearing allegiance to the King of Spain, Charles III upon receiving the land grant. Captain Archbold had even participated in the slave trade controlled by the English before his arrival in Old Providence (Robinson 1996).

Philip Beekman Livingston Senior, originally from Scotland, was a seaman and merchant. He married Mary Archbold, a daughter of Captain Francis Archbold. They had extensive fields of cotton, large herds of sheep and cattle. Philip Beekman Livingston Jr. was born in Old Providence, January 16, 1814. After he was grown, he went to Jamaica, and while there, his mother requested his return to Old Providence to free the slaves. He fulfilled this request on August 1st, 1834, retaining a portion of land for his family. When he established in Saint Andrew, he also freed his slaves there on August 1st, 1838. It can be ascertained that Livingston's actions initiated abolition in the archipelago. After Phillip Livingston and his mother freed their slaves based on their moral and religious principles, they set an example that led to a process of gradual emancipation of slaves on the islands. J. C. Robinson states that in 1853, the President of Colombia, José Hilario López, emancipated the remaining slaves with the proclamation of the abolition of slavery. However, natives of Providence and

Saint Andrew Island celebrate the former date of August 1st (1834 and 1838, respectively). Philip Beekman Livingston Jr. was also the first landowner to assemble the freed slaves' children to teach them to read and write on weekdays and on Sundays to teach them Bible lessons. These children's parents joined in later on. Philip Beekman Livingston Jr. married Ann Elisa, ex-Governor Thomas O'Neill's daughter, on the 7th of December 1839.

LOUIS-MICHEL AURY

In 1818 Louis-Michel Aury, a French adventurer, arrived in Old Providence with some 800 men and a fleet of 14 vessels. The inhabitants Aury found on Old Providence were described as colonists and planters, the majority being English from Jamaica. Among them, there were many Blacks who cultivated coffee, cotton, corn, bananas, cassava, sugarcane, tobacco, potatoes, sweet sap, pineapple, mango, papaya, oranges, watermelon, pepper, and coconuts. Louis Aury acted as a privateer operating out of Old Providence between 1817 and 1820. He received 18% of booty taken by his Old Providence-based vessels; the rest of it was distributed to officers and crews. Many ships were raided by the Frenchman's marauders. The British acknowledged and approved their privateering since commercial relations between Jamaica and Old Providence were of a friendly nature. Aury was even reinforced with 150 British soldiers from Jamaica for the fortification of the island due to privateering profits. He also recruited other men from Port-au-Prince, St. Thomas, and New Orleans.

Among the recruited, there was a young Italian engineer by the name of Agustin Codazzi, who helped with the expansion of the channel between Old Providence and Ketlena performed by Aury not long after his arrival. The Spaniards had already opened the channel to fortify the island of Ketlena sometime in the 17th century by breaking the ravine of the channel almost to the level of the sea, in the construction of the forts. However, the channel took Aury's name. Codazzi later moved to Bogotá, and became the founder of the Instituto Geográfico that carries his name. At present, there is a wooden bridge between Old Providence and Ketlena set on floating tanks in the middle and with both ends resting on solid concrete ground and posts.

Aury had established a friendship with Simón Bolívar and had offered him aid with an army of 800 men and 14 vessels, but this did not come about. To the contrary, in 1821 Bolívar manifested to Aury that the cause of the independence of Nueva Granada (now Colombia) had reached the condition where it no longer needed the support of corsairs who were only degrading its flag before the rest of the world. Aury was far from accomplishing his political dreams.[11] Some of his men perished on board his ships in Old Providence harbor due to a hurricane just after his arrival in 1818. His plan for aiding Simón Bolívar was not successful; and the worst of it, he fell from his horse in the southern part of the island on August 20th, and died as a consequence of this accident on August 30th, 1821.

After Aury's death, most of his men left Old Providence to seek their fortune in other parts of the Caribbean. However, some of them decided to settle in the island in order to pursue a more peaceful life. According to history, after all the different attacks on the island, life remained peaceful thereon. Louis Peru de Lacroix, a Frenchman who had served as Aury's secretary, assembled the people on Old Providence on June 23, 1822, to swear allegiance to the constitution of Cúcuta, which was the first constitution of the Republic of Gran Colombia. It may be surmised that had Aury not died in that year he would have kept control of the island but there would have probably never been an annexation, since by that time Simón Bolívar had acridly refused Aury's support; after repeated rejections, their presumed friendship had practically broken up.

No one mentions what language was used to perform the allegiance of annexation on that day. Since Aury's secretary Louis Peru de Lacroix convened the local assembly, it is possible that it was done in French. Moreover, English was obviously spoken by most longtime residents, so it could have been performed in that language as well. If Governor O'Neill in Saint Andrew in 1803 said that the Saint Andrewans only spoke the English language, then it may be supposed that the same language was also spoken almost exclusively in the island of Old Providence at the time of the annexation 19 years later. (It must be kept in mind that O'Neill governed Saint Andrew before Colombia's independence from Spain.) The inhabitants freely participated in this act of allegiance. Following the ceremony, the Gran Colombian flag was hoisted. The flag flown was the red, blue and yellow vertical in equal parts with a white star of five points in the blue segment, being the nearest to the pole. A similar ceremony of annexation

---

[11] For the political ambitions undergirding Aury's extensive exploits in the Caribbean see Jaime Duarte French (1988). (N.E.)

was also held in Saint Andrew on the 21st of July of the same year (1822).

Even though the people of Old Providence and Saint Andrew pledged allegiance to the Constitution of Cúcuta in 1822 and became a part of the Gran Colombia, they never wanted to change their culture and their language, which was the English language.[12] They remained loyal to Anglo-Saxon culture and Protestantism. They wanted to maintain their connections with the Anglo-Saxon world, especially England, the United States, and Jamaica. This attachment was not welcomed by the Gran Colombia government; it was confusing for the Colombian Government at that time representing the empire inherited from the Spanish culture. Therefore, their worries were how to obtain loyalty to a republic where Spanish culture was dominant. In 1835, the population of Old Providence was approximately 342 of which about one half were slaves. It can be assumed that most of the 800 men who accompanied Aury, plus the 150 British soldiers from Jamaica and the other 394 accompanying McGregor, did not remain on the Island. The fact, already mentioned, that some of Aury's men perished on board some of his ships in Old Providence harbor due to a hurricane the year he arrived (in 1818) must be taken into account. After the annexation, Lt. Colonel Jean-Baptiste Faiquere, a Frenchman who Aury had appointed Providence's governor, was made the first Colombian military commander of the islands for 5 years and was later replaced by Antonio Cardenas from Cartagena.

The islands of Providence, St. Andrew and Corn adhered to the constitution of the Republic of La Gran Colombia.[13] This resulted in their formal incorporation, in 1822, into the republic as the canton of "Islas San Andres" under the jurisdiction of the Province of Cartagena. In 1824, during the government of the military chief Antonio Cardenas, the seat of government of the canton was transferred from Old Providence to Saint Andrew. This jurisdictional administration through Cartagena lasted until 1868 when it was

---

[12] According to current linguistic studies the vernacular language of the three islands comprising Colombia's only overseas department, San Andrés, Providencia and Santa Cataline, is Creole English (classified by linguists as Western Caribbean Creole English). However, in the linguistic consciousness of most islanders, their creole vernacular is not necessarily considered a distinct language from standard English, they regard it to be part of what is generally understood by "English." See Marcia Dittmann (2013). (N.E.).

[13] The Republic of Gran Colombia included the territories of present-day Colombia, Ecuador, Panamá, Venezuela, and parts of northern Perú, western Guyana and northwestern Brazil until 1831, when it was dissolved and the República de Nueva Granada was established, which directly evolved into present day Colombia as it lost big chunks of territory, among them Panama. (N.E.)

passed to direct administration from Bogotá until 1888. In that same year, it was returned to Cartagena as the "Province of Providence." The government of Cartagena neglected the islands, causing the islanders to lodge complaints constantly without any positive results until this day.

It is said that in 1877, when Old Providence was devastated by a hurricane, the governor of the island notified the president of the United States of America instead of the president of Colombia. The obvious presumption is that there would be a quicker and more effective aid coming from the U.S. than from Colombia, given that commercial cultural and linguistic ties with the northern country were stronger in many senses. Moreover, the islands were not, and are still not well attended by Colombia. Even when literacy was much higher in the islands than in Colombia, very little Spanish was used. Although most people spoke Creole English, a significant number of individuals were fluent and literate in standard English. English in general was absolutely dominant. This was irritating to the Colombian government, causing them to fight and try to eradicate the English language from the islands. Historian J.C. Robinson (1996) states that in 1878 the Corregidor of Old Providence, Arthur Hawkins, was fired from his office "por ignorar totalmente el idioma Español" (for totally ignoring the Spanish language). This can be credited since there has been persecution against the English language in the islands (more on language politics further ahead). In 1912 the islands were constitutionally declared as "Intendencia de San Andres y Providencia." It was administrated directly through the Ministry of territories in Bogotá and an "Intendente" (local administrator) appointed by the president of the nation.

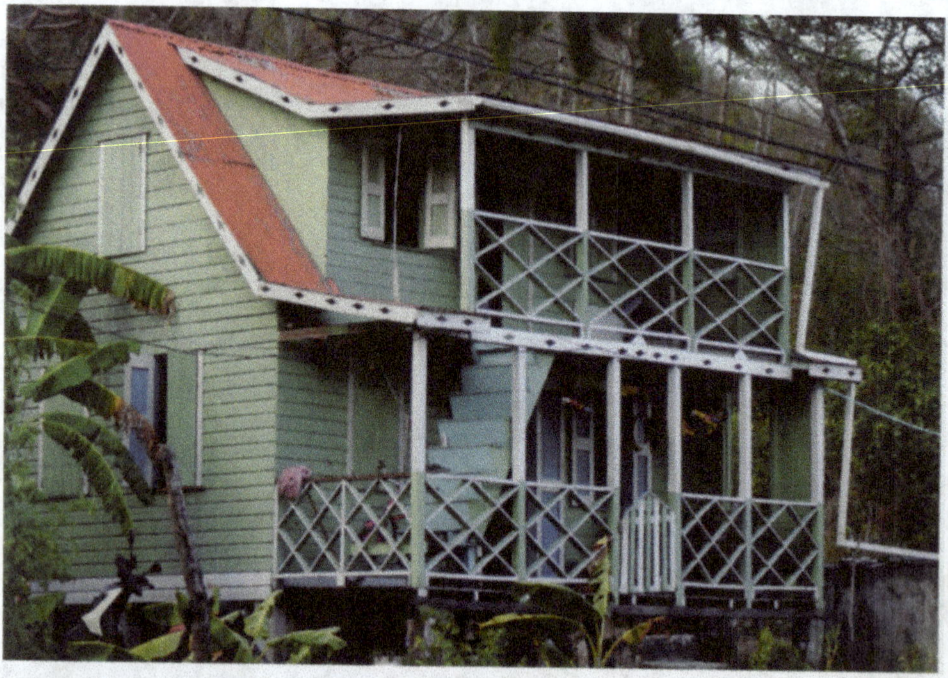

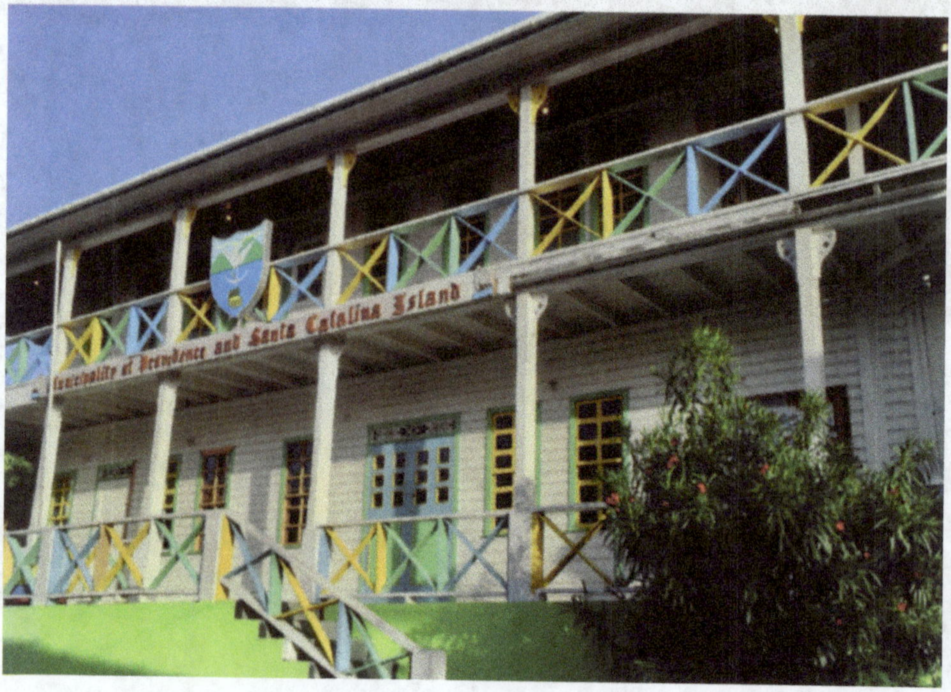
and Santa Catalina Island

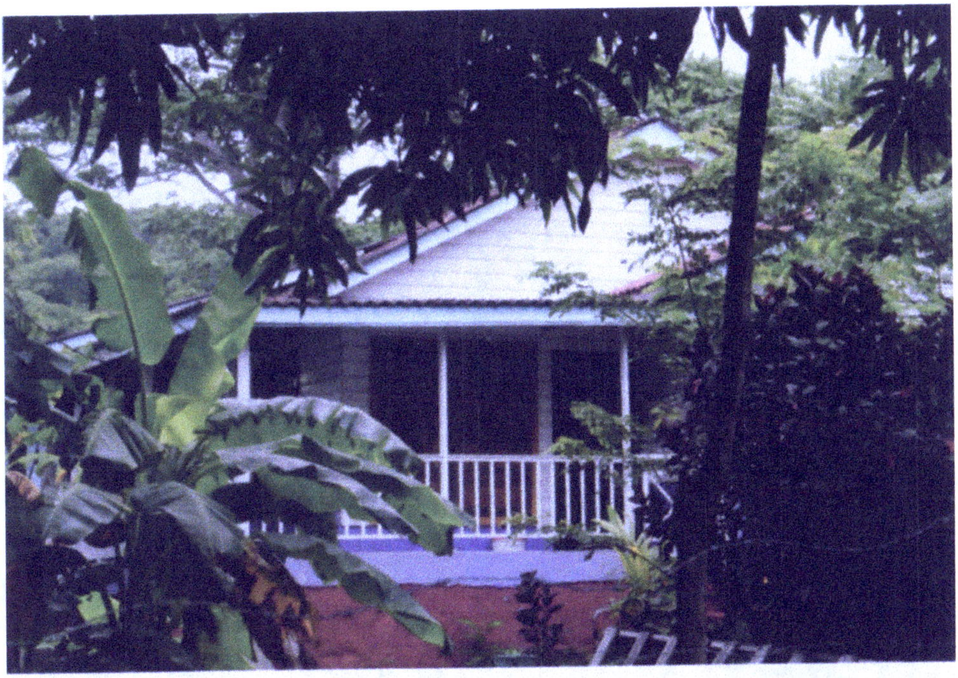

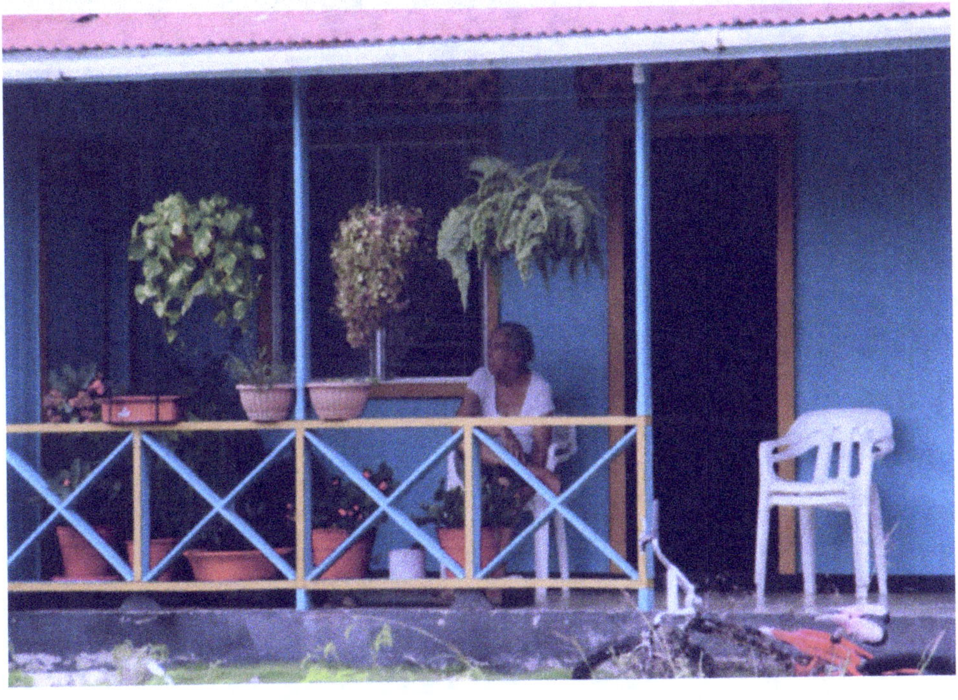

Clamor of the Islands

Religion on the Islands

Even when there is no precise record of the origin of religion on the islands, we could presume it would be that of the Puritans, provided that they were the first settlers on Old Providence. The Puritans as a corporate community left Old Providence Island in 1641 when the Spanish military took charge. It is possible that there was a priest with the Spanish as it was the custom of the Crown to have a confessor with their expeditions. However, Thomas O'Neill, an Irish born Catholic who in 1789 came with the Spanish as an interpreter, was appointed governor of Saint Andrew (and Old Providence) in 1795. On assuming this position, he requested that one or two priests be sent to the islands, especially since the residents had promised to become Catholics as a part of the bargain made with the Spanish Crown, which had permitted them to remain on the islands (Parson 1964). Alexander Exquemelin (1967) refers to a church where Henry Morgan had the women locked up after taking possession of Old Providence in 1670. In 1835 there were no priests nor pastors as attested by Collette when he wrote: "it is to be regretted, that in a remote corner of the western hemisphere, there should be so many persons without the advantages or means of Christian instruction; and it is rather a matter of surprise that missionaries, either of the Protestant or Roman Catholic Church, have not found their way to a place so well calculated, in every respect, to ensure success to their labors." (Collette 1837: 352). Because of the different interventions of the English, Spanish, Dutch and French on Old Providence it could be that in different periods distinct religious groups of a specified denomination taught their religious faith.

Referring to the celebration of the islands' adhesion to Gran Colombia, it is said that a Spanish priest, one Fr. Luis Jose Brillabrille, offered a prayer and sang a Te-Deum of thanks (Robinson 1996). Parsons (1964) says that in the descriptions of the ceremonies of annexation on Old Providence in 1822 there is reference to a church, possibly French Catholic, but whatever it was it seems to have ceased functioning with the departure of the buccaneers.

Baptists

As mentioned above, Philip Livingston Jr. was the first landowner to assemble the freed slave children to teach them to read and write during weekdays and to study the Bible along with their parents in 1844, on the island of Saint Andrew. The first established church on Saint Andrew was the Baptist, organized in 1845 by the American Baptist Board of Home Mission, persuaded by Philip Beekman Livingston Jr., a native of Old Providence whose father was originally from Scotland, a seaman and merchant married with Mary, daughter of Captain Francis Archbold. Livingston Jr. was educated abroad, and after being rebaptized in the Baptist faith in Manhattan, USA, the church licensed him to preach on New Year's Day, 1845. On one of his voyages to Jamaica, he was ordained into the Baptist Ministry in Kingston. After returning from Jamaica to Saint Andrew, he dedicated his time to the church and its ministry. Later, in 1855, one "Miss Abel," traveled from Saint Andrew to Old Providence to teach and preach to people recently converted to the Baptist faith by Pastor Philip Beekman Livingston. She organized the First Baptist Church on Old Providence in the southern neighborhood of Bottom House.

Roman Catholics and Adventists

English speaking Roman Catholics began their activities in 1902 with a Josephite missionary by the name of Albert Stroebele. He was joined by Eusebio Howard (known as "uncle Sabe)," who had already split from the Baptist Church pastored by his brother Simon Howard Jr., and converted to Catholicism. In 1910, the Catholic Mission in Old Providence was officially assigned to the Josephite Order headquartered in Baltimore, a branch of the main order located in England. Not long after, the brothers John and James Albert were sent to Old Providence by the order in Baltimore. These two brothers founded two more churches, one in Salt Creek (Lazy Hill) and the other in South West Bay. Nuns were also sent from the Josephite order to strengthen the mission, which grew successfully. These missionaries respected the Baptist and Adventist churches, their customs and culture, and would even attend special services when invited. Services were in English. It is said that they all lived as one people.

The Adventist church began their activities in Old Providence in 1902 with Frank J. Hutchins, a missionary lay preacher who also practiced dentistry. Two religious booksellers, J. B. Haughton, and Mateland also accompanied Hutchins in his missionary work. The Gospel was preached from the deck of "The Herald," a ship anchored off New Westminster, now known as Old Town. They made 14 converts.

In 1912, Mill Hill missionaries from England replaced North American Catholic priests. This was due to political conflicts between Colombia and the United States over the independence of Panama. Colombian authorities became increasingly suspicions of the United States' involvement in the separation of Panama. All American citizens became suspects including the Josephite missionaries. Among those that were sent away the most appreciated by islanders were James Rogan and Richard Turner, who were always mentioned by the older folks. These missionaries, apart from controlling the public schools, organized their own Catholic schools and obtained scholarships for boys and girls to further their studies in Colombia. The American and English priests spoke English, as did the islanders. The people in Old Providence have always claimed to be descendants of English, Scottish and Irish settlers, as well as of African slaves. Such conviction and the common use of the English language made it more comfortable for both the natives and the Mill Hill missionaries, who found that the people were closer to the Anglo-Saxon world than to Colombia's Spanish heritage. In 1926, by mutual agreement between the Josephite order in England and the Colombian government, the Spanish based branch of the Capuchin order replaced the Mill Hill missionaries in Old Providence. This was done due to the anxiety of Colombia to hispanize the island people. But with the Capuchin priests, everything went the other way for the island people, who suffered a tremendous change in every sense. Before giving details of what took place during the years of the Capuchin mission, the author will provide excerpts from their book *Cincuenta años de misión cumplida* justifying what was done during their years of "civilizing" the islanders:

> The Catholic faith has never considered its mission in Colombia as a foreign interference of the Church or the Holy See in the internal or sovereign affairs of a country. To this purpose we ought to remember that the initiative of the Catholic mission in Colombia was taken in its days by the civil authorities, rightfully constituted by law 72 of 1892, which was well explicit: "give rights to the executive power in order that, in accordance with the ecclesiastic authority,

it proceeds to establish Catholic Missions in the territory of the Republic in places that are considered convenient".

It was not, then, the Church, but rather the executive power that was authorized to establish missions in places that it esteemed convenient. The Bishops and the Holy See, subsequently, would only be the collaborators of a mandate or a governmental initiative. Being as it was, an essentially cultural mission, the Government confided to the leaders of the mission the direction of primary public schools and the inspection of education establishments in the territory (Idem, art. 9). This was not dealt with as an irritating privilege. It was a serious responsibility and, on occasions, the only alternative.

The Holy See created the "SUI IURIS" (Origin Law) of Saint Andrew and Old Providence by decree of the Sacred Consistorial Congregation, obtained under the authority of Pope Pius X on the 20th of June 1912, assigning English priests of the St Joseph school of Mill Hill in England (The Josephite). The first expedition arrived in Saint Andrew at the beginning of 1913. Ecclesiastic Superior James Fitzpatrick and the Fathers Richard Turner and H. Keans were the Priests who took canonical position of the mission. In the mid-1915 Reverend James Rogan, an Irishman, arrived in Saint Andrew. In 1920, after Father Fitzpatrick returned to London, Reverent Richard Turner took over as Superior. The Mill Hill Mission was in the Archipelago until March 1927. At this time the Colombian Government wanted to change the Mill Hill Mission in order to establish a religious and cultural mission like those operating in the Nation in accordance to the history, customs, and Spanish language of Colombia. For this reason, the Holy See had commended the Mission of Saint Andrew to the Capuchin order by decree No.1945 of the Sacred Congregation on May 21, 1926. The Reverend Eugenio de Carcagente was designated Ecclesiastic Superior of the new Capuchin order. Before leaving for Colombia, he arranged with Monsignor, Luis Amigo for the foundation of a Capuchin nunnery in Saint Andrew, which was conformed in Colombia by direct conversation with Madre Victoria de Valencia, the general commissary. In January 1927 a religious community was founded in Saint Andrew. They took charge of the girls' school and in December of said year the Capuchin nuns gave Christmas gifts only to girls attending classes and catechism.

Religious Persecution

There was a complete environmental change in the islands with the arrival of the Capuchin order replacing the Josephite order, following lengthy negotiations in 1926 and the mutual agreement between the Colombian government and the Josephite order in England. As mentioned above, the Colombian government was anxious to bring about the complete colombianization of the people of Old Providence and Saint Andrew using religion and language as the main instruments of acculturation. The Capuchins were of Spanish nationality and spoke only Spanish. The Josephite missionaries of Baltimore and Mill Hill made their headquarters in Old Providence, but the Capuchins settled in Saint Andrew. The Capuchin order's strategy was to first attempt to destroy the native cultural foundations and later replace them with what they considered to be true "civilization." Ultimately, the intention of the Capuchins was to completely eradicate all forms of religious belief different from theirs, whether Baptist or Seventh Day Adventist, because to them these were mere "sects." To accomplish their goal, the Capuchin priests selected education as the best means of bringing about conversion to Catholicism. They believed that once conversion to Catholicism took place, colombianization would follow since the two were closely linked.

The urge of the Colombian government to convert the islanders to Catholicism seemed desperate; they placed an experienced person to accelerate conversions. Mother Victoria de Valencia, who was then the general commissary in Colombia, sent Father Eugenio de Carcagente of the Provincia Capuchina de Valencia to the island of Saint Andrew on May 21, 1926. He was considered a clever missionary. In the following years seven Capuchin nuns joined him. Initially, they established a Catholic school for girls directed and administrated by the nuns. They were assigned to do their best to change the teachings and culture that the children received at home. Pastor Philip Beekman Livingston had already organized a number of native schools in 1850 while sharing God's word among the people of Saint Andrew (Parson 1964). The Reverend Noel Julian La Rosa Gonsalves, a Canadian Baptist, was sent to Saint Andrew in June 1926, but as was predictable, he was not appreciated by the Capuchins. The Reverend was aware of their sagacity at gaining people according to their mission. Later, the Roman Catholic Church signed a contract with the government as inspectors of public education. Things started to change radically. As inspectors, the Capuchins ensured that only practicing Catholics were employed as teachers. They blatantly turned the public schools into centers of Catholic teaching. In those schools they railed against the Baptists and Seventh Day Adventists, thus seeking to impose obligatory Catholic religious practices on all students.

These efforts at conversion to Catholicism represented a significant change for the islanders. Catholics, as a rule, were expected to know the rudiments of the Catholic liturgy (done in Latin at the time), attend mass on Sundays, confess whenever they could and be sure to baptize and raise their children as Catholics, even if only nominally so. Under the Capuchins, Catholics were also expected to speak Spanish, be loyal and patriotic towards Colombia, and to act and behave like their compatriots on the mainland. Colombianization was now strongly felt in both islands. Given that neither the nuns nor the Capuchin brothers knew English, the students were forced to learn Spanish. All subjects were taught in Spanish out of context, without taking into account, not only that the primary language of the children was English, but also that they had no previous knowledge of Spanish. As a consequence they memorized the lessons without any understanding of what they were all about. This author can remember how, being a little boy in 1948, he was made to memorize all the lessons and even recite them in school with no idea of what he was saying. Students were regularly punished if they spoke English in the classrooms. Many were locked up in darkrooms at the Bolivariano High School and the elementary schools in Saint Andrew because they dared speak in their own language.

The Capuchins persuaded the local government to support their objective when the national government of Colombia began spending considerable funds to improve education and other public facilities. The fact that the administrative head of the archipelago was appointed by the President of Colombia helped in this. Only Roman Catholics were employed in the construction of school buildings. On account of penury, many individuals in Baptist families joined the Roman Catholic Church to obtain work. These were called "job Catholics" because they were not really converted.

The great majority of the children in the public schools were from non-Catholic homes, but all the teachers were Catholics and most of them were nuns. Children were taught the symbol of the cross, to be devoted to the saints and encouraged to take fresh flowers every morning to decorate the images placed in the schools. They were introduced to the mass and other Catholic rituals. Children of non-Catholic families felt frustrated because they were told that the Baptist church was the devil and that there was no salvation out of the Catholic church. Students did not do the parade on the 20th of July celebrating the independence of Colombia until the arrival of the Capuchins in 1926.

The Baptist leaders' repeated protests had no positive result. The answer was simply that "the Apostolic Catholic Church has the rights, under the constitution of the Republic of Colombia, to supervise education." There was nothing that the Baptists could do but revive their own private schools and work to preserve their faith and the English language. The Baptists started a private school in San Luis, located between the north and south ends of Saint Andrew Island. They enlarged the school on May Mount hill (next to the First Baptist Church). They charged tuition although children at these schools were generally from homes that could not afford to pay the expenses. For many years the students from Baptist schools were not invited to participate in the Independence Day parades and festivities; neither were they favored when seeking governmental scholarships to study on the continent. There was a severe pressure put on non-Catholics to make them surrender to the Capuchin order's mandates.

Since the arrival of the Capuchin order there has been a continuous persecution of islanders to obtain their complete colombianization and conversion to Catholicism. It grew worse in 1953 and 1954. In 1953 Baptist missionaries were forced to abandon their work on both Saint Andrew and Old Providence. This was due to a new missions agreement signed on January 29, 1953, between Pope Pius XII and the acting President of Colombia, Roberto Urdaneta Arbelaez. This accord further restricted all Christian activities other than Roman Catholic in the areas designated as mission areas. On March 1, 1954, Prefect Friar Gasper de Orijuela, chief prelate of the Catholic Mission on Saint Andrew ordered the three Baptist and two Adventist schools to be closed. He charged that they were not following the curriculum of the ministry of education. The result was that almost six hundred children were out of school with no way to continue their education (Turnage, 1977).

Turnage drew the conclusion that "the Treaty of Missions, supposedly signed to facilitate Christianization of the pagan Indians [in colonial times]," was used in an effort to eradicate the protestant community on the islands of Old Providence and Saint Andrew. A great deal of tension developed between Catholics and non-Catholic groups, because of the power to direct and supervise education according to the agreement signed by the missions granted to the Apostolic Prefecture. Moreover, native islanders of both Saint Andrew and Old Providence were being persecuted and harassed in every aspect. Things became so critical that in 1953 there were confrontations between natives and immigrants from the Andean region of Colombia due to the forceful spread of Catholicism and the Spanish language by the Capuchin order.

In 1956, there was a conflict between the Baptist school and Father Eligio de Aguadasuar-Cuasiparroco, who was the Inspector of Education in Old Providence. He charged that the Baptist schoolteachers were not capable of doing their job because they had no pedagogical training. Faced with such adversity, the pastor at that time, Rev Bert W. Archbold had his mother-in-law, Mrs. Gutierrez, who was a pedagogue, take over the Baptist school to solve the problem. Thence the school avoided persecution. This event was really a confusing situation for the people who had been living a peaceful religious life, according to their belief. It was something similar to the persecution of the churches throughout the first century in antiquity. The Colombian state was like a ferocious beast pursuing its prey without mercy. The people felt helpless without any means whatsoever of defending themselves from such monstrosity. It was like living in hell. The people were treated like wild animals; pictures were shown of children with uncombed hair with a bow bone in it as to mean that they were not civilized people and therefore they would have to be tamed. The fact was that for the Colombian state, these people would have to come under their ruling conditions, "do or die."

Today, everybody can surely say that the plans of domination of the Capuchin order and the Colombian government have been completed in approximately 80%. After they won the battle raising high their banner, many others came in later to make religion a business instead of a mission to win souls. We can sum up as follows the main features of this overall process:

a) The new religious leaders suppressed English in both its standard and Creole variants.

b) Religions different from Roman Catholicism were persecuted and treated contemptuously.

c) A national and religious ideology was forced upon the people.

d) A new language was imposed on the people with unjust punishment and degradation.

c) The people were considered by their persecutors as uncivilized and were treated as such.

f) Non-Catholics were displaced in their own territory, especially when seeking jobs.

g) Governmental pressures and persecutions were exerted strictly against non-Catholics.

Before closing this section, the author of this book would like to refer to an incident that occurred in Saint Andrew Island not long after the arrival of the Reverend Noel Julian La Rosa Gonsalves, commonly known as Reverend Gonsalves; an episode that should never be forgotten but rather be highlighted in all histories of the Islands. Loren Turnage relates the following:

ATTEMPT AGAINST REV. GONSALVES

Some day before the San Luis celebration, the committee of festivities invited pastor Gonsalves to be one of the speakers, along with Doctor Simon Howard, an attorney. Gonsalves accepted and prepared an address entitled "The Onward March of Democracy." On the special day, a large group including the Intendente and his wife and several officials were assembled. Dr. Howard spoke first, followed by Rev. Gonsalves' speech on democracy.

During the fifteen-minutes presentation, dealing with such a popular subject, the patriotic feeling of the crowd, and the emotions exploded with a loud, prolonged applause as Gonsalves ended with the words: "As you gaze upon the red which typifies the blood shed for Colombia's Independence, remember that it says to you: "Be brave!" Long live the sovereign Republic of Colombia!

Before the applause had died out, the Intendente invited Gonsalves to accompany him to the banquet hall. They entered together. Around the large table distinguished guests were seated. The Intendente took the seat at the head of the table, and next to him was his wife's seat. To Gonsalves' surprise, he indicated the seat next to him. The glasses were filled with wine and the Intendente rose with the dignity of a chief executive to propose a toast to the President. The glasses were lifted in unison. Gonsalves, being a total abstainer, raised his glass, but did not drink the wine. This was observed by the Intendente, who became enraged. He blurted out in a furry, "What sort of foolish religion is this that you cannot drink to the health of the President of the Republic?" Meekly, Gonsalves replied that he was sorry but that he did not drink wine, even at home. The doctor (lawyer) Abel Francis, seated next to Gonsalves, interposing himself to relieve the tension, said, "Oh, that's all right; I'll drink it for him." He gulped the contents of the pastor's glass and sat down. A few moments later the doctor uttered a strange shriek and fell to the floor screaming and cursing. Soon he was without control, and several men had to subdue him. Pandemonium broke out. In the commotion, Gonsalves slipped out and had his chauffeur drive him to his home on the hill.

The doctor who had drunk the poison intended for the pastor hung between life and death for three full weeks, but he lived. It was never known who put the poison in the pastor's glass.

Another attempt was made a few nights later, which showed the pastor and his people how serious the enemies were. One night upon leaving the Sunday evening service in North End, six men of the congregation closed around Gonsalves and said they would accompany him home that night. No reason was given. When the car reached the bushy part of the Perry Hill section, from each side of the road two men with raincoats over their heads rushed to the car. Discovering that the car was crowded with several men, they hastily retreated. The pastor's many questions were answered only by, "Oh, that's all right. They are endeavoring to frighten somebody." The pastor was seen inside his bolted door before the car left. Perhaps some of the men stayed around the house all night.

That same night Dr. Simon Howard was attacked by three men disguised and armed with slabs driven through with large nails who jumped on him in the dark. In the vicious attack, the lawyer's hands were broken, his head and body were terribly lacerated and punctured, before the people heard him and came running to his rescue, his son declared.

Neither the mayor, the police chief, the municipal Judge nor the Intendendente Jorge Tadeo Lozano, could find the attackers of Dr. Howard. However, the circuit judge came to the island, he studied the case and made four arrests, but the men were exonerated. Dr. Howard gradually got worse and it was necessary to take him to Panama to save his life. The circuit judge, who had done the investigation, became mysteriously ill and was taken to Panama where he died in the hospital. It was rumored that he had died of poisoning. (Turnage 1977: 59-60)

Violence was not known in the islands before these events, and this can be confirmed by consulting Father Cristobal Canales' description of the people in Old Providence. He was one of the first Capuchin priests to arrive there. He said:

The people are very peaceful and naturally honest. But the worst thing is that these natives are in every way Yankees. This explains their cold nature, which we shall change with our apostolate to make them love Colombia and the Catholic religion." He even described their "cold nature" by saying: "No-one comes, not even one young man, to help with the mass." He continued: "All the Colombians who have visited me, were very nice and loving everywhere and mostly with us. Only the Colombians speak Spanish and the islanders speak English. (*50 años de misión cumplida* 1976)

This declaration by the missionary gives the natives more proof that they were forced into an imposed culture, causing division among themselves. In other words, the islanders have been abused all along the line until this present time. Even when religious persecution on these islands is not as it used to be since non-Catholics and Catholic churches have been joining hands to proclaim the Gospel, still there are misunderstandings hidden somewhere in the corners. It is of much hope that very soon there will be a complete unity of Christian love among all those who are really redeemed by the blood of the Lamb of God regardless of their denomination.

There are incidences that cannot pass unseen or be ignored once we have complete information of plans that were studied and enforced within the years. The author of the book *50 años de misión cumplida* states that the Church did not arbitrarily come to the islands, but that it was rather an initiative of the Colombian government. No doubt it was!

What took place in the islands with the arrival of the Capuchin's order was not just an accident, it was a course of action that was already planned and was to be enforced in due time. This means that Colombian authorities had programmed all these occurrences many years before the arrival of the Capuchins as it will be analyzed on further pages.

REPORTS OF A COMMISIONER FROM BOGOTA IN 1911

Santiago Guerrero, who was a commissioner sent from Bogotá to the islands of Saint Andrew and Old Providence in 1911 to study the situation of the islands and their inhabitants, made a most despicable and disrespectful report about the islands and their peoples to the Colombian minister of government.[14] In his report he degraded the people in an unforgiveable manner. The commissioner stated:

---

[14] Archivo General de la Nación, *Informe del prefecto al Ministro del Interior.* Sección 1. República Ministerio de Gobierno, Sección 1, Tomo 696. Quotations of documents originally written in Spanish are translated by the author (N.E.).

On Saint Andrew as well as Old Providence there does not exist anything that constitutes civilization and progress of the people. Everything there is submerged in a deep and lamentable backwardness. Those islands do not even merit the name of town, because they are not. The most unfortunate town among us has streets regularly designed, schools directed by teachers more or less competent, a government building, a Catholic Church and finally they have at least a cemetery. On these islands this does not even exist. Those who die there, if they are owners of land, they are buried on it. And of those who do not have, some are buried in the public highway and others at The Point, a place which does not have any kind of security and the bodies are left to the mercies of the hogs and dogs that go there to satisfy their hunger.

On the islands everything is there to be done, starting with the teaching of their inhabitants that they are Colombians, since many of them ignore this. The religion, the customs, the language, everything is absolutely contrary to ours. To observe something of the region in order to say that it belongs to Colombia, it is necessary to leave the islands, look at them from afar and confirm oneself by thinking that those lands are an integral part of our territory. But on the inside, there is nothing that shows that that land is an integrated part of our territory; there is nothing that manifests that that region belongs to Colombia since the last 109 years.

On my arrival at the archipelago I found its inhabitants, more than usual, profoundly dissatisfied and complaining about the present government of [the department of] Bolívar, that seems to have extremely applied more violent measures than was accustomed by its predecessors in governing the islands. The dissatisfaction that I refer to was perfectly justifiable according to my point of view. This was due to the increase of taxes on exportation causing the merchants to become desperate.

[...] The present archipelago of Saint Andrew is made up of the islands of Saint Andrew, Old Providence, Saint Catherine and the cays of Roncador, Serranilla, Quitasueño and some others of less importance. As it is well known, these islands, from the year 1886, constituted the Province of Providence of the Department of Bolívar, Saint Andrew being the capital. It can be said that the islands of Saint Andrew, Old Providence and Saint Catherine are those that in true, form the province, because the cays are completely abandoned.

According to reports the present population of Saint Andrew today is 3,125. The island is divided into the following sections: Saint Andrew, Sprat Bight, School House, Rock Hole, Point, San Luis, Harmony Hall, Cove, Brooks Hill, Barrack, May Mount, Flowers Hill and Bay. Of these points the most important are: San Andrés for being the settlement of the authorities and near the beach; and San Louis, for being the place where the principal houses of commerce of the island are located.

Until now, there is not an agreed plan in force to outline the places where houses can be built for the islanders; and therefore, the town does not have symmetry. Each individual builds wherever he wants, having therefore the buildings widely separated so irregularly, that at present it cannot be said that there is a compact village. The vast numbers of coconut palms under which the constructions are arrayed in an elegant disorder, present at first sight a panorama of incomparable beauty.

Despite being harsh and lying in these statements, particularly concerning the dead, Santiago Guerrero somehow acted as defending counsel on certain issues. He complained against the governor of Bolívar for abusing the islanders with an exaggerated tax on the exportation of coconuts that was increased from $0.60 to $2.00 according to decree No. 487 issued at that time and approved by the governor of Bolívar. The rising of the levy was affecting the islands' merchants in such a way that they manifested their desire to be governed directly under the national government. In writing to the national government he said that he explained to the islanders that this government loves and protects them as it does with the rest of the country and its people; that the minister of government had presented to Congress in its latest session the project of law for the creation of the national intendancy in the islands, a project which not even the islanders had information about. He pointed out to the people the purposes of the project, which were to reduce taxes, to invest the money from the income tax in the archipelago, to build schools, fund Catholic missions and provide scholarships for students to go to schools in Cartagena and so forth. All this was done, he said, to show the natives that the national government looks with interest on that important region. With this report he said, "I believe I have proceeded as a Colombian and as an agent of the Government."

What is to be understood in Mr. Guerrero's expression—"The national government looks with interest on that important region"—is that as a matter of fact, its land and marine resources have always been the target of the Colombian government. But the Saint Andrewan indigenous,[15] as a people, have never

---

[15] In this book the terms "natives," "indigenous," "islanders," "raizales," and "aboriginals" refer to people that are born in the islands, that are descendants of islanders, and make part of their culture and community. The term "raizal" is used in contradistinction to other designations used for afrodescendant populations belonging to other regions of Colombia, such as "afrocolombianos," "afrodescendientes," and "negros," with the particularity that light skinned individuals with genealogies traced to the West Indian population of the islands are also, without question, regarded as raizales. On the other hand, "paña," "pañaman," and "pañawoman" refer to Spanish speaking people from the Colombian mainland (N.E.).

been of any interest to the Colombian authorities and will never be thought of as a population that is the center and soul of these islands. Therefore, it can also be understood why the people were once treated as "wild animals" and today are displaced and ill treated psychologically, spiritually, emotionally and economically.

In 1911, the newspaper *El Porvenir* from Cartagena, referred to the employees sent to Saint Andrew by the governor of Bolívar stating: "for a very long time the employees sent to the islands by the governor of Bolívar did not do anything but extort and offend the people in the islands even in their homes." One of the offenses the journal might have referred to is the incident in which the prefect went to Reverend Livingston's home with Mr. Forero Herrera, who served as interpreter, to press the pastor not to sign the petition for the creation of the island intendancy and therefore influence his parishioners to also abstain from signing it. The secretary of the prefecture also did the same with some of the "important people" of the islands. Mr. Julius Robinson in Old Providence, who was the mayor at that time, was also discriminated and fired from his job for writing a congratulation to the director of the recently organized newspaper *The Searchlight*. A similar case took place with Mr. Cleveland Hawkins, who was a schoolteacher.

Since the nineteenth century, the indigenous people of these islands have been complaining and begging the national government to better their conditions. However, the government has never and will never do anything on behalf of our people. As proof of that event the author encloses a copy of a petition of complaint to the national government in 1912. With respect to the creation of the intendancy there is no doubt that Mr. Guerrero really had a hand in it. There was a letter sent to the minister of government in Bogotá, from Cartagena, on the 17th of January 1912 by Mr. Rodrigo Sanchez, who was secretary of government in Cartagena, stating that "Mr. Santiago Guerrero, who was in the island as an inspector of census, was working along with Mr. Eugenio Garnica collecting signatures from the natives of the islands, asking the national government to establish an intendancy of the islands, with the pretext that the governors of Bolívar had never attended to the interests of this province properly." Be whatever this was, in the people's concept, it was to be for better and not for worse. Finally it was created and approved successfully. A copy of the petition is hereby reproduced, in English.

Providence, March 26th, 1912.

The Municipal Council of Providence

CONSIDERING:

1-That for 26 years these islands have been constituted into a Province of the Department of Bolívar;
2-That during this long interval of time the Government of Bolívar has not done absolutely anything for their welfare or progress notwithstanding the substantial sums in American gold they have produced and that have increased the departmental treasury;
3-That due to the awful administration these islands have had from the Government of Bolívar, a general dissatisfaction prevails among its inhabitants; and
4-Interpreting faithfully the unanimous feeling and wishes of the people it represents

DECIDES:

1-To respectfully ask the Congress of the Republic, through his Excellency the President of the Republic, the approval of the project of law presented by the Minister of Government in the past year creating a National Intendancy and
2-To congratulate his Excellency the President of the Republic and the Minister of government for having presented spontaneously the alluded project to the consideration of Congress in their last session.

TO BE COMMUNICATED

The vice president
Alejandro G. Archbold

The President
Cleveland H. Hawkins

Vocal
Franklin Jr. Howard

Vocal
Ephraim Archbold

Vocal
John Archbold

Members of the board of directors

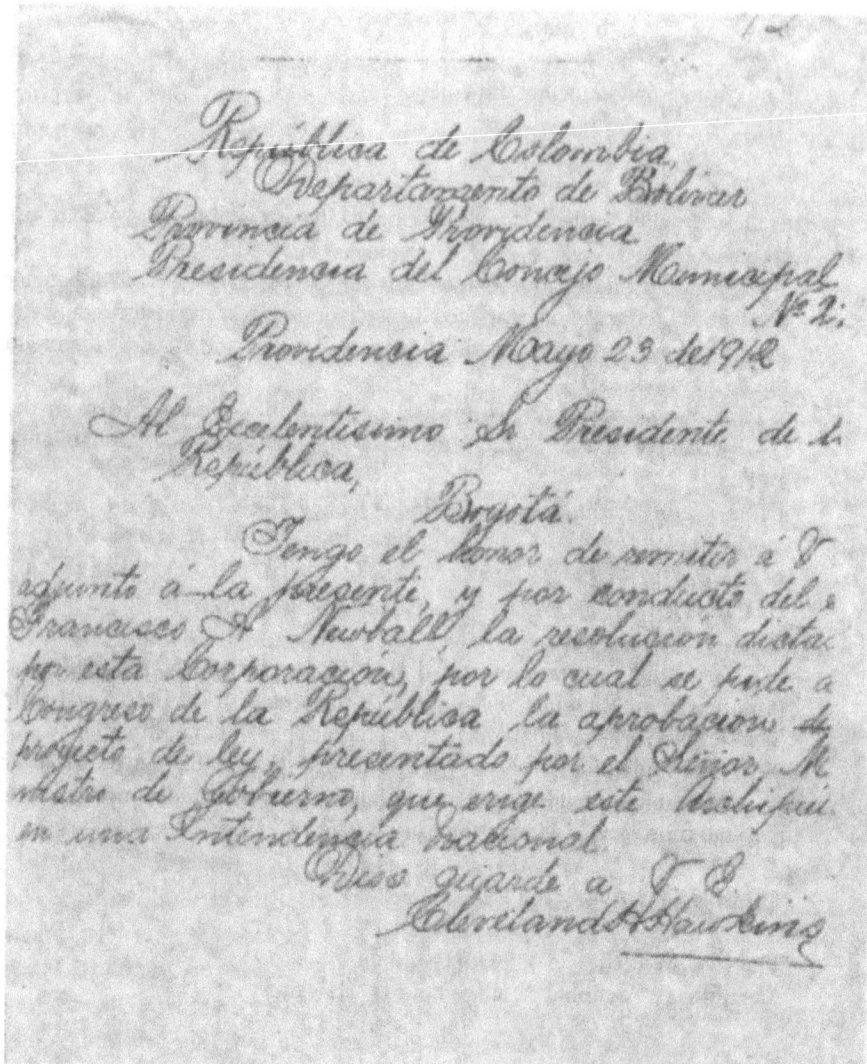

The following is a facsimile copy of the cover letter sent to the President of the Nation by Cleveland H. Hawkins, President of the Municipal Council.

Republic of Colombia Department of Bolivar

The Province of Providence
Presidency of the Municipal Council No.2:

Providence, May 23, 1912

To his Excellency Mr. President of the Republic,
Bogotá:
I have the honor to forward to you and by means of Mr. Francisco A. Newball, the presently enclosed resolution approved by this Corporation, in which it asks the Congress of the Republic for the approval of the project of law presented by the Minister of Government to establish this Archipelago as a National Intendancy.

May God Protect You,

Cleveland Hawkins

What changes and benefits did the established Intendancy bring to the archipelago of Saint Andrew, Old Providence and Ketlena?

The wonderful islands of Saint Andrew, Old Providence and Ketlena that were in the 17th century inhabited by English Puritans, were now coveted by a nation that would soon be using not only intellectual strategies, but also force of power to suppress the primitive Christian faith and the popular language of a small group of inhabitants who inherited them from their masters. Due to the domineering desire of the Colombian state to transform the very souls of these inhabitants there was a continuous struggle and desperation in the mind of the rulers. One of the observations and recommendations made by the education commissioner was that the creation of new schools and the immigration of Spanish teachers to control such schools were indispensable. Therefore he recommended printing a little textbook in Spanish and English to distribute freely among the adults and children so that they would learn the Spanish language quickly. The little textbook was never printed and will never be, throughout the ages.

Even when Guerrero mentioned that the teachers were incompetent to manage the two public schools in the islands, it was not because they did not know how to teach, but rather, because those native teachers were not versed in the Spanish language, since most of them were of West Indies culture as the rest of the population. On the other hand, he was worried about those students of better economical conditions who traveled, at the expense of their families or other benefactors, to the United States of America in order to further their studies, with serious detriment to the general patriotic feeling.

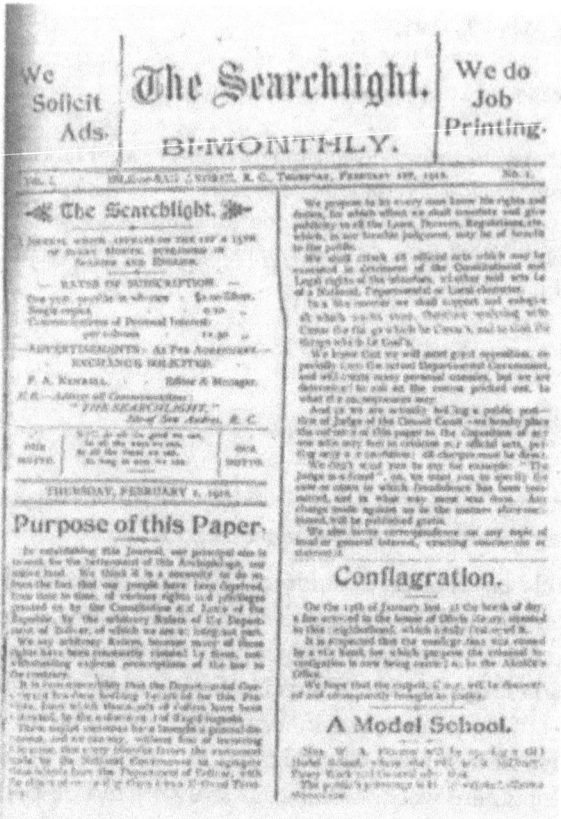

There was a director of the schools in Old Providence, one Romero from Cartagena who, according to Guerrero, was very ignorant even when he thought himself to be very illustrious and competent. Guerrero said that such teacher did not even know the territorial division of the country. On the other hand, Mr. Guerrero approved of Mr. Alejandro J. Archbold's capacity, who was a teacher at the school in Rocky Point. He also recognized the cultural background of Mr. Cleveland Hawkins, who was also a businessman and a schoolteacher. Another person who was also recommended was Mr. Francisco A. Newball, a man of recognized elucidation who knew the Spanish language perfectly and had also performed the duties of various important posts in Saint Andrew, such as circuit judge. Moreover he was elected deputy to the assembly of Bolívar for the province of Saint Andrew. He was also the founder and editor of the local newspaper *The Searchlight*, which was the first newspaper published in Saint Andrew Island.

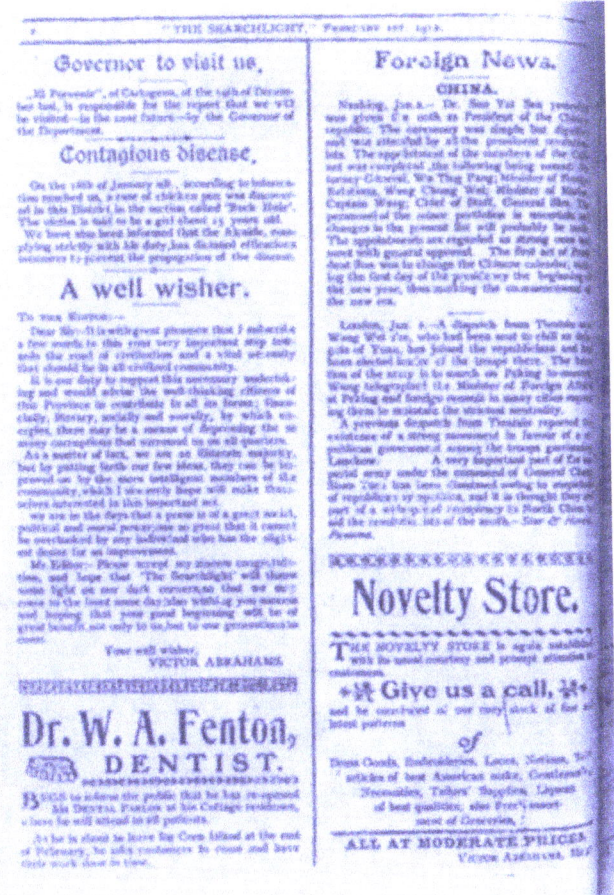

Many others were also recommended for secondary public services because of their outstanding capacity, even when not versed in the Spanish language, such as: Felix A. Howard, Polidoro Martínez, Victor Abrahams, Joshua Pomare, Ephraim E. Archbold, Lorenzo D. Howard, Daniel J. Bent, Oswald L. Robinson, Sam A. Newball, John James, Alejandro Archbold, Messhel Forbes, Federico Archbold, William E. Taylor, Julio Robinson, Wallace Hayes, Holfermes Forbes, William B. Forbes, M. Velez Forbes, Persival R. Robinson, Floran C. Macariz, Enríque Vélez and Arthur Ramírez. The real problem was not that there were no islanders to do the job. It was just a complicated situation for a national government that breathed anxiety for a land possessed by Afro-Caribbeans, who in the government's mind represented only an obstacle to complete control of the territory.

IRVING HOWARD HOWARD

These people who inhabited the islands, speaking a language that was not the Spanish language, who professed a religion that was not the Colombian religion soon became a thorn in the nation's shoe that was to be removed in the near future with discreet tactics in a very cunning way. It is very curious to see all the strategies that were put in practice. Mr. Guerrero did not just stop there, with the schools, but he also advised the government to employ islanders on Navy ships, based on their skills as seamen, so that through such means they could be colombianized. He mentioned Federico Archbold, captain of the ship "El Cartagena," who became fluent in the Spanish language. He was a man from Old Providence, contented with his job, but he left because of low payment. "He now resides in Old Providence," said Mr. Guerrero. He also insisted that a garrison of the military or the police be established to confront the serious problems that arise each day with risk of losing the islands. "Because of the insatiable grudge with the Yanquees, they are always ready to take possession of the islands, and since some time ago they have been looking forward to the opportune moment to do so. Frequently American newspapers talk about the necessity and convenience to establish a U.S. naval base in the islands since their positions are admirable for their closeness to the Panama Canal"—said Mr. Guerrero.

In tune with Mr. Guerrero's prejudiced concept concerning native abilities, the Saint Andrewans were to be considered "inept." It is unfortunate that islanders were tarnished like this by a government official like Guerrero. For this reason it is of great importance to include in this section the accomplishments of Mr. Irving Howard, a native from the island of Old Providence, inasmuch as they are recognized by records of the Ministry of War in 1937, which state the following:

> IRVING HOWARD. Was born on Old Providence Island.
> Parents: James Bartolome Howard and María J. Howard.
> Date: December 9th, 1905.
> Married: With Elvira Soto de Howard.
> Children: Henry, Olga, Irving, Mariany, María Stella.
> Descendant of Benjamin Odel Howard.

He was admitted to the Air Force in the decade of the 1930's . He died in the decade of the 50's. He was an aircraft designer and a competitive pilot (1930-1940); he designed the famous Howard-DGA airplane in Texas, U. S. A.

In the decade of the 1940's, he was on board of the "Catalina 613," commanded by the chief of the squadron of transport for the National Air Force Rafael Valdés Tabera, commissioned by the National Government to study the route from the interior of the country to Saint Andrew and Old Providence in order to find a better way of approaching and linking those isolated regions of the country. On board the Catalina were: Lieutenant Antonio Mejia, one of the most experienced and most skillful pilots of the F.A.C. (Colombian Air-Force), who was piloting the airplane; Lieutenant Luis Casablanca, who was assistant of the headquarters of the squadron of transport; Sub-lieutenant Max Camargo; Captain John Carroll from the Air Mission of the U.S.A.; Lieutenant Vesto Taylor, official of the infantry, a native from Old Providence; navigator Alférez Gómez, from the base in Cali; radio operator Sánchez and the mechanic Germán Londoño, and Rodrigo Salas; Irving Howard and John Archbold (also natives of Old Providence) from the technical class of the military aviation. All flew without setback leaving from the base of Madrid (Bogotá, Cundinamarca) to Soledad, Barranquilla and after four hours hydroplaned on Saint Andrew harbor. (Summary taken from the Documentary Center of the Bank of the Republic, Saint Andrew Branch.)

President Olaya Herrera asked that Irving Howard join the crew of the presidential airplane, because the Providencian spoke English as a native language, so he could practice English with him on international flights.

Captain Howard joined the Air Force on the 1st of January, 1935. He was promoted on June 1st 1935 as 1st mechanic. He retired from the institution according to resolution no. 142 on the 1st of January 1949, due to relative and permanent disability.

The fear of losing the islands has always obsessed the Colombian government and is best expressed by officials like Commissioner Guerrero, so there is never lack of material regarding that issue. The illustrious commissioner analyzed the physical and spiritual atmosphere of the islands and, unsurprisingly, he was overwhelmed by the percentage of non-Catholics. He spoke of some 88 Catholics as opposed to 3,036 Protestants. He asserted, "The islands are given to Protestantism." He recognized Rev. T.V. Livingston to be an honorable man who was looked upon with respect and authority. He also mentioned that Rev. Livingston had a liking for the American Nation, undoubtedly because he was educated there and because with that Nation he also had the greater part of his business. So Guerrero said: "He has a close link of union with that country that did so much harm to Colombia, from which new abuses must be expected." To the above statement, he added, "It would make sense to establish a Catholic mission in Saint Andrew only if it could be directed by Colombian priests who can speak English." He thought maybe at least this way religion could be guaranteed to preserve national union.

As it can be seen, one of Guerrero's worries was the close relationship between the islands and the United States. He apparently saw as a threat the fact that Rev. Livingston was an influential leader who was married to an American woman, concluding that the islands should be possessed by sufficient colombianizing forces to eradicate anti-Colombian influences tied to the United States, a country considered to be, if not an enemy, potentially detrimental to Colombia after it "took" Panama in 1903. Nevertheless, Mr. Guerrero did not mention eradicating the English language. He rather suggested the immigration of Colombian priests with sufficient knowledge of English who could easily understand and be understood by the local people. He seemed to realize (at least on this occasion) that if the people were treated with some measure of dignity and respect there wouldn't be so much discontent and resentment against the Colombian government.

When Mr. Guerrero was sent to Saint Andrew, it was not so much to find out about the needs of the people, but rather to observe and analyze their idiosyncrasy in order to figure out the best way to accomplish a complete colombianization or some form of population substitution if it was necessary. However, drastic measures would not have been to Colombia's convenience because of the close relationship that the islands sustained with the United States and for plain fear of angering the country that had had the power to just "take" Panama, a big chunk of the national territory, by backing separatist

Panamanians. Therefore, other strategies would have to be devised to acquire a complete dominion over the people and the islands.

To everyone who visited the islands, their civility was as evident as light. Mr. Guerrero also admired such civility when he talked about the order and seriousness that reigned during the voting for the Municipal Council in Old Providence. He also admired the response given by Mr. Julius Robinson, Mayor of Old Providence, to the Governor of Bolívar, Sr. Gómez Recuero when he was asked to inform his political affiliation to the prefecture. Mr. Robinson stated: "Fortunately here among us, the political passion has not entered to divide us. The only political affiliation we have is to be honest workers." What great contrast between island rulers in those days and the rulers of today! Was it really worth changing such a culture for the imposed one? Was having lost such civil rulers the achievement of colombianization?

It is clear that from Mr. Guerrero's visit to the islands that his struggle and push was for the Colombian government to hasten the conversion of the people to Catholicism and the imposition of the Spanish language. So, from this perspective, it was clear why he felt fulfilled in 1926 with the presence of the Capuchin order.

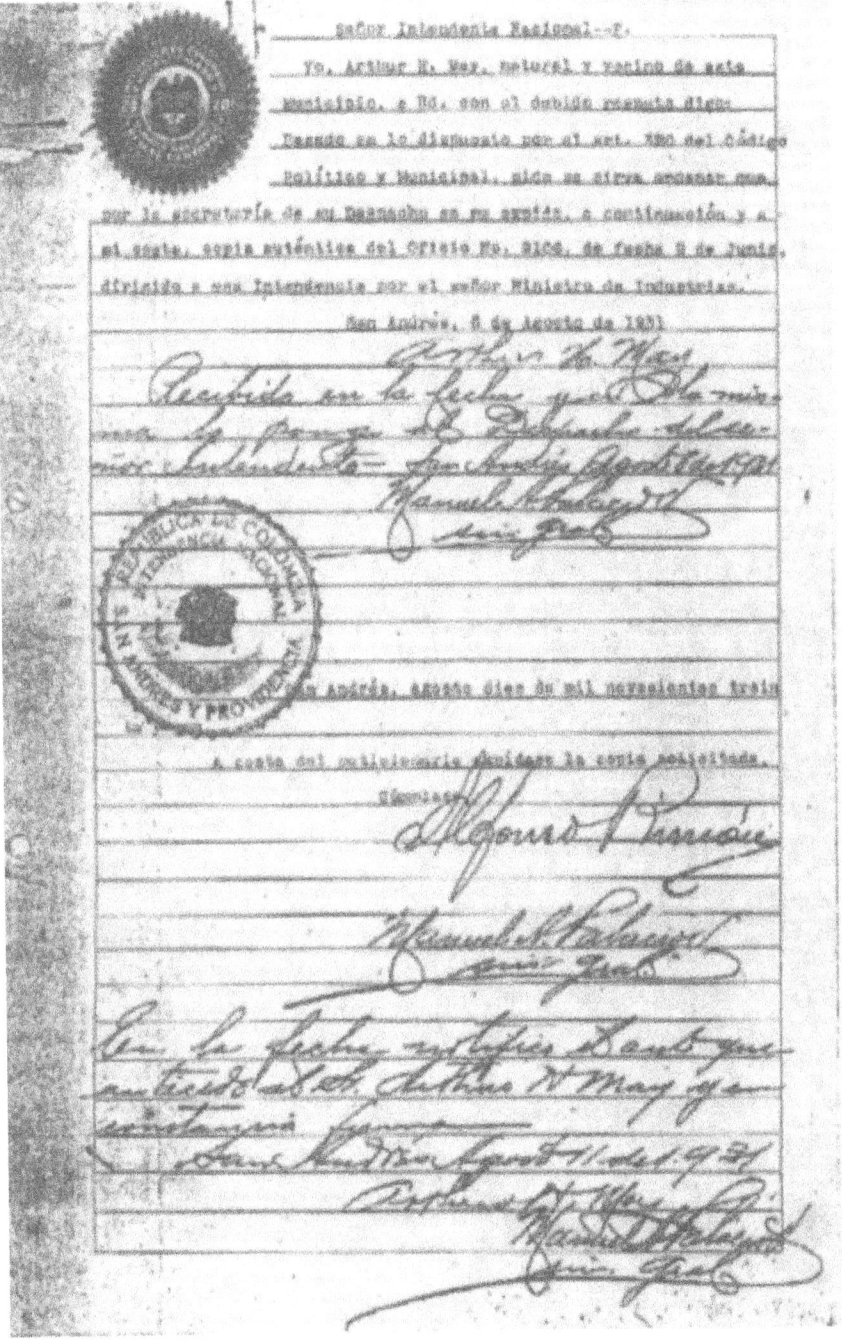

En cumplimiento a lo ordenado por el Señor Intendente en el auto de fecha cinco de los corrientes recaído a la solicitud del Señor Arthur M. Hay paso a expedir la copia solicitada que a la letra dice: "República de Colombia.--Ministerio de Industrias.--Departamento Agricultura.--Sección entomología.--Número 2.106.--Bogotá junio 9 de 1.931.--Señor Intendente de las Islas de San Andrés y Providencia.--En relación con la plaga de las coqueras que ha aparecido en San Andrés,tengo el gusto de manifestarle que este Despacho,apenas tuvo conocimiento de la existencia en Trinidad,de un insecto llamado Criptognatha nodicera,que tiene la cualidad de destruir los parásitos-escamas que destruyen las palmeras,comisionó al Consul de Colombia en esa Isla, para que, asesorándose de un entomólogo, averiguara la mejor manera de recoger y remitir al Archipiélago el aludido insecto.--En relación con esta Nota,el Consul en TRINIDAD,nos hizo la comunicación que le transcribo en seguida:--"Señor Ministro de Industrias.--Dep.de Agricultura.--Bogotá.-Me acuerdo con lo prometido a S.S.en mi nota N°45,de 7 del mes en curso,tengo el honor de enviar a S.S., junto con el presente oficio,la nota N°C.A.252,de 13 de este mes,firmada por el Profesor H.A.Ballou,Comisionado de agricultura del Colegio Imperial de Agricultura Tropical, relacionada con un cable reciente de S.S.para este Consulado,el cual me fue entregado anteayer,con un retardo inexplicable de cinco días.--Como lo verá S.S.en la referida nota,del Profesor Ballou,la recolección de los insectos entomófagos denominados Criptognatha nodicera y su envío a Cartagena,no es un asunto tan sencillo como lo presupone el citado cable de S.S.de 7 del presente mes,pues requiere el contrato de los servicios de un entomólogo que los recoja,cultive y lleve a su destino,cuidándolos en el tránsito,con un gasto total que el profesor Ballou calcula en cuatro cientas libras esterlinas (£400),además de la venida de una goleta especial que los conduzca a San Andrés y Providencia.Como el viaje de las goletas es muy incierto,por estar sujeto a muchas contingencias,me permito insinuar a S.S.la idea de contratar aquí una goleta que tenga motor,lo cual la independiza de la acción de los vientos en caso de que le sean contrarios.--Por carecer de autorizaciones expresas no he hablado todavía con Mr.W.L.Cupby,el entomólogo indicado por el Profesor Ballou para llevar a cabo la recolección y transporte de los insectos a referencia.--El presente oficio va por vapor alemán "Teutonia",que sarpa hoy,recomendado al señor Comandante del Resguardo de Puerto Colombia,para que dicho funcionario lo remita a S.S.por hidravión.--Soy de usted muy atento,(firmado) Francisco Palacio Fortus--Consul de Colombia en Trinidad.-".--Como debido a las actuales circunstancias fiscales el Gobierno está imposibilitado para hacer,por el momento,estos gastos, este Despacho pide a usted haga un llamiento a todos los interesados en la industria de las coqueras,para obtener de ellos,ya que esto redunda en su propio favor,paguen los gastos que ocasione la introducción del benéfico insecto a las coqueras infestadas de San Andrés,estos gastos juntos valen aproximadamente seiscientas libras esterlinas (£600).--Si usted lograra interesar a los cultivadores de cocos a la realización de esta empresa,y se reuniera el dinero necesario,el Ministerio se encargaría de realizar prontamente este negocio.--Embarcaré a usted envío lo más próximo posible a ese Departamento,el informe del entomólogo doctor Nateck, sobre las plagas de las coqueras de la Isla;y si acaso se encontrara allí bien un concepto sobre la eficacia del entomófago Criptognatha nodicera en el combate contra las escamas o peste de las palmas.--Soy de usted muy atento,--(fdo) Carlos Durán Castro.--Jefe del Departamento de Agricultura.-"

Es fiel copia de su original y la expide a favor del interesado en una foja útil y escrita,hoy once de Agosto de mil novecientos treinta y uno.

In compliance to what has been ordered by the Intendant in his "auto" of the [illegible] instant, as a result of a petition forwarded by Mr. Arthur [illegible] May, I [illegible] despatch the copy solicited which goes as follows: "Republic of Colombia.- Office of the Ministry of Industry.- Department of Agriculture.- Section of [illegible].- No. 2106.- Bogotá, June [illegible], 1931.- Intendant of the Islands of San Andrés and Providence.- Relative to the plague of the cocoa-nut palms that has appeared in San Andrés, I take pleasure in manifesting to you that [illegible] has recently had the knowledge of the existence of an insect called "Cryptognatha nodiceps," in Trinidad, that has the power to destroy the [illegible] that destroy the palms, and has commissioned the Colombian Consul in that island to consult an Entomologist so as to discover the best means to gather and to remit the alluded insect to the Archipelago.- With regards to this note, the Consul in Trinidad communicated with us, and stated as follows: "Minister of Industry, Department of Agriculture, Bogotá.- In accordance to what has been promised to his Lordship in my official letter No. [illegible] of the [illegible] instant, I have the honor in remitting to his Lordship, jointly with this official letter, the letter No. C.4, [illegible] of the 15th instant, signed by Professor [illegible] Salleu, Commissioner of Agriculture of the Imperial College of Tropical Agriculture, letter that bears relation with a recent cablegram from his Lordship to that Consulate, and which was delivered to me day before yesterday with an unexplainable delay of five days.- His Lordship will observe [illegible] Prof. [illegible]'s letter that the accumulating of the entomophagus insects called "Cryptognatha nodiceps," and their shipping to Cartagena is necessary, as is presumed according to your cablegram of the 7th instant, it requires an Entomologist who will gather them together, procreate and carry them to their destination, taking care of them during the transfer, with a [illegible] expense, according to Prof. [illegible]'s calculation, of four hundred ([illegible]) pounds sterling, besides a special vessel to take them to San Andrés and Providence. As the voyages of sailing vessels are uncertain, you would allow me the privilege to recommend the idea of contracting a motor-vessel from [illegible] which would make it independent of the action of the winds, in case of contracting.- I have not spoken as yet with Mr. [illegible], the Entomologist recommended by Prof. [illegible] to make the collection and the transporting of the insects in reference, due from my deficiency of the proper authorization to do so.- The present official letter goes by the German steamship [illegible] which sails to-day, recommended to the Chief of the Port of Puerto [illegible], so that he may forward it to his Lordship by air-mail.- I am Yours [illegible] servant, (signed) Francisco Palacio Portus, Colombian Consul in Trinidad.- As the Government is unable to shoulder such expenses, for the time being, from the actual financial circumstances, this Despatch asks that [illegible] call on all the interested ones in the cocoanut industry, as this is [illegible] favour, so that they may pay the expenses of the importing of the beneficial insect to the cocoanut-palms infested in San Andrés; all these [illegible] amount approximately six hundred (£ 600) pounds sterling. [illegible] would be fortunate enough as to interest the cocoanut planters in the [illegible] of this enterprise, and the money necessary should be accumulated, [illegible] would undertake the fostering of this matter immediately.- I therefore [illegible] you to remit to this Despatch, at your most early convenience, the [illegible] the Entomologist, Mr. [illegible], on the plague of the cocoanut in the Island, [illegible] he is still there, get his concept with regards to the [illegible] of the entomophagus "Cryptognatha nodiceps" on the combating of the [illegible] pests of the palms.- I am, Yours truly. (sgnd) Carlos Durán Castro, [illegible] the Department of Agriculture."

This is a true copy taken from its original, and I hereby despatch it [illegible] of the interested party, in one well written sheet, to-day [illegible] of [illegible] the year one thousand nine hundred and thirty-one.

(sgnd) Manuel A. Palacio,

Secretary-General.

Big Commerce

What Mr. Guerrero did not mention in his comments was how the people lived independently through their commerce and related activities. There were merchants in the island of Saint Andrew who were very prosperous, like for example, the Rubinstein and Sons Stock-Company managed by Arthur May, the largest in the island, which was located at the Gaff (known today as San Luis). They had their own currency with the company's name inscribed. This money was not used to trade with in other countries but was perfectly used for shopping in the island just as the Balboa is used in Panama. This store or mega market would supply other shops in the island, especially in the North End section.

After the exportation of coconuts had reached up to 14 million a year, a disease that had killed practically all the coconut palms on the Atlantic coast of Colombia, also contaminated the island of Saint Andrew by means of cargoes, especially yam and potatoes which were packed in discarded packages and containers. In 1929, this disease hit the island so hard that within approximately two years most of the islands' coconut palms were destroyed. In 1931, Arthur May made a petition to the government in Cartagena for help, but no help was offered. Store owners who benefited from Rubenstein and Sons's activities were Julio E. Gallardo, Alejandro Rankin, Bernard Rigneir, Jay Lung, Terence Howard, Frank Smith Edward and Pinkey Jay.

The Free Port

Was the free port just a coincidence or the fulfillment of a plan?

Doctor Dilia Robinson, a sociologist, in her study "The Other Face of the Tourist Paradise"(1974), states that due to the violence unleashed in the interior of the country in the forties, the national government forgot Saint Andrew and Old Providence. So much so that the Saint Andrewans, desperate because of the difficult moment its economy and people were going through, decided to join another country. Faced with this situation, the central government decided to occupy itself with Saint Andrew and this is why on the 14th of November 1953, the President, Lieutenant General Gustavo Rojas Pinilla, personally visited the islands and announced the creation of a free port. Whatever was the immediate cause of this impetuous visit and announcement, overall it worked as part of the plan drawn by the national government. Upon the president's arrival in Old Providence there were no hotels on the islands. He stayed at Mr. Victor Ray Howard's home for 24 hours before returning to Saint Andrew. After returning to Bogotá the President appointed and nominated Maximiliano Rodríguez Pardo, a man from the Andean region, as military intendant of Saint Andrew, Old Providence and Ketlena. At that time the Caja Agraria in Saint Andrew was the only bank. However, due to increased commerce allowed by the free port the Banco Popular was also established there. Before the arrival of General Gustavo R. Pinilla the Veinte de Julio was the only real street in North End, Saint Andrew.

The free port was initially believed to be of great benefit to the natives but, unfortunately, it turned out to be to the contrary. The author of this book would venture to say that no one really knew what a free port was about, or the consequences it would have brought. In one way or another it has brought condemnation to the islands and their occupants. Prejudice toward the native population and attempts at its exclusion, translated into historical, political and administrative neglect have thwarted the development of a proper free port economy.

From the beginning of the 1920's the Colombian government has purportedly been making efforts to bring about the political and economic integration of the archipelago into the nation. These efforts, however, do not come with a real investment in the people, but have included attempts to have islanders abandon their traditions, language and religion in order to replace them with a supposedly Colombian identity that really resembles that of the Spanish *conquistadors*. When Rojas Pinilla spoke of the free port maybe some, or most of the people who were harassed by customs officers whenever the merchandise came from Colón, Panama, thought it would be a relief to them. Many islanders working in Colon in those days used to send certain things to their families or relatives. Products like corned beef, ham, yellow cheese, smoked sausage, other canned stuffs and also clothing. Many times the boxes containing the merchandise were torn and the articles stolen by custom officers that behaved like real pirates arguing that the stuffs were illegal. (But it was legal to satisfy their greed.) Then, hearing of the free port most of the islanders perhaps thought of a complete relief from those bandits who were living from the people's merchandises. Nevertheless, in hindsight, it is obvious that the free port has caused much more damage than the customs officers who ransacked the merchandise in those days.

THE DOWNFALL

The downfall of Saint Andrew and Old Providence is due to the abuse of the national government and the ignorance of the natives. These two elements come from way back in the past. The scripture says, "Our parents ate the grapes and set our teeth on edge." It is stated that when the Spaniards found America's Indians, they enticed them with beautiful colored cloth, beads and "looking glasses" (mirrors) in exchange for their gold. A similar trick took place in Saint Andrew centuries after. The national government set the trap and the greedy shortsighted ones were caught. Natives cannot say that there was no one who could see or understand but they can say that bribery goes a long way and greed is its support.

"Uncle Joe," a columnist of the local press, warned everyone in the early fifties and sixties about the dangers lying ahead. However, just like today, there were many who closed their eyes and their ears. Those seeking personal interest were unconcerned about the suffering of the majority; they were not ignorant or helpless. An attempt to struggle for collective survival was made by a reduced number of conscious people, but it did not prosper because of the "idea" of Judas: "I got the money, and let the Master defend himself." It is hard to believe that natives counted with such low-minded, self-centered leaders at the time when real struggle was needed. Faces can only be seen and words of promises be heard that sometimes are only meant to reduce the sufferings of the humble and to regain the extinguishing faith. But the fact remains that no one knows what is hidden deep down in another person's mind. As Jesus once said, "they are wolves in sheep clothing." In the early nineteen fifties, when the free port was announced by President Gustavo Rojas Pinilla, the people were asked not to sell or give away their lands. Notwithstanding, the big worm of "civilization" lurched toward the islands and signs of chaos gleamed through a dark cloud of unconsciousness. The government recklessly started taking land for building roads and hotels all over the place (such as the Abacoa and the Isleño) without studies of feasibility or any assurance of economical retrieval. There are numerous roads built today that were not needed but rather contributed to the diminishing of spaces that could be used for other beneficial purposes. Many lots of land used for building the airport were never paid for. As thousands of coconut palms were destroyed for the mentioned purposes only 20 Colombian pesos (0.30 USD approximately in those days) were paid for each tree. Most of the land occupied by the government was not paid for at all. Some landowners who refused to sell their land lost it because the payment money was placed in the bank but was never drawn by the landowners. Undoubtedly, they were not informed about it.

For most people it was a total disaster while for a few others it was like awaking into a new world of eternal bliss. Saint Andrew was just stepping into the abyss of its doom. Those who were in the position of saving the island were only concerned about getting some of the fat and disregarding the rest of it. The island was under a military government and the opposition of a minority made no effect. The disorder began causing indignation in the farsighted ones but induced an ephemeral "happiness" in the shortsighted ones. The airport imposed and built by the Colombian state caused conflict among the people because some natives agreed while others did not. However, the Military Intendant, Maximiliano Rodríguez Pardo, who was nicknamed "Pa," decided that the airport was a must by hook or by crook. No one could have thought of a future disorder and panic as what is now seen at present. A part of the above mentioned coconut palms were destroyed in the North End to allow for an airport runway from sea to sea. Hotels, stores and roads sprung up creating a new commercial area.

How many of these new stores were owned by natives? Just a couple, since the original ones were replaced very soon by foreign owned business. Syrio-Lebanese immigrants owned most newly established stores. The Colombian government sponsored these and other foreigners in order to displace a Black ethnic population that it historically distrusted. Moreover, the newcomers discriminated against ethnic Blacks in order to gain racial privileges in the country of arrival. It was like the Gold Rush down there in the U.S. It was a time bomb set up to extinguish the indigenous people.

As mentioned, many islanders thought that the free port was the best thing that could ever happen to the islands. Everything seemed to be blooming; it was "spring time." However, a few prudent Saint Andrewans began to sense the danger and were protesting in different ways. Dr. Federico Newball and "Uncle Joe" saw the situation as the Pharaoh's dream with the "seven fatted cows and the seven leanly ones." For some indigenous people it was the "land flowing with milk and honey." It was like the proverb, which says, "Eat, drink, and be merry, for tomorrow you die." Foreigners began pouring in like raindrops. Colombian mainlanders, many from the Andean region of the country, foreigners from the Middle East and Europe began to arrive in significant numbers. As usually happens, not all fortune seekers were inclined to thrive on honest work.

The first hotel, the Abacoa, was built near the beach in Sprat Bight in 1955, owned by Maximiliano Rodríguez, also known as Max Rodríguez (the intendant nominated and appointed by General Gustavo Rojas Pinilla). Mr. William Taylor or Willy Taylor, as he was called, was part owner and administrator. There were only a couple of native employees, including the author of this book. At that time there were a few mainlanders who came to the island of Saint Andrew and were engaged in carpentry and masonry. Those who came from the Middle East were merchants. The discriminating racial culture fostered by the Colombian state encouraged them to assume arrogant attitudes toward the islanders. With the establishment of the free port, the newly arrived merchants sought space to set up their stores. Some of the immigrants wanted to buy land, others wanted to rent, but native people did not know what to do; so the clever foreigners offered more money than what sellers would ask for. Saint Andrewans were astonished by what seemed to them an extraordinary amount of money. Many sold their lands, others resolved to build two-story houses in order to set up residence upstairs and rent the downstairs as storefront locales. The amount they could get for such rentals seemed a fortune. The aliens prospered rapidly. Many acquired large lots of land for a relatively small amount of money.

As it was and will always be, traitors joined in cunningly deceiving their fellowmen for a few Colombian pesos. How did this happen? At the time most native landowners did not know Spanish and they used interpreters, because according to the Colombian law, starting from then, all documents had to be made in Spanish. Land with original documents made in English with measurements in yards and feet had to be put into Spanish using meters. This was a very good opportunity for the evil-minded money grabbers. Landowners renting their lands and/or locales at this point had to pay an interpreter to do the job, who in many cases was a scoundrel, even though a native. Instead of helping his fellowmen, he betrayed them by receiving money from the tenants (Turks or continentals) to distort the document. When the period of time intended by the owner was expired and he went to renew the contract, he would then discover that he had unwittingly signed a sales-document instead of a lease or rental, and unwillingly lost his property, because he did not understand the

Spanish language in which the document was made. The unfortunate native landowner surprisingly found himself on the street without land, money, nor locales to set his own business.

Eventually, control over commerce was in the hands of foreigners. I, the author of this book, feel that islanders were very much faulted for the enormous chaos they brought upon themselves, affecting everyone, because they, being on the scene at the right time, with lands in the right location, with homes, friends, relatives and sufficient money to set up better stores than those that were already in service, chose to sell their lots for what were apparently very high prices at that time. Only Willy Taylor had enough vision to start the hotel Abacoa, which became a giant in the local hotel industry. As a matter of fact, the foreign merchants were not interested in the participation of islanders in the new economic structure; they only wanted their land.

BIG SALE

It all began with the presence of some white skinned ladies who would entice, sweeten-up the islanders' ears or entertain inexperienced men seeking a nightstand. A week's pay was not enough to cope with the entertainers, therefore this also contributed to the sale of some nice pieces of land. I elaborate on this further ahead, but suffice it to say, that in those days, islanders had the opportunity to uplift themselves and go into good business, but seemingly, they were too occupied idling. Others thought of taxicabs as the most luxurious business. Some of these were the famous "wifers." On this basis some good pieces of land were also sold. The land buyers observed this and they wisely embraced the opportunity to get what they wanted. Even though there were some people who sold their lands to school their children on the mainland, Colombia, or elsewhere, most of the land was not sold for the latter purpose.

As Saint Andrewans lost their land, more and more they were displaced from the center of town or forced into lots behind the buildings erected to administrate the commercial and tourist trades. From proprietors, islanders were transformed into chambermaids and taxi drivers backing grips at the airport. Saint Andrewans became mere spectators due to the free port and rapid growth imposed by fiat. In the first stores established by the Syrio-Lebanese they employed a few natives who were soon replaced by Colombian mainlander girls upon their arrival in Saint Andrew. At that time most clients were Spanish speakers coming from Colombia, therefore storeowners wanted clerks who knew Spanish. Merchants from the Middle East residing in Saint Andrew learned Spanish quickly and attended their clients themselves with the help of a few Spanish-speaking clerks. However, soon after their wives, relatives, compatriots and so on came over to the island, many of the initial clerks were dismissed.

It was known from that time onward that most Syrio-Lebanese businessmen did not like black people and that they lived among them only because they could not have organized any sort of colony by keeping away from the indigenous population, perhaps on account of the distribution of the obtained lots, and the scarcity of space in a small island. They sorted the best lots in Las Americas, Sprat Bight and Sarie Bay (districts in the North End section used for farming in those days). All front lands were sold to foreigners with the exception of a small portion that was rented by a limited number of very prudent islanders, some of who also established their own business. For example, in those days two residential hotels were established. One in 1957, Hotel Colombia, owned by Mr. Tenneson Brown. The other in 1958, Residencia Herrera, owned by Mr. Longino Herrera and his wife Lucille de Armas. (It is exactly where the Inpescar is now located.) Mr. Tenneson Brown was a very hard-working man along with his wife. The first few continentals from Colombia that came to the island of Saint Andrew, some to work in construction, were very friendly and learned English or Creole so as to get along with the natives, since Spanish was not much spoken in the island. They associated with the natives. Maybe, their good behavior was due to concern that they would be ill-treated by the native majority if they went off tract. They joined "fair and dance" parties, a general tradition of organizing social gatherings that was still on the go, when string music was still used for dancing. However, eventually the outsiders began to take hold of more and more property and business, and as they grew in numbers, they began to push the natives aside.

Vessels Owned by Natives

This is the *V.J. Victoria*. Photo by Franklin Howard.

This is the *Persistence*. Photo by Jay Edwards.

Part of Saint Andrew Bay. Photo by Philip Philips.

Horses carrying coconuts to the docks. Photo by Philip Philips.

A seaplane anchored in Saint Andrew harbor. Photo by Philip Philips.

The *Goldfield*, picture by Jay Edward.

Captain Palmerson Coulson

A few islanders were still working on boats going to Cartagena (Colombia), Colón (Panama), and sometimes to other ports in Nicaragua. Natives owned important vessels. These were not very big, but could suffice the islands. Captain James Rankin owned The Remro (propelled by sail), the Winsco and the Princesa (both propelled by fuel engine). Some four natives from Old Providence owned The Victoria, a company boat that ended up with Victor R. Howard and James C. Howard. Captain Palmerson, who was known as Captain Pally, owned the Persistence and Deliverance, that was sold some years later to Alejandro Rankin, known as Captain Bye, also owner of the Goldfield. Julio Gallardo senior owned the Cisne. Captain John Bull (Antonio Bryan) owned the Merit-Well. Captain Ulrich Archbold owned the Arcabra. All these vessels had native owners and existed long before the free port and even some years after. Unfortunately, they began to sink one by one and were not replaced. The Arcabra's real route was Saint Andrew, Old Providence and Colón. The Goldfield only sailed between Saint Andrew and Cartagena. In 1954 a big boat was confiscated by the Colombian coastguard and was donated to the islands. The name of this boat was Providencia and her route was Saint Andrew, Cartagena and Old Providence. With the importation of more goods from Cartagena and Barranquilla, and also from Miami, more vessels were needed. Commerce began to grow and apparently the native vessels that were still on the run were insufficient. Unfortunately, by the late sixties there were not many boats owned by islanders. With the dredging of Saint Andrew harbor and the construction of a dock, bigger boats were able to enter and cargoes were easily discharged.

Long before the Colombian Navy pretended to teach the islanders anything about the seas, there were many captains from Saint Andrew and Old Providence who were great sea wolves. In fact, the Colombian Navy came into being with some of our native captains. The following list contains some of the well-known names who were real veterans traveling the seas in sail ships. Almost all of these captains have passed away.

From Old Providence

Teriso "Mico" Alamía
Celestino Alamía
Elkaina Archbold
Enrique Archbold
Jonathan Archbold
Lisandro Archbold
Marshall Archbold
Marvin Archbold
Orvil Archbold
Sheridan Archbold
Ulric Archbold
Antonio Archbold Howard
Eduardo Britton
Baldwin Britton
Antonio Bryan Sr.
Antonio Brayan Jr.
Ethalson Bryan
Kiddison Bush
Elsworth Connaly
Amos Duffis
Cleveland Hawkins
Eliseo Hawkins
Endicot Hawkins
James C. Howard Sr.

From Saint Andrew

Eric Abrahams
Victor Abrahams
Calton Bent
Henry Bradley
Palmerston Coulson
Selso Davis
Elton Faquiare
Candelario Garay
Climaco Garay
Irwin Hooker
Lowel Hooker
Rupért Hudson
Samuel May
Smuel May Jr.
Dudley May
Altimeau Martinez
Walton Martinez
John Mitchell
J. Mathewson
Enrique Palacio
Ernesto Palacio
Joshua Pomare
William Rankin
Stephen Steele

Cap. Roosevelt Robinson (1904-1980)

Cap. Orville Archbold (1902-1978)

Cap. Segasta Robinson (1898-1960)

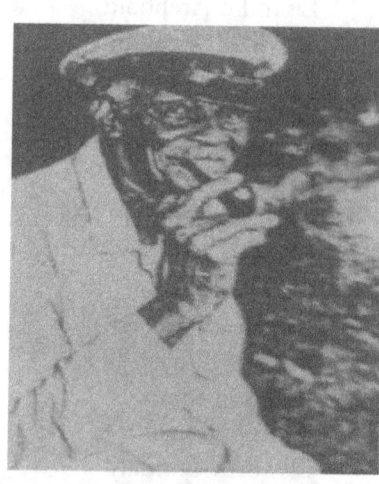
Cap. Lowell Hooker

Cap. Leopoldo Robinson (1897-1971)

Cap. Hilton Robinson (1900-1972)

Cap. Alejandro Rankin (1903-1973)

Cap. Theodore "Tim" Robinson (-1915)

Cap. Frederick Robinson (1861-1932)

Cap. Victor Abrahams (- 1913)

Cap. Franco Robinson (1901-1983)

Cap. Ulrich Archbold (1909-1997)

Clamor of the Islands

Cap. Elsworth Connoly (1893-1964)

Cap. Antonio Archbold Howard (1937-2014)

James C Howard Jr
Frederic Robinson
Oreste Howard
Willie Howard
Fenton Hooker
Alvaro Huffington
Alford May
Alban Mc.Lean Joseph
Alston Newball
Antonio Newball A.
Daniel Newball Sr.
Daniel Newball Jr.
Lemuel Newball
Maxwell Newball
Nicolas Newball
Rudolph Newball
Timothy Newball
Alejandro Rankin
James Rankin
Franco Robinson

Marthie Stephens
Henry Stephens
Eustacio Suarez
John Suarez Sr.
John Suarez Jr.
James Taylor
Barnabas Watson
Transiano Williams
Juan Suarez Howard
Daniel May Robinson
John Lever
Hilton Robinson
Leopoldo Robinson
Rosvelt Robinson
Segasta Robinson
Theodore Robinson (Tim)
Ronald Taylor Jr. (Maly)
Leon Wilson

Before the construction of the dock, native vessels used to anchor at a considerable distance from the shore and canoes or catboats took the cargo to the relatively small wharves existing then. With the facilities for big boats, a bigger volume of merchandise was brought from Miami and from Colón, Panama. After the extinction of most of the native vessels that were not replaced by their owners, foreigners brought in bigger boats. One Mr. Bello brought three boats and these vessels blocked the traffic for other boats traveling from mainland Cartagena to Saint Andrew, except for the Goldfield. There were no boats then to take Cargo to Old Providence directly from Cartagena. Arcabra was still on the Saint Andrew-Colon-Old Providence route, but never went to Cartagena. Cargoes brought from Cartagena to Old Providence were first discharged in Saint Andrew, and then put on a smaller boat going to Old Providence. At that time there were only about three small boats going to Old Providence. Later, with the loss of the Arcabra and the Betty Be (in the 1970's) all merchandise would stop first in Saint Andrew whether coming from Cartagena or Colón. In most cases these cargoes would be deposited in warehouses on the Saint Andrew docks before going to Old Providence. These extra expenses for warehouses and freight, made the cost of living much higher in Old Providence than in Saint Andrew, in fact, somewhat exaggerated.

One important exception should be mentioned. The Doña Olga III, a small boat of just about 45 tons owned by a native lady from Old Providence, Olga Henry, sometimes transported cargo directly from Cartagena to Old Providence. The problem was that no other boats could take cargo from Cartagena to Saint Andrew, since this vessel practically monopolized the route. Unfortunately, the Doña Olga III was lost in 1990 going from Cartagena to Old Providence. Two deaths were registered.

BIG ENTERTAINMENT

Before the great change that took place with the establishment of the free port, life in Saint Andrew was completely normal, quiet, relaxing, and everyone lived harmoniously with nature. A high moral standard was observed throughout the islands and Sunday was a day of rest, not a day of spree to drink rum and to make scandal as it is today. People need to be aware that not every change is for the better. Undoubtedly this has been the worst change the archipelago could ever experience. As I mentioned in previous pages, in the late 1950's and early 1960's when the Devil was setting Saint Andrew on fire, a few ladies were brought from somewhere in Colombia by one Maria Elena, who wanted to entertain some men inexperienced in the sexual life. These half white or yellow skinned ladies with curly and straight hair were enough to drive the young men and even older ones to an insatiable sex diversion. This sort of entertainment required money since it was also accompanied with drunkenness and whatever goes along with sexual activity in a cabaret or whorehouse. Even when some additional money had begun circulating in the island with the free port, most islanders were not making enough to keep up with the exorbitant demands of an uncontrollable wild life. This was never seen before on the island because native girls in those days would never under any circumstances engage in such a depraved behavior.

As mentioned above in the section "Big Sale," those so-called "good times" caused a few pieces of land to be sold. It seemed as if the natives were not really conscious of what it meant to have a piece of land. With the taste of a new "flavored life", things did not stay right there. Even after Maria Elena had left the island, the seeds were already sown and prostitution grew uncontrollably. All this had led to the establishment of prostitution rings in the North West section of the island. The main whorehouse was called "Elefante Blanco." This type of "entertainment" has become the opium of immorality for the present generation. One could venture to say that while people were clapping their hands and merrymaking as the president announced the making of a free port, God was turning his back upon this land and its people. The curse of God has darkened the island with corruption, revelry and whatever stunk before the Almighty.

In the early 1970's, the "easy money" began its move. The bottom line was: "let's go for big money". Those who could not go on the "trips" (traveling the seas with marihuana deliveries) did not forget the land selling. If in the mid 1950's thirty or forty thousand Colombian pesos was a good hit, then in the early 1970's, millions was the talk. By 1978 and later years, big money was being offered to seamen for the "trips" and to land owners for their lands. Mafias here, there and everywhere were inducing and enticing the native islanders as "mules" into the business. Islanders were not mafia, neither did they buy or sell drugs in those days. They were used only to take it from one place to another, for which they were paid. The game was "take the sea for it or get rid of that good piece of land for 40, 60 or even 90 million pesos." The real bomb exploded! A demand for money was now felt to keep up with the "best," offered by casinos and discotheques. All these entertainments were like satanic tricks blinding the people's eyes and deafening their ears to the warning of a few prudent advisers. It did not take long for the ominous consequences to become manifest. By the late 1970's an equal number of strangers or aliens were coping with the natives and by the early 1980's they were obtaining privileges. This is to say, demanding preference in jobs, politics, business, and administration, pretending that the indigenous were incompetent. The natives were too kind hearted and philanthropic to draw a limit line and stop the spreading of anti-islander prejudice which proved to be the greatest menace to the islands and their people as is being described in these pages.

What was Taking Place in Old Providence During These Disasters in Saint Andrew?

While Saint Andrew was on the "go-go" and in its swing, Old Providence was still considered in the dark, "behind time and uncivilized." The author recalls talking with one of his co-workers, an outstanding professor, Frank May, at the Centro Colombo-Americano in Cartagena in the mid-seventies, and hearing him remember his wonderful time in Old Providence during the mid-forties. He would say, *"If civilization is what Saint Andrew has come to, would to God Old Providence never get civilized."* When General Gustavo Rojas Pinilla promised to "modernize" Saint Andrew with the free port, Old Providence was also contemplated in his plan, but fortunately, the ruling people in Saint Andrew forgot about it at that time. While airlines like Taxader (Colombia) and Lloyd (Costa Rica) were landing in Saint Andrew on an unpaved runway, a small twin propelled hydroplane, Sahasa, was sea landing in Town's harbor (Santa Isabel), Old Providence Island. Passengers were taken from the hydroplane to the wharf by canoes or catboats. There was a new road cut from Boncas Hill to Old Town, where vehicles could travel. A piece of road was paved from Town to the convent, having the road divided, paved on one side and unpaved on the other. Vehicles could also travel from Town to the end of Bailey. This was not paved.

At that time, with the paving of some streets in Old Providence, a little economical help showed up for the Providencians. Crushed rocks were used for the paving of the road. However, this was not done by machines, but by people who broke rocks with sledgehammers and even with hammers to the size needed for the mixture of the concrete. At that time (1956) broken rocks were sold for 0.20 cents a can or one peso a barrel (5 cans). Big rocks were also sold by the meter for filling the unnecessarily elevated piece of road in front of the park constructed in Town by Mr. Goldsmith. Those who were building brick houses would also buy rocks to use in the foundation. A group of men were sent from Saint Andrew to Old Providence to build the road. These were bulldozer operators, truck drivers, masons, and even men to mix the concrete, which was also done by hand and not by machine.

Right here it is worth emphasizing that not even for the mixing of the cement were the Providencians taken into account. Discrimination was still on the go. However, with the intercession of a noble man from Old Providence a few men were employed and are now on pension. A few months later the pavement came to an end when the cement for paving in Saint Andrew was finished and the one thousand bags lying in the basement of Ms. Antonia's house (in Town), were asked for and sent to Saint Andrew, leaving Old Providence just as it was for the following years. This suspension of road paving also influenced negatively on the rock breaking and selling in Old Providence. Those engaged in such activities were affected economically in one-way or another. Similarly, in 1958, the electricity plant was dismantled and taken to Saint Andrew, leaving Old Providence in darkness for a few years.

It was common knowledge that tourists who arrived in Saint Andrew in those days and wanted to know Old Providence, would be taken around "the rocks" (that is the northwestern part of Saint Andrew island) by native taxi drivers and told that the highest part of the mountain was Old Providence, that the people there were savages and dangerous. Therefore, it was not recommendable to go up there in the woods. Colombians traveling to Saint Andrew as tourists did not know anything about these islands so they would assume that there was only one island named "San Andres y Providencia." Even ministers of government still ignore that these islands lie fifty miles apart in the Caribbean Sea. One minister of health provided a jeep to Saint Andrew for ambulance service, ordering that it was to work during the morning in Saint Andrew and in the afternoon in Old Providence, ignoring the seaway separating both islands with a four to six hours trip by engine boat. This misconception prevails as a means of keeping down Old Providence. There were no hotels, cabins, motels, or anything of the sort in Old Providence for some time after the free port was developed in Saint Andrew. The first hotel was established by an Italian who laid the foundation in South West Bay too close to the beach so it was destroyed by a heavy North West wind. North-West winds used to blow between the months of October and December. This Italian, whose name was Silvano Novaglia, left the island after marrying an island girl and never returned.

Many people from Old Providence went to Saint Andrew in the late fifties and early sixties seeking jobs and staying at their relatives' homes. Some returned, but others did not. Old Providence's population was to remain relatively stable for some decades, with a median of approximately two thousand inhabitants. The people in this island were considered docile, tranquil and cooperative, but most of all conservatives in a cultural, though not political sense. Commerce was on its go in Saint Andrew, many stores were selling electrical household appliances, and there were also hardware stores. Cabins, hotels, guest houses were springing up there. But since these services and materials were not to be found in Old Providence, things were normal and the environment remained for some time at its best. However, in the mid-seventies land selling activity picked up in Old Providence, although not for businesses, rather for house building.

In November 1969, an airstrip capable of accommodating jet planes had been inaugurated in Saint Andrew. This meant that the airport was transformed. Only in 1986 did Old Providence acquire the minimum safety facilities of an airport for small planes carrying 12 passengers. Until then, Providence's "airport" had a short runway accommodating twin-engine planes, but no passenger or cargo terminal, no control tower, no lighting and no navigational instruments. Moreover, the site was plagued by crossed winds. This explains why most natives had continued to use freight boats to go from one island to another until then. At that time there were not many tourists traveling to Old Providence. As soon as minimal facilities were provided, land selling increased significantly. Then substantive lots were sold to the "mafias" who offered big money. But in spite of this, it seems as if the Providence people are aware of the danger posed by undesired investors. Even though there is a considerable influx of continentals in Old Providence today, they are far from outnumbering natives. Most of the continentals residing there have taken native mates and have assumed their customs. Investments by outsiders has not displaced the native population or affected public order to the extent of Saint Andrew. The difference is so noticeable that Old Providence today attracts a type of tourist that prefers tranquility instead of the "big entertainment" services offered

Clamor of the Islands

in Saint Andrew. Changes that have taken place in Old Providence will be mentioned in the section "The Present Situation."

THE BOMB

Quite a few indigenous people are still with their eyes tied and are not seeing things the way they are, and keep, unfortunately, fumbling around with the bomb, which is set for a given time to blast to pieces those thinking that it is a sort of toy. Islanders were always looked upon as a group of passive people and, most of all, as a people who are willing to sacrifice their very souls by carrying the mark of peace. When tombstones were being smashed to pieces and cemeteries destroyed in Saint Andrew, everyone was so peaceful that a chorus of "amen" was humbly whispered for peace's sake. The only one who stood up against it and fought to the end was Dr. Federico Newball, when his mother's tomb was destroyed just because "Pa" (Max Rodriguez), the intendant, said so or wanted it to be so. This guy, "Pa," had everyone walking in line. It was as though he was seeking revenge from a Black ethnic group. Under his watch, those who came from elsewhere would always be addressing the natives as Negroes. No one was hurt because he/she was black. It was simply that the term "Negro" (in Spanish) was being used to discriminate them.

It seemed as if among natives themselves they were suffering a kind of complex when parents would always say: "you have to raise your color or go for a better hair." All this variety of ideas caused some natives to cling to the Spanish with straight or curly hair and a semi-white or yellow skin, causing a mixture of race. Because of convenience and pleasure, there were not many legal marriages. When continentals started to pile in, labor prices began to freeze and the natives sought a way to make more money. This caused the outsiders, who were having a very hard time where they came from, standing on a worse economical ground, to embrace the opportunity, to work for whatever wage was offered. Meanwhile, some natives wandered around and were qualified as lazy. The situation grew worse and all the big and medium enterprises began employing Spanish speaking Colombian continentals. The slogan or bottom line has been: "Saint Andrewans are lazy, don't want to work, and moreover, they are incapable;" therefore, this has gone throughout the land and it is the concept of many non-natives. Even though natives, that is, Raizales might not be lazy, they are given to conformism.

Because of the concepts toward the natives observed by the non-natives, more people came in to replace the so-called "lazy Saint Andrewans." This started in conformity on the part of the indigenous islanders and thus brought a sort of discrimination on both parties. Amidst all these confusions land selling revived to keep the pockets bulging. Education, sickness, pleasure, vices or whatever the cause was, the loss of lands to outsiders continued its way and lessened the space for natives. If the decade of the seventies was "harvest time," the early eighties were not left out. However, from the late eighties up, things started to become darker and a notable change was both seen and felt throughout both islands. Politics has played a very important role whether in favor of or against the natives. Since politics is known to be a very tricky affair, it has drawn the more clever ones to its corruption. Everyone wanted a seat in the big yard of politics and applied to the majority of newcomers for votes even when it has a more negative advantage for the natives. During the author's absence from the islands for many years, he was told that people were brought from the mainland, Colombia, during the political campaigns to vote in Saint Andrew and many never returned to their homeland.

These voters were offered house spots to build their shanties to start out with. These immigrants would also get jobs working on construction, and with their little earnings, remodeled their shanties transforming them into houses made of bricks. It seems as if a great deal of people who have come from the mainland brought by certain politicians to obtain a great number of ballots, really made it. By these means, these politicians would become very famous. This strategy used by the politicians has led the islands, especially Saint Andrew, to their political, economical, moral and spiritual destruction. The immigrants who came in on a political basis, after settling also brought in their nearest relatives and friends. This influx of Spanish speaking people from the Colombia mainland increased the dominance of that language.

THE LANGUAGE PROBLEM

The exclusive influence of Spanish has been so far one of the natives' problems. At the end of the 18th century, the Governor of Saint Andrew Island, the Irish-Catholic from the Canary Islands by the name of Thomas O'Neill, who we already mentioned, strongly urged Cartagena officials to send more Spanish soldiers, priests, school-teachers and petty officials to the island to hasten the process of assimilation. Since Colombian legislation had urged from the year 1926 that elementary and secondary schools instructions be exclusively in Spanish and that, in the 1950's, place names on the islands be changed to their equivalent in Spanish, apparently the majority of natives have been indifferent to such an idea. Notwithstanding, now a day the influence of the Spanish language has been so intensified that even the names of districts have been changed from their original English names to pseudo Spanish names. Historian J.C. Robinson affirmed that in the year 1878 the Corregidor of Old Providence, one Arthur Hawkins was dismissed from his office for completely ignoring the Spanish language.

Decrees forbidding the use of local place names have not obtained a 100% success. Before the free port, natives almost completely refused to speak Spanish, but instead tried to better their English. From 1792 a "Real Orden" addressed to the Viceroy of Nueva Granada suggested that some Spanish families be settled among the islanders in order "to introduce our language and customs so that in time they will be able to consider themselves Spanish."

The presence of soldiers was also a pretext, because, besides military purposes, it was also intended to reinforce the language hoping they would marry island girls, forcing them and their children into the language. What the soldiers did not accomplish when they were sent some years later, those that have come in the twentieth century and the present continentals of today, along with the policemen, have really made it. One can see that as of today the task of language replacement is carried out by continentals looking for equivalent names in Spanish to replace those that were given in English more than one hundred and fifty years ago. Worst of all, it has reached the limit when native surnames are changed disrespectfully from Marteen to "Martinez" and Pomare to "Pomares." Forbes is no longer pronounced as in the English form, but in its Spanish pronunciation, as "For-bes." People who come from the coast of Colombia, especially Cartagena, many of them living on the lots they have obtained, organize their little shanties, and give whatever name they think of, taken from any of the slums in Cartagena. For example, Swamp ground is what the continentals have changed to "Cartagena Alegre;" Rook, is Vietnam or Torrices, and Gaff is not even mentioned any more but the whole thing is San Luis. There are many more cases like these. These places in the islands which had their original names in English, even when they were not inhabited they were used for farming.

The islands of Old Providence and Saint Andrew have been struggling ever since the days of the Puritan settlement to maintain afloat the English language and elements of an Anglo-Saxon culture amidst all storms of opposition and imposition. If governor O'Neill did not achieve his goal, the Colombian government along with the "Capuchinos" have had an 80% success. Even though it is believed that it is very difficult to extinguish a people's culture and language, the natives of both islands cannot deny that they have lost more than 70% of theirs.

The loss of the English language among the youth in the island of Old Providence is really discouraging. At present, Spanish is displacing what English-based creole is used in the island. The problem is, as it is in Saint Andrew, that younger people do not want to speak their own native language. In Fresh Water Bay, for example, there is more Spanish speaking than either Creole or English, as informed by Mr. Arenas. There are more Spanish employees than Raizales (indigenous), because there are more continentals inhabiting that area. The problem is just that the Colombian continentals living on the islands whether single or married will not learn neither Creole nor English, thus forcing the Raizal (indigenous) people into the Spanish language that is, if the Raizal want to get along with them.

At present, all public schools teach in Spanish, and all public events are rarely done either in English or Creole, but only in Spanish. There has never been anyone who went to either island and learned the native language since apparently there is no need for it. It is almost impossible for anyone to live in Saint Andrew without knowing the Spanish language, except that a person wants to be completely isolated. Even when it is not exactly the case of Old Providence, however, it is not far from being so. For example, I, the author, have never seen or heard any public event performed in the native language. Instructions in the schools are never given in English; neither is the English language nor Creole used by the teachers in the classrooms. Even in meetings celebrated among natives, the Spanish language overpowers the Creole language. Are the people aware of this language conflict? Are they really doing anything to promote the original language? If a meeting is held where 50 indigenous and 2 continentals are present, it is carried out in Spanish for the sake of the 2 non-English speakers. Islanders do not appreciate their own tradition handed down from their ancestors. There is a notable tendency of the people to incline to other people's customs and culture and a declination from their own tradition. This inclination is what brought most of the indigenous people to what they are today, "spaniardized natives." Notwithstanding, thank heaven there are still a few older native islanders and even younger ones who are struggling extremely hard to keep their culture, religion, language and tradition.

In the year 2001 there was a program for two or three schools to have English from the very primary level. However, it was just a daydream. The aged natives are totally uninformed of what is going on in the country and the islands of San Andrew, Old Providence and Ketlena (St. Catherine), because all news broadcasting is done in Spanish. The local radio stations are in Spanish except for one or two religious radio programs in the island of Saint Andrew. There is now a local radio station in Old Providence. It's semi-bilingual. There was a half an hour program on Saturdays by Lolia Pomare carried out in English, which was suspended, due to her ill health. There was an English program of great interest to the natives named "People and culture," directed by Dr. Fidel Corpus and Dr. Diego Livingston (both lawyers), on the local TV station on Sunday evenings. This program broadcasted many enlightening historical facts. There were other topics brought by native people, like the lawyer and historian Mr. Wall Peterson. For one reason or another, this program was suspended, and was never renewed, leaving its audience in complete suspense, with no hope. Bill Frances and professor Juvencio Gallardo directed another program called the S.O.S. Variety Show, which has also been discontinued owing to professor Gallardo's illness. Many good programs have been lost. At present, there is a radio station with most of its program in Creole and English, called the "Good News" located at Harbor View, in Saint Andrew and is sponsored by the Baptist Association. A news section is also televised partly in creole on the "Voice of the Island."

BILINGUALISM IN THE ISLANDS

What is bilingualism? Linguists have been giving different concepts about it and each one would give a definition according to his experience acquired in a certain region agreeable to their circumstances. In accordance with the Webster Dictionary, bilingualism is basically the constant use of two or more languages. It has often, if not always, been the powerless, oppressed linguistic minorities who have been forced into bilingualism. When two or more groups speaking different languages come into contact with one another, the less powerful of the groups must often learn the language of the most powerful. Bilingualism is often associated with a subordinate position. It has been observed by linguists that the position of minority languages is under threat throughout the world. English is everywhere recognized as a global dominant language, nobody would think of it as being under threat of extinction, but ironically, there are situations in which it is an oppressed language. Such is the case in the western Caribbean, where standard English is inseparable from English-based Creoles spoken by discriminated Afrodescendant minorities. In Providence, Saint Andrews (Colombia), Colón, Bocas del Toro (Panama), Greytown, Bluefields, and Corn Islands (Nicaragua) for example, English *has been and continues to be* a minority language inasmuch as it is the *mother tongue* of ethnic Blacks.[16] Although English is reputed to be a global, world-dominant language, the truth is that the English spoken by Blacks is a subordinate language in those places; it is subordinate to Spanish in the first place and also to the English variant learnt and spoken by white creole elites and foreigners.

In the case of Saint Andrew and Old Providence, Spanish, which in colonial times had been a second language imposed on the people of African and indigenous descent, has now become a "strait-jacket" that threatens the development of our community. It is true that English-based Creole is the *primary language* of Providencians and Saint Andrewans (as well as other communities in the western Caribbean), but so is standard English too, because it is the literate expression that corresponds to the oral vernacular of native Creole speakers in the region. We can say that Creole is the primary oral language of native islanders while Standard English should be their primary written language.

What is a "Creole?" It is a new language created by mixing features of different languages to the basic grammar and vocabulary of a dominant language in such a way that it becomes the vernacular, living tongue of a community of people with different language backgrounds. In this way, English was the base upon which Creole was created to eventually become the mother tongue of Africans with different language backgrounds taken to the West Indies during the slave trade in the 17th and 18th centuries. This means of communication was pleasant

---

[16] The term *mother tongue* is supposedly an old fashioned, romantic way of referring to the language that is the primary source of communication of an individual or a community. It is presumed to be the ground of being through which the heartbeat of the community of speakers is felt. I do not totally discard the notion of a *mother tongue*.

in the islands to everyone using it not only as their language, but also as their identity. Bilingualism is growing weaker in both our islands and the borrowed or imposed language is being empowered day by day. The implementation of bilingualism in school has not been a matter of choice, but of force.

Law 47 of 1993 in its articles 42 and 43 guarantees that Spanish and English commonly spoken by the native community are official languages in the archipelago department and that teaching must be bilingual, respecting the linguistic expressions of the Natives.

Law 70 of 1993, in its article 35 reads as follows: *"The programs and services of education assigned by the State and the black community must be developed and applied in cooperating with it so as to respond to its particular needs and must include its history, its system of values, its linguistic and dialectal forms and all its other social, economic and cultural aspirations."*

Laws 47 and 70 appear to be a remorseful action on the part of the national government after it had historically imposed the Spanish language and culture on the indigenous people of the archipelago. But these laws and articles are only stains on a piece of paper that have no value because they have never been applied at any time in the islands. This is to say that the famous bilingualism is still wet behind the ears. The strategy of unilateral colombianization has already damaged the very being of the people so much so that there is very little if anything to be done to recuperate what has all but disappeared with the storm of colonialism. Creole has been so discriminated by Colombians living in the islands and elsewhere in the continent that many Saint Andrewans and Old Providencians have put it away replacing it with Spanish. Nowadays, only a minority of native islanders use the mother tongue in their homes. The situation of standard English is even worse for native islanders because it requires a level of formal education in the language to which they do not have access, the irony being that elite Spanish speakers in the mainland do have access to many private schools that emphasize English while the establishment of these type of schools is strongly discouraged by authorities in the islands. Local efforts to establish English dominant private schools have met incredible obstacles placed by authorities. Meanwhile, the English taught in public schools does not meet standards and is only taught as a second language, which does not meet the needs of islanders who are native speakers of English (that is, in its West Indian and Creole variants). When the original language becomes weak in the home it values, it is overpowered by the language used by the vast majority.

This is the present situation of the natives of the Archipelago of Saint Andrew, Old Providence, and Ketlena where most people seem not to care about their situation morally, physically, economically or spiritually.

The existing bilingual program receives such an insignificant official support that it is practically ignored. Notwithstanding the laws mentioned, there is no one to encourage or enforce this program on schools. What do bilingual schools mean? Does this mean that the English language must continue to be taught as a second language as it has always been? Then if this is so, obviously all schools in Colombia are bilingual, because all schools without exception teach English as a subject, and as a second language, just as it is done in the archipelago, with the aggravation that the teaching of English in public schools generally does not meet minimal standards. At the moment, the only subject that is taught in English in the islands is English. All other subjects are taught in Spanish, just as it is done in the rest of the country. Therefore, there are no bilingual schools on the islands.

According to the law mentioned above all public services including governmental affairs must use both languages. But, what about the policemen giving their services among a group of people who are not Spanish speaking? Is it fair? Are the policemen tolerable with those who do not understand them, or are they very harsh? Well, the fact is that the natives are insulted and mistreated if they do not go along with the Spanish or refuse to cooperate with it when facing policemen from the Colombia mainland or the Andean region. Should not these policemen learn the language before coming to the islands? Isn't this an abuse and mockery of the laws made by the Colombian nation itself? The fact remains that the nation psychologically is still putting pressure on the Raizal (indigenous) to show that they have the power to do whatever they want to do to the people and with the people.

Hotels and stores disregard English completely. There is just maybe a 3% of stores with English speaking employees and probably 1% of hotels with someone who speaks English. When English-speaking tourists visit these stores, communication is terrible and tedious. This situation causes the clerks or owners to feel somewhat frustrated. However, minutes later when the English-speaking tourists are gone and the Cachacos (those from the Andean region) are in, the frustrated employees and owners are restored once again to their natural feature with the Spanish monolinguals. However, in spite of this confusing situation enterprises regularly refuse to employ Saint Andrewans, just because they are Black, even though being bilingual.

There are religious services in English in both islands for the few aged and middle age faithful that are still not acquainted with the Spanish language and are striving to preserve the English language (in both its Creole expression and the Standard, that is always present though used intermittently). The fact is that the national government forced radio and TV stations to be in Spanish and militarized the island just as it was planned in the past. In 1991, after returning from abroad, the author of this book came to Saint Andrew and personally visited a few hotels and discovered that the English language was null. There was only one receptionist who spoke English in all of the following hotels among everyone he visited in North End: Hotel Casablanca, with one; Hotel el Isleño, with one young man surnamed Archbold, and Bahía Sardina, with a young lady from the Hill district. Other English-Creole speaking employees from the islands, if there were any, would be engaged in other activities and be in the back. In 1996 there were 22 teachers working at the "Colegio Cajasai": 8 natives and 14 continentals. Eventually, this same school has increased its number of employees, because there have been more students. So at present, the number of teachers has increased, but as for natives, the number is stable. The Bolivariano high school, has 17 native teachers and 27 continentals in the morning, and 6 natives and 26 continentals in the afternoon; the Sagrada Familia high school, has 5 natives and 20 non-natives in the afternoon; the Adventist high school, has 30 employees of which 7 are natives and the rest of them (23) are non-natives.

What is very surprising is that most of the indigenous youth and some of the middle age parents don't even speak or want to speak either English or Creole. In governmental offices and hospitals natives do not speak anything but Spanish. At times, no one can really tell who is indigenous and who is not. The indigenous parents will speak neither Creole nor English to their children or grandchildren, except for a few aged individuals who really do not know the Spanish language. Therefore, there are many children who even though being of native parents and grandparents do not know any English or Creole whatsoever. Then, what will be the future of the islands' English and Creole? The question is: Do those giving the news on local radio and TV stations use English (and/or its Creole variant)? No! But then, why don't they do it if both the speakers and the audience are indigenous? If the national government agreed that Creole be accepted and used in all its phases in the islands, then why don't they use it on the radio and TV stations? Could this be interpreted as discriminating the Creole? Well, maybe there is an explanation to this. A majority of the personnel is Spanish speaking, therefore majority carries. It is so hurtful to know that there are still so many people on both islands who really are not so much acquainted with the Spanish language but in spite of the so-called bilingualism neither English nor Creole is heard most of the time. No matter how important the news might be, a significant part of the audience who doesn't speak Spanish as its primary language will go mostly uninformed. Then the famous bilingualism so much promulgated by the national government is only a fake. It is of no use trying to recuperate spilt milk. Because of this confusing situation a few religious groups through struggles have managed to deliver religious programs in English on a radio station and a television program done here and there by enthusiasts and so on. In further pages the reasons for these complications with the language will be developed, taking into account the "Secret Plan" mentioned at the beginning of this book.

What we are analyzing here is the cause of these disastrous situations and the inconformity of a minority indigenous people. Some of the situations might have been provoked by the natives themselves, but most of the problems are caused by the abuse of the newcomers and the carelessness of the unambitious natives. These things are what a few of the native people are annoyed about and who knows in the future could cause serious problems. Even when it appears as if there is no one on the outside paying attention to the critical situation, the author will provide the reader with an opinion on the island's conditions written by former president of Colombia Dr. Alfonso Lopez Michelsen for *El Heraldo*, (December 26, 1999) which reads as follows:

S.O.S. FOR SAINT ANDREW AND OLD PROVIDENCE

In my capacity as Chancellor of the Republic and having belonged to the Foreign Affairs Advisory Commission for more than 35 years, I have fairly complete information on the situation of the Archipelago of San Andrés y Providencia, elevated to the Department category by the Constitution of 1991. There is a widespread version that we have a lawsuit pending with the Republic of Nicaragua. It is not true. In 1928 the Treaty of Esquérra-Bárcenas was signed, through which the so-called Costa Mosquitia, which has been Colombian property since time immemorial, was recognized as part of Nicaragua by Colombia. In turn, Nicaragua recognized Colombia as the sovereign of all the islands and islets located west of the Meridian 82, that is, San Andrés, Providencia, Santa Catalina, and other minor keys and islets. What is still in dispute is the delimitation of marine and submarine areas, according to the interpretation of the scope of the allusion to the Meridian 82, in light of Maritime Law.

I wish the problem of the Archipelago consisted in a legal dispute, susceptible of a peaceful airing of the different means contemplated in International Law for this class of conflicts; but it's not like that. The problem in San Andrés is not Colombia's dominion over the Islands, but that of the native and continental inhabitants over a disproportionate area to keep them in normal conditions. A brief recount of the origins of the problem and the point we have reached, will save me the work of drawing conclusions different from asking the Public Authorities and all Colombians, to open our eyes opportunely about this monumental error of management outside the metropolitan territory of Colombia.

The archipelago counted with less than a thousand inhabitants when it was declared a free port. Its thousand inhabitants, most of who were of Anglo-African origin, spoke English and professed the evangelical religion. In honor of the truth, San Andrés was one of the best conditioned districts in Colombia, with a rate of almost zero illiteracy and with a discipline superior to that of the rest of the region by virtue of the practices of Protestantism: Today, the archipelago has a little more than 80,000 inhabitants, and of the three governors chosen by popular election, after the validation of the new Constitution, two are in jail, Maflin and Manuel, and only Simón González, a native of Antioquia and first governor, is exempt from charges. Insecurity, mainly armed robbery, has dominated the Islands.

The analysis of the process of deterioration cannot be simpler and more dramatic. When the free port was established, compatriots from all latitudes came to the island in search of fortune. Shops, hotels, spas and other places of recreation proliferated, because, through the port of San Andres, all kinds of goods exempt from customs duties could enter Colombia to be sold in the interior in the so-called San Andresitos. The native population knew little about business, and the capitals of the inhabitants of San Andrés were insufficient for large-scale operations, such as those that make the island a tax haven.

The "Pañamanes", as the continentals are called, took over the island, dislodging the Raizales, who are presently reduced to a secondary position, in which the only thing they have left is the land outside the urban perimeter. Population growth is so disproportionate that it reaches the scandalous figure of 2,600 inhabitants per km^2, lacking the most basic public services, but, mainly, drinking water, which is installed to supply a demand of 40 liters/second, while the real demand is 169 liters/second. Then, as another of the hurricanes of the Caribbean, the economic opening has razed the island with the passage of a large number of domestic and consumer goods that are really destined for a continent that is located 500 miles away. The hotels, with a mediocre occupation, the empty business premises, the idle labor, denote the gravity of the economic situation, many times more distressing than the rest of the country, where at least it is suspected that there will be light at the end of the tunnel, but, in San Andrés, with 50% unemployment and no possible future, what can be expected?

For different reasons, people continue to arrive, even if measures are adopted to lower the population density, such as Article 310 of the Constitution and Decree Law 2762 of December 1993. But the problem is not one of rules, but one of action. It consists in seeking a different economic activity for the inhabitants of San Andrés and in controlling the flow of immigrants from the Continent. Otherwise, an anti-Colombian sentiment, which is by no means pro-Nicaraguan, is taking over the island, overwhelmed by its own contradictions. It would seem a small problem in the face of the seriousness of the total situation of the country in matters of public order, economy and unemployment, but, in this case, there is an additional factor, because what is involved is our sovereignty over the Archipelago, and we can not ignore the consequences that a massive uprising against the authorities would bring, if it does not have a goal or program, and is totally anarchic.

How about an East Timor-style conflict, where two ethnic groups would face each other: English-speaking Anglo-Africans and Continentals of Spanish and Syrian-Lebanese descent? May the hand of God lead Colombia!

Everyone is conscious of these facts mentioned by Dr. Lopez, and it is true that anything may happen among these people. Analyzing carefully Dr. Lopez´s concept, there is no doubt that the anti-Colombian feeling is really sown in many Saint Andrewan hearts, notwithstanding the presumably beneficial laws issued by the national government to protect the people. One reason for this is that these laws are being enacted in a very hesitant and unconvincing manner. Moreover, because of the possible conflict that was foreseen by Dr. Lopez and of which national authorities are aware, there has been a constant piling in of policemen, soldiers, anti-revolt squads and equipment to fight against the ancestral people and to impede any kind of protest besides marching in the streets. When Dr. Lopez wrote his piece of advice, he mentioned 50% of unemployment, but today, that number has increased by approximately 15%, because of the uncontrollable increasing population. Now please look at the following, written by the same former president in 1977 during his presidential administration, which shows the government's cynicism:

> In the case of Saint Andrew and Old Providence a certain degree of integration has been achieved from a juridical, political and even economic standpoint, but not from an ethnic, cultural, or social standpoint. Therefore, the incorporation of the Archipelago into Colombian nationality has not yet been achieved, since this implies the gradual elimination of existing diversity for the construction of a homogenous body.
>
> Administration of the Regional Educational Fund (FER) by island Protestants could hinder this integration, so it is important that the National Government nominate a Catholic as its representative, preferably the "Apostolic Prefect." Every support should be given to the Colombian Religious Orders represented in the islands in the various schools and hospitals.
>
> Instead of making Saint Andrew and Old Providence into a center of "Patois" speakers, ways must be found to turn them into a center for spreading Colombian culture.
>
> The presence of the military forces should be increased for the purposes of guaranteeing national sovereignty [...] and would also serve to deter any separatist movement that might be attempted.

With respect to the above quoted affirmations, Dr. Lopez's desire was partly accomplished, because at that time, Mr. Nunnolly Pusey Bent, who was a Catholic, even though being an indigenous islander, was appointed head of the FER.

How could anyone really trust the "beautiful" words spoken by the rulers with the intention to convince a people who had innocently put their trust in them? Are they giving any sort of hope for a humble people who are completely frustrated and have been deluded year after year? Ii is to be understood then that there should be no more space for storage of deceit in the hearts of the indigenous people who have humbly humiliated themselves before a mocking nation. There are abuses on every side. Undoubtedly 90% of the indigenous or Raizal, as they are called by the Colombian state, have no idea whatsoever of these things that are going on in the nation. In other words, what the nation is still doing against them. Should things like these be broadcast so that the people everywhere can know that the Colombian state is still not satisfied with all what they have done and are still doing to a minority after persecuting them against their religion and language, hoping that they will further along see their identity completely erased and be one hundred percent Spanish and Catholics? The people are not anti-Colombian as some continentals are saying, but rights need to be recognized where it is due.

The following is an anonymous flyer distributed in 1994 during a political campaign, undoubtedly written by a Spanish continental:

> Mr. Pañaman, remember: All of us Colombians have the right to live in peace without having to put up with insults of a few embittered natives self-nominated as "sons of the soil." Let's remind them on election day that the difference consists in that we came to this beautiful territory by our own means on DC-3, DC-4, DC-6, Constellation, Electra or by jet, while they arrived in chains. Ask such "sons of the soil" why do they attack the free port so much, how many of them have become professionals in the continent studying with their own money? The majority, if not all, studied with and are still enjoying the scholarships taken from our taxes, or with loans they never pay back.
>
> Ask them if opportunities in the continent were denied them. If anyone has been discriminated. Colombia wants peace. The Paña (Spanish speakers) reside and want to continue living in Saint Andrews, but we are not going to permit a little group of "AVIVATOS" that are continually fooling other islanders to take away what we have gained with our sweat and sacrifice. Neither will decrees or threats work. The best answer is that on the 30th of October "Paña vote for Paña."

Regarding what Dr. Lopez said in his newspaper column as to the possibility of a conflict, the author of this book continues to believe that it is somewhat inevitable and that everyone should be aware of such a lamentable possibility. As it is known, the government has been trying in every way to stoke division among the natives so that they may become weaker and, according to this divisive scheme, the veiled incorporation of islanders into the police is being activated. The soul of the problem of Saint Andrew is in overpopulation, economy and space. Due to overpopulation space is reduced to its minimum. So many people clustering in a small portion of land suffocate the very air. This stifling even brings an unhealthy environment. Overpopulation is not caused by the indigenous people, but by the outsiders. With an economy at stake, there is not much hope for survival. The few people that are being employed are precisely non-natives. Even though the silly author of the stupid anonymous tract seemed to ignore it, indigenous islanders were here centuries before the Paña and were known to be God-fearing people with a peaceful life, high moral standards, and good principles. Deep down discrimination is obvious.

Those who, like the writer of the anonymous libel quoted above, discriminate against islanders, with their presence and corrupted mind, proud look and greed for money, have brought disgrace upon the native community. Precisely because of these rogues the island has sunk into the depths of poverty, crowned with immorality and theft. Unconsciously, the writer of the anonymous libel admitted that the indigenous have been here for centuries, and that they, the newcomers, have no right to displace the natives. They have a right to apply for immigration, and to be considered for permanent residence inasmuch as the limited space and resources of the islands allow, but this immigration has to be controlled by islanders and should in no way become a threat to their survival as a society and a culture. The type of ignorant discrimination exhibited by the anonymous libel is precisely what must be analyzed here, which will take the reader to the causes and reasons why the situation of our islands today is getting more critical due to unhealed wounds in the very souls of the sensible true-hearted indigenous people who strive for a better future.

THE PRESENT SITUATION

To get into the heart of the present situation, one has to look into the past, and analyze the situation that brought about the conflicts in both Saint Andrew and Old Providence, before and after the free port. It can be seen from the sociologist Dr. Dilia Robinson's point of view: one of the factors that caused the central government to declare a free port in both islands was "the people's decision to join another country."

If one should look back on the happenings of the past years and compare them with what is going on in the islands today, it would really be overwhelming. After one recalls what the islands and their people were or used to be, with what they are today, it is almost unbelievable. The fact is that these situations need to be put into a balance and examined very carefully. The reader of these pages will be the arbiter.

In the late seventies and early eighties natives were losing their lands by selling them while others were serving as "mules" for the mafias to keep afloat. Today, it is well known that some of these indigenous individuals have gone from "mules" to drugs dealers. To be too ambitious is just as bad as not being ambitious at all.

In the past years some people sold their lands to get money to spree and to "have a good time;" others, did it to school their children away from the islands. However, as it is seen today, some people, especially in Saint Andrew, have to be engaged in land selling because of the high tax that is imposed on these unproductive lands. When the old folks from the 1930's and up to the late 1940's were exporting grains and fruits, above all coconuts, land tax was very low, almost nothing. Now, as it is today, land taxes have gone so high on unproductive lands that they are sold just before being confiscated by the government, because of unpaid levy. Those who have taken it for granted to run drugs to get rich have become like the buccaneers in the 16th and 17th centuries. Some have lavished their booty, others have made mansions that have been confiscated by the authorities; others have returned to sea for more, but reached the land of nowhere, while others are behind iron bars.

As the seas near the islands and keys become more and more infested with coast guards and helicopters flying all day long, things have changed for both suppliers and consumers. Packages of coke are not found drifting along the beaches and seashore as they used to be just a few years ago. Natives have become violent. Shooting and killings have occurred because of drugs that have been on the scene. Should these people be criticized and despised, or be treated with pity? Who knows! The only truth that is known is that there are no jobs for no one and people are pressured economically and many are going ship-out to avoid starvation.

There is no better to come and as things grow worse in every aspect some people are comforted with "there is nothing we can do." Doctors working in hospitals after being owed for a semester have to apply for ship-outs on tourist ships. Many have already gone, and for others, it will not be long when they too will also be gone. Parents have sacrificed their living to school their children in universities out of the islands, but most of them after becoming professionals and returning home spend one year or more looking for a job in their professional field, none to be found. These young professionals have no other option but to leave the islands to seek for jobs elsewhere or try for a tourist ship. Islanders are becoming lesser in number owing to such causes, while continentals are filling their spaces (in part thanks to the purposeful lack of control of the OCCRE migration services—see section about OCCRE ahead). Given that the shipping companies require English, continentals are not going that way. Funny, eh! To leave the islands and work on the ships one has to know English, but to stay and work in Saint Andrew, Spanish is the required language.

However, certain things need to be looked at, things that connect native discontent to a desire for separation from Colombia. In the decades of the 1950's and 1960's there was a pushing aside of the natives by the immigrants. It was noticed then that the continental Colombian merchants would employ continental Spanish speakers, while the Syrio-Lebanese, generally called Turks, would handle their own business or work with one of their relatives, and whenever they hired anyone apart from their relatives, it would be a continental so as to learn from them the Spanish language.

Sometime between the years of 1967 and 1968, the separatists idea of the creation of an independent mini-state was promoted. According to information which is obtained from the very serious resource known as "The Secret Plan," (see citation at the beginning of this book and addendum at the end), there were about 10,000 potential votes for separatism. In 1973 *Cromos* magazine published that according to Mr. Dudly Thomson, the Jamaican Foreign Minister: "Saint Andrew should be independent. Saint Andrewans speak English, they are Black, Protestant and descended from Englishmen and Antilleans. Colombians are white or mestizo, they speak Spanish and they are Catholics." He also asked the question: "Is there any reason to believe Saint Andrewans are part of the Colombian Nation? Every people has the right to choose the moment it wishes to be free."

Here I quote an extensive excerpt of a paper on the same issue presented by professor Dulph W. Mitchell. I ask the reader to bear with me in this multiple page qoutation. Mr. Mitchell's paper is titled...

Why We the Raizal (Earliest Surviving Inhabitants) of The Archipelago of Saint Andrew, Old Providence and Saint Catherine Are Not Colombians! (And need to struggle for our independence)

(Permit me to clarify that what is laid out in this paper applies only to the descendants of the aboriginal islanders (the earliest surviving inhabitants of our territory and does not refer in any way to the offspring of mixed parents —a Raizal and an alien— or aliens and their children, who have all the right to choose, claim or decide to which nationality they belong.)

How can we be Colombians when as the rightful owners of this territory located 480 miles from Cartagena, the nearest Colombian port, being an indigenous ethnic group who acknowledge and affirm ourselves as a distinct and unique people with a historical background and continuity to the original settlers of the Raizal Archipelago of Saint Andrew, Providence and Saint Catherine and our history, language, actions, attitudes, customs, beliefs, culture, traditions, way of thinking, diet, general cosmogony, cosmovision, and idiosyncrasy are all so entirely different?

The Colombian State's historical assumption of the "*1822 spontaneous adhesion of the inhabitants of Saint Andrew, Providence and Mangles to the 1821 Constitution of Cucuta*", not to Colombia as a State or nation, did not change in any way our forefathers or our nature of being the autochthonous citizens of our Archipelago of Saint Andrew, Providence and Saint Catherine. The fact that our forefathers supposedly adopted the Colombian citizenship did not miraculously convert or transform them, nor us, into natural Colombian beings. We the descendants of the first settlers on our territory were born within the Colombian State under certain circumstances of citizenship, but this condition does not transfigure or causes any change in our ethnological *and cosmogonical characteristics as a different people from the Colombians.*

An example of this is: if a Raizal baby was born of Raizal parents among an indigenous community, this does not convert the newborn into an indigenous being belonging to the specific indigenous people. That newborn baby is still the son or daughter of the Raizal couple, and is therefore, a Raizal by origin. The Colombian Administrative Litigious Tribunal supports this in its Sentence of March 5, 1998, as follows: *"The contrary interpretation that a native is everyone who is born in a place is not acceptable because this fails to acknowledge the constitutional antecedents mentioned. Every Raizal is a Saintandrewan but every Saintandrewan is not a Raizal. Pretending otherwise, would be like assuming that by being born in the Huitoto or Embera territories one is indigenous when one is not a member of those communities."*

The Raizal Archipelago, until the signing of the Esguerra-Bárcenas treaty in 1928, encompassed the Corn Islands and portions of the Atlantic Coast of Nicaragua, so determined by Royal Order of November 30, 1803, issued by Carlos IV, king of Spain, and later ratified in 1805, in reply to a request submitted to him by the inhabitants of the Archipelago, which, signed by "SOLER," in the respective part, states as follows: *"The King has resolved that the islands of San Andres and the portion of the Mosquittia Coast from Cape Gracias a*

Dios, inclusive, up till the river Chagres, be segregated from the General Captainship of Guatemala and be dependent on the Viceroyalty of Santa Fe..."

Here, we need to bear in mind that in 1803-05 what is now known as Colombia was not an independent country, but was still under the Spanish jurisdiction. Colombia became independent 14 years later in 1819. Moreover, the Order of 1803 was withdrawn on March 31, 1808.

As is presumed from the Royal Order of 1803, mentioned above, before the existence of Colombia as a State, our Archipelago appeared as a possession of Spain and at that time was under the jurisdiction of the Captainship of Guatemala.

There occurred, however, during that period, a series of evictions between the Spanish and English and apparently Spain was overcome by England, which country finally ended up as the main occupant of our territory in the 17th century, from where, apart from our African heritage, a considerable amount of our idiosyncrasy, characteristics, traditions and customs are oriented.

Moreover, we cannot overlook the fact and reason why the English were occupying the territory, as is historically recorded:

"On December 1, 1793, a fleet anchored at the port of Saint Andrew (San Andrés), commanded by Captain Tomás de Ramery, with the mission to make a census of the population, exportations, and importations as well as to explain to the people about the scope of the Agreement that the inhabitants would make with Spain. This Agreement would permit the people of the territory to live on the islands, if they agreed to accept a Governor appointed by Spain, confess the Catholic faith, erect a church building and maintain it along with a priest on their account, accept and pay a teacher to teach them Spanish and obey the Spanish laws. The people of the territory agreed to these demands and a Minute was taken. This proves that Saint Andrew (San Andrés), Providence (Providencia) and Saint Catherine (Santa Catalina), the Great and Small Islands of Mangle, were received directly by the residents of the territory at that time. The census, dated January 3, 1793, states that on January 1st of that same year, the total population of the Archipelago was apparently 391 inhabitants, including 281 enslaved blacks, these, evidently, being the majority." (Quotations from: *Complemento a la Historia Extensa de Colombia*, Volume IX, "Nuestro Archipiélago de San Andrés y la Mosquittia Colombiana," authored by Enrique Gaviria Liévano, published by Plaza & Janes)

In 1810, the then Governor of the Raizal territory, Thomás O'Neill, at the time of his retirement, gave land titles to the people of the territory, and therefore set in legal standing the possession and ownership of this territory to the people who resided here and, as far as we know, history has not proven with absolute clarity that this territory has ever been conquered or fully held throughout the period of colonization by any specific nation or State, except being recognized as part of the Mosquitia Coast.

San Andrés, and Providence-Saint Catherine experienced a brief period of autonomy as from 1818 till 1912 (each island was an autonomous territory with its own respective town council). The Raizal People lived almost completely independent of the Colombian State. Economically self-sufficient, they developed their own economic, religious and educative institutions and their way of administrating justice. This local independence occurred after the settlers ousted the English Captain, John Bligh, who in turn had evicted the popular Thomas O'Neill, an Irishman who governed our Archipelago on two occasions on the behalf of Spain.

The supposed adhesion to the Gran Colombia in 1822 of our ancestors, the first settlers and their territory, including a vast portion of continental Central America, as recorded by the Colombian Academy of History (1, page 93), is registered as follows:

Aury dies in Bogotá (sic) by falling from a horse, and soon after that one of the most important events occurred in the history of our archipelago. It has to do with the spontaneous adhesion of the inhabitants of San Andres, Providence and Mangles to the 1821 Constitution of Cucuta." And continues on pages 94-95, stating: "There is no doubt that, if we examine the procedure of the inhabitants of the Archipelago, in the light of today's International Rights, we find them exercising a genuine act of 'free determination of peoples.' Two important resolutions of the General Assembly of the United Nations and a 'consultative opinion' of the International Court of Justice accept the association to an independent State as an authentic expression of that right: Resolution 1514 (XV), on the independence of colonial countries and peoples, as well as "that which refers to the friendly relationship of peoples freely expressed about those peoples to which they become annexed. In this same manner, the International Court of Justice has stated its 'consultative opinion' concerning the Western Sahara. All of which requirements are fulfilled in the voluntary, spontaneous and free act of the inhabitants of Saint Andrew (San Andrés), Providence (Providencia) and the Corn Islands (Mangles)..." (Quoted from: *Complemento a la Historia Extensa de Colombia*, Volume IX, "Nuestro Archipiélago de San Andrés y la Mosquittia Colombiana", authored by Enrique Gaviria Liévano, published by Plaza & Janes)

In relation to the Royal Order of 1803, we refer to the "Excerpt" from Mr. Federick Chatfield's (English Diplomatic Representative in Central America-1834-1852) letter of April 15, 1847 to Viscount Palmerston (received July 8) that stated:

The pretensions of sovereignty assumed by New Granada to the whole of the Mosquito Territory will, I conceive, be found upon examination quite irregular, and rest merely on the Royal Order of San Lorenzo of 30th November, 1803, separating for military purposes from the Captaincy-General of Guatemala the Islands of Saint Andrew and that part of the Mosquito shore from Cape Gracias á Dios inclusive towards the River Chagres, and making them dependent on the Vice-royalty of Santa Fé de Bogotá; which order was never carried out into effect any more than the decrees are allowed to have been which the Government of Spain has issued at different times in a view to regulate the internal affairs of the American province generally, after they have declared their independence of its rule.

The Royal Order of San Lorenzo above alluded to is, I conclude, the only act upon which the New Granadian Government attempts to found a claim to the Mosquito Territory; and it is strange that a measure of such importance as that order seems to involve—the transferring of a vast tract of country from one Government to another—should not have been provided for in a formal manner by a Royal Cédula, or Order of the Sovereign in Council, instead of by a simple ministerial notification or instruction, which the Royal Order of San Lorenzo only amounts to.

The main point is, whether the New Granadian Government has a just claim to any part of the Mosquito King's territory, or to any part of that of Central America: and I request to lay before your Lordship such particulars as I have been able to collect respecting the origin and effect of the Order of San Lorenzo of 30th November, 1803; trusting that what I shall state will appear to Her Majesty's Government a sufficient ground for declining to recognize the right of New Granada to an extension of territory beyond the boundaries on the Central American side, as they existed previous to the independence of both countries of Spain, since it is demonstrable that New Granada has never acquired either a military or civil jurisdiction over the Mosquito and Central American territories, nor any title to treat for the division or appropriation of States which do not belong to it. (Quotations from: *Correspondence Respecting The Mosquito Territory* – Pages 2-3 – No. 5 – Elibron Classics)

And, moreover, apart from Mr. Frederick Chatfield's letter to Viscount Palmerston, referred to on page 6, we have in our files copy of a letter of October 21, 1822, obtained from the Public Records Office, London, Ref. CO137/153, folio 251 (signature illegible), which states:

In reference to my letter to you of the 19th of March last, inclosing copies of some dispatches from Rear Admiral Sir Charles Rowley, respecting a piratical establishment formed on the Island of Old Providence, I am commanded by my Lord Commissioner of the Admiralty to transmit to you, for the information of Lord Balhurst, a copy of a letter from Sir Charles Rowley stating that the Colombian Government has taken possession of Old Providence and its dependencies.

These observations leave some very dubious thoughts in our minds, and, we the Raizal People, up till today, do not know under what conditions our forefathers agreed to that annexation. We are still ignorant to the knowledge of the circumstances under which we remained with the Nueva Granada when the Gran Colombia was disintegrated. We are told by Colombian authorities that the referred Annexation Document signed by some leaders of our territory that supposedly legalized the adhesion of our territory to the Gran Colombia in 1822 is now apparently lost.

We, as the Nation we had been, were supposedly to be a Nation within a Nation, however, this has not been the case, at a certain time we were designated by the Colombian State as "Intendencia, Nacional de Colombia" (1912), then "Intendencia Especial de Colombia" (1976), and finally "Departamento de Colombia" (1991), and so, today we are just as another Department of Colombia, but worst off than any of the others, in the sense that we are now forcibly reduced to a minority in our own territory, not able to design or decide our own future, under a system of "false-democracy" that is contrary to our cosmovision, and regulated by a Central Government that dictates our destiny, our life.

After 1822, the Raizal People began to suffer and this has continued until today, 188 years of a continuous colonialism by the Colombian State (1822-2010), a total genocidal imposition on a people, our people, who are established on this archipelago since approximately 1624 (some 450+ years), when our ancestors were brought to these islands and started to build up a peaceful society, composed of Puritans, colonizers, mainly English, Dutchmen and Africans, and succeeded in the building of such a society. They suffered and resisted nearly 200 years the wars of conquest and colonization between the European powers for the possession of America, and the Caribbean; in the midst of the wars, our ancestors never ceased their desire and process of edifying themselves as a people, with a religion, a language, a culture, and common roots, in spite of the changing claimers of our archipelago.

A bloody Caribbean sea is the historical witness and evidence of a repeated transfer of possession between Spain and England during those first two centuries of our existence. But, when the spirit of freedom started to flow in America, when the people of the area decided to carry no more the chains of oppression of the European colonialists, then free nations started to emerge in America.

Here, we also need to bear in mind that in 1803-05 what is now known as the Republic of Colombia was not an independent country, but was still under the Hispanic jurisdiction, and until the signing of the Esguerra-Bárcenas Treaty in 1928 the Raizal Archipelago encompassed the Corn Islands (Mangles) and portions of the Nicaraguan, Costa Rican and Panamanian coasts. Colombia only became independent 14 years later in 1819.

The puzzling question here is: If our archipelago was already a possession of Colombia, since 1803 as Colombia claims, why was its adhesion necessary? On the other hand, our history is different. It was not until 1818 (July 18), when the French Commodore Louis-Michel Aury, born in Paris about 1788, the first Governor of the province of Texas and Galveston Island, under the Mexican Republic, freed the archipelago (Providencia), definitely from Spain and also from Europe, freed from the inhuman oppression of colonialism, and established, as the first independent state of Central America, a successful settlement with an economy thriving on captured Spanish cargo. The people of the United States of America had started this chain of freedom, in 1776, followed by Haiti (1804), Providencia 1818, Nueva Granada (Colombia) in 1819, as well as many of our surrounding neighbors, such as Nicaragua and Venezuela, that were freed from Spain in 1821.

You may notice with careful attention the fact that the Raizal People were liberated in 1818, before Colombia (1819), Venezuela, Ecuador, Panama, Nicaragua, etc., some of whom were freed 3 years later after us, in 1821. (Luis Aury took Providence Island with 800 men aboard 14 vessels. A year after, the troops Aury awaited from Jamaica arrived under the command of British General Gregor McGregor who took control of the Island of San Andres.)

Take note also that, our Liberator was not Simón Bolívar, he nor any of his troops did not ever set foot on our archipelago. Moreover, Louis Aury, after freeing the Raizal archipelago, made several efforts to enter the struggle by offering his troops and naval force to Simon Bolivar in order to help in the liberation from Spain, but his offers were rejected and unsuccessful.

During this time, there occurred, a series of evictions between the Spanish and English and apparently Spain was overcome by England, which country finally ended up as the main occupant of our territory in the 17th century, from where, apart from our African heritage, a considerable amount of our idiosyncrasy, characteristics, traditions and customs are oriented. Therefore, Saint Andrew, Old Providence, and Saint Catherine experienced a brief period of autonomy as from 1818 till 1912 (each island was an autonomous territory with its own respective town council). The Raizal People lived almost completely independent of the Colombian State.

On August 1st, 1834, Philip Beekman Livingston, grants freedom to his mother's enslaved people and, sharing a portion of his family's property with the newly freed slaves, kept what was left for himself. Later, on August 1st 1838, he also granted freedom to the enslaved workers in Saint Andrew Island, then, went on to found the "Protestant" Baptist Church and school in the year 1844.

Something we need to bear in mind is that, our ancestors who were not brought here directly from Africa, arrived on these islands by way of Jamaica and other Caribbean areas, their origin had absolutely nothing to do with Colombia in any way. Therefore, let's take into consideration some international examples:

a) Since 1898, Puerto Rico has been under the dominance of the United States, that's a very long time, are the inhabitants of Puerto Rico then North Americans, I should say not, they are Puerto Ricans, aren't they? Of course, they are. Today they are seeking their independence.

b) Since 1893, Hawaii has been under the dominion of the United States, are the people of Hawaii, North Americans, no, they are Hawaiians. They are now seeking their independence.

c) The Cayman Islands have been under the British dominion since 1670 (339 years), are the citizens of the Caymans British, no, they are Caymanians. They also are seeking their independence now.

d) The Falkland Islands are under the dominion of The British, since 1833, are the people from the Falklands British, no they are not, they are Falklanders or Kelpers. In relation to the Falkland Islanders' identity, and to support my opinion on this matter, I quote: Lewis Clifton, Speaker of the Falklands Legislative Council: "British cultural, economic, social, political and educational values create a unique British-like, Falkland Islands. Yet Islanders feel distinctly different from their fellow citizens who reside in the United Kingdom. This might have something to do with geographical isolation or with living on a smaller island – perhaps akin to those British people not feeling European." Notice that the Falklanders consider themselves as "fellow citizens" of the British people and not "British."

During the last few decades the political dimension of Falklander identity has evolved around the campaigning for recognition of the Islander right to self-determination since 1968. Britain's recognition of that right after the Islanders turned down the so called 'leaseback proposal' put forward by the Foreign and Commonwealth Office in 1980, and the new Falklands Constitution enacted in 1985, which vested the political power in the elected Falklands Legislative Council rather than the old style colonial governors.

A specific regional aspect of that identity evolution are the human relations the Islanders traditionally maintain with Chile and Uruguay, and indeed the well known Islander rejection of the Argentine sovereignty claim:

"In the Falkland Islands a national identity dynamic also exists: it is constructed upon the Islanders' desire not to deal with Argentina." (Quotations on Falkland Islands taken from: *Wikipedia, the free Encyclopedia*)

Are we any different from the abovementioned people? Whose countries are all on the UN List of territories considered by said organization as colonies which have the right to be decolonized? Since 1803, as Colombia claims, our Archipelago is under the dominion of this State, does this make us Colombians? We must consider this as negative. We are Saintandrewans, Providencians, Saintcatherinians, or whatever, but certainly not Colombians.

Let me put it a little more clearly in the following manner: Our supposed citizenship would be Colombian, or rather, we could be considered as "fellow-citizens" to the Colombians, due to the respective, particular, and historical circumstances of our forefathers free adhesion to the Gran Colombia, remember not to Colombia as a State or Republic, which action was later usurped by the Colombian State, but, nevertheless, we have our own distinct and different identity as Saintandrewans.

As Saintandrewans, we need to emancipate our minds from the erroneous and false teachings which for so many years we have been bombarded with. Generally, when we talk about slavery and emancipation it refers to how the physical and body structures are affected, when people are forced to do hard labor with little or no pay, etc., but there is another very serious condition which affects humanity more profoundly and that is the enslavement of our minds, which we seldom or hardly ever talk about. This enslavement of the mind does not only exist in our Archipelago but it also permeates itself around the world, especially among Black people.

All of this has to do with colonization. It is a fact that in this 21st Century we are not enslaved but we are a colonized people in our own homeland, for in addition to colonizing our Raizal Territory, Colombia has also colonized our knowledge, understanding and mind, not just to impose their own, but also to disconnect us from our African heritage and culture. Why has Colombia done this? Because people who are cut off from their heritage and culture are more easily manipulated and controlled than people who are not.

Our struggle is based on three specific aspects: Self-Determination (Freedom), Reparation and Sustainable Development (Restoration). What we are speaking about, then, is genuine freedom. Freedom means liberty, self-determination, independence or free will. Reparation means the act of making good or compensating for loss, damage or an injury. Restoration means returning to a normal or healthy condition.

Human rights are the basic rights and freedoms all humans are entitled to, often held to include the right to life and liberty, freedom of thought and expression, and equality before the law.

We certainly had our original names, religion, culture, history, language and identity erased from our minds. Today, many of us are still blind to the fact that mental genocide was committed against the African slaves and their descendants, which final goal is deculturalization and miseducation, a strategy to implant Eurocentric values and to erase the Africancentric values in our minds. We fail to understand that the institution of slavery was a weapon of mass destruction; used to psychologically extirpate the slaves' minds and so because we do not know our history the lapse is causing us great harm.

Mental genocide or "*mentacide*" is the deliberate and systematic annihilation of a people's mind. The process of destroying our original name, religion, culture, history, language and identity, which has not been given back to us. What good is freedom or what is freedom, if we do not have human rights? Until we come face to face with our own reality and realize who we are, we will continue not only to be blind but also to remain with our minds entirely enslaved and colonized.

After observing this long excerpt of Professor Mitchel's paper, I am obliged to complement with some historical facts: In 1936, a Colombian commission from the Chamber of Representatives visited the archipelago, supposedly to help find solutions to the problems the people were facing then. The following are excerpts from the comments made by several of the islands' leaders at that time:

Dr. Timothy Britton:

Since, as a matter of fact, on the Archipelago English is commonly spoken, the instruction system implemented in the schools [...] up till today, is rather irrational: The system that is being followed consists of preparing what is called a "program," by putting together portions of history, grammar and geography, etc., written in Spanish, which the students must learn in order to present a test. Can you imagine the problem of a poor schoolteacher, making great efforts to have those students, who do not understand Spanish, learn by such programs? The best result that can be obtained is that the children, as is natural, will learn such parts by memory, and will be able to repeat them perfectly, but in the same manner as a parrot would do it, without understanding the meaning. In summary, the years go by and the children do not learn either English or Spanish, and much less the subjects of the programs. It is necessary, then, to rationalize the studies, in conformity with the precepts of modern pedagogy, taking into consideration the circumstances of the language.

Dr. Carlos Federico Lever:

The reorganizing of the education system on the Archipelago is necessary and urgent. It is of utmost importance to do away with the old methods of teaching. Teachers' salaries must be increased. Competent teachers must be selected, if only it could be those who can speak both English and Spanish.

Professor Vernon W. May:

Several years ago, during the conservative administration, the government signed a contract with the church to establish on these islands a mission whose primary objective was to civilize us [...]. This attitude of the government deeply affected the heart of the most insignificant sons of the Archipelago. The circumstances, honorable congressmen, that the dominant language, the religion professed by the majority and the peculiar customs of these islands not being in agreement with those of the rest of the republic, is no justified reason for us to be considered as uncivilized. If this concept would be fundamental, if this criteria should be accepted, as the conservative administration has declared it, I affirm that this can also be applied to the inhabitants of Germany, of England, and the United States of America.

Dr. Bedel Duffis:

That we are not patriots? Say if we are not those sons of the Archipelago who were the first to march to the borderline, in defense of national sovereignty, against the Peruvian aggression, whose patriotism and abnegation were shown in the Amazonian zones, as an expression of Islander patriotic fervor. That we are a savage people is an insensate judgment, since it is well known that the island people have never shown any savageness in the course of our history. The first settlers of these islands were civilized, and say what they may, our society has never degenerated.

Mr. Silvano May, Vice-President of the Municipal Council of Saint Andrew.

Perhaps for religious reasons the government has incurred in the error of its relationship with the islands. It seems as if the impression prevails that catholicizing the Islanders is colombianizing them. There will never be any favorable results of approachability of this section to the rest of the country, as long as the religious matter is not discarded. We the Islanders are Protestants and we will continue being Protestants.

Mr. James Hayes, Municipal Judge

How many competent Islanders have had to abandon their homeland in search of work in foreign lands; Islanders whose parents have spent the last cent in sending them to study in one of the various schools of the country. Yes, they have had to do it due to the mistreatment and persecutions on the part of many governors, liberals or not. And I show the proof: Where is the Islander who participates in the intendential government, that is, occupying a post that is of any value? Where is the cooperation on the part of the mainland liberals in favor of the Archipelago? Where is the equality preconized by the liberal constitution? We have not experienced it here as yet, and in the way things are marching, they will never reach us, unless we put a final stop to the present occurrences with all our hearts, spirit, interest, sincerity and abnegation. I will not leave my native land as some other countrymen have done, until we have obtained for the Archipelago all that it deserves.

Mr. Hayes also stated that a mainland countryman once said: "This is ours, we have it in our hands...let us do with it" —To which Mr. Hayes added: "If he could have said that, what then can we say? This has always been ours and now more than ever we certainly declare it as belonging to us; let us do with it as we please!"

Can the Raizals say the same thing today as Mr. Hayes said at that meeting? Are the people of today exercising their rights as they should?

On January 1, 1912 a complaint letter of petition signed by 250 members of the archipelago's population, was sent to Carlos E. Restrepo Restrepo, President of the Republic of Colombia, and his ministers, which states in its 5th and 6th points:

5th. Finally, we wish to submit that the laws of the country, cannot be possibly carried out, there cannot be any regard paid to any system of Government, based on rewards and punishments, in the nature of things; for the authorities themselves, are the leaders in evil, at least in gambling and immorality. This we most sacredly affirm, and we might add that on this very account, we are at this time, in more peril of robbers, etc. than ever we have been.

6th. We further beg to state that we have before forwarded through our representative, the Late Rev. B. Livingston, two petitions, and whereas we believe notice has been taken of them, and replies made, no such replies have ever been received.

In view therefore, of our grievances herein presented, Your Excellency, Mr. President, and you fathers of our "common republic", be it known to you that we are weary of this present government over us, and will have to take steps of ourselves to gain freedom, from this yoke of oppression, should you ignore our Petition, and not help us, as much as we would deplore such action.

In 1912, the Colombian state's response to the former petition, apparently based on Guerrero's report (seen on former pages), in spite of the above petitions made by the Raizal People for a "participative and equitable government", was the creation of the Intendencia Nacional de San Andrés y Providencia by Law 52 of October 26, apparently done with the only spirit of colonizing the archipelago. With Law 52, the Colombian state deliberately started implementing an official policy of colonization and colombianization of the indigenous (Raizal) people, just as it is shown in articles 13 and 14 below.

The law provided funds for mainland Colombian families "of four or more" to immigrate to the archipelago for residence and inter-procreation purposes (Article 14). Law 52 also placed public education under the control and administration of the Catholic church which would then require that all the education offered in the archipelago should be implemented in Spanish, totally disregarding and undermining in this manner the already established English schools that were in function long before, especially the First Baptist School.

Law 52, which is still in force, was a clear and flagrant violation of cultural, religious, traditional and human rights. Articles 13 and 14 of Law 52, respectively establish:

> 13 - As soon as this Law comes into force the Government shall enter into agreement with the Ecclesiastic Authority so that a Catholic Mission shall be sent to the Intendancy under whose charge the public schools can be placed.
>
> 14 - The Government is authorized to offer free passages on the national ships to families of four or more who desire to go to the Archipelago to establish their residence there.

In April 21, 1927; regarding the aforementioned Law 52, the intendant, doctor Jorge Tadeo Lozano, in his report to the Colombian state on the conditions of the indigenous territory, informed:

> The condition of the inhabitants is more or less full of anguish due to the almost absolute lack of work and the enormous density of the population (it can be well said that this is the most populated region of the [national] territory; it

has reached its limit). In this respect and taking into consideration the lack of work force on the mainland of the Republic and the good salaries that those employed in public works are favored with, I have opened up an inscription process so that all the people of the island who wish to improve their condition, go over to labor in public works, with good payment, transportation and hospital services on the government's account. This process can be developed because the Ministry of Public Works really needs workers. The Islanders, whether from love of the land, or from their recent deceit experienced by the offer of work in Nicaragua, or because they are satisfied with life without much labor, have been slow in registering themselves and that is why up till now the number of people inscribed is relatively small. Since Law 52 of 1912, which established the Intendancy imposes the promotion of immigration to the Archipelago, regarding the condition that has been mentioned, the prudent thing would be to promote emigration to the mainland, more so, when on the island the lands are totally inhabited and cultivated, and materially there is not even a fourth of uncultivated land available.

It is very interesting to consider the expressions used by the intendant, Dr. Lozano in his letter to the Colombian state: "Immigration and Emigration." In his report he confesses that Law 52 imposes immigration to the archipelago and in his concept the island of Saint Andrew is therefore to its limit or capacity as far as population is concerned. According to his "benevolence," he is offering the best solution to help unemployed islanders, which involves their emigration to continental Colombia for jobs. This, then, means that the Raizal people would abandon their lands giving the continental immigrants occasion to possess such territory. However, it did not work according to his plan, because even though the people were not rich, they were satisfied with their life style, also proud of what they had and who they were.

This proves how almost everyone in the government of Colombia over the past hundred years has been trying in his own cunning way to expel the indigenous from their own homeland from the moment of their adhesion to such nation. Dr. Lozano was also convinced that the island was almost completely cultivated, which means that the people were farmers and loved their land. However, the Colombian nation has put every effort to accomplish their pernicious plan in spite of the people's protest from the very start until the present day.

In 1946, Dr. Carlos Federico Lever, Raizal intendant, was abruptly removed from office, because he refused to follow the erroneous Colombian state's system of government and publicly spoke out, on behalf of the Saint Andrewans, against the negative policies and injustices that were being implemented upon them by the central government. This is what generally happens to any indigenous public server who has the courage to criticize publicly the Colombian government.

The practice of the Colombian state of not tolerating positive opinions in favor of the natives was again demonstrated fifty-six years later when, in 2002, history repeated itself and the indigenous governor of the archipelago, Dr. Ralph Newball Sotelo, was also brusquely suspended and finally removed from office for defending his people and not going along with the Colombian government's mistaken procedures.

It is good to observe carefully here that during the two main periods of the Colombian colonialist project with the islands, similar situations ensued with two different indigenous intendants/governors who had the courage to break the silence and speak out against the oppression levied on the indigenous people by the Colombian state: One of them was Dr. Federico Lever, in 1946; and the other was Dr. Ralph Newball Sotelo, in 2002. Both of them opposed all forms of oppression and corruption originating from the Colombian state that affected the archipelago and its indigenous inhabitants. Moreover, in the 1950's, under the administration of captain Maximiliano Rodriguez Pardo (Max), many indigenous leaders were harassed, maltreated and jailed, because they spoke out and expressed their opinions publicly against the Colombian government's evil system. Some of these were: Mr. Harold Forbes, Mr. Graciano Pomare, and Mr. Dan May, among many others. A man nicknamed "Soaky", was tied to a horse mounted by intendant Max and dragged along the street. Although the central government did nothing about it, Max was finally rejected and ousted by the indigenous community itself.

The above cases only go to prove that for more than 97 years the people, under the oppression of the Colombian state, were saying the same things they are saying today, so to think that they could certainly work out a bargain with that state, is a mistake. Instead of getting better, things have gotten much worse and there is no apparent prognostic of any positive improvement in the near future.

In 1960, based on the UN Charter (Articles 73-74), Resolutions 1514 and 1541 were issued, and Colombia, as a member of the UN is obliged to comply with them, as follows:

> Article 73 - Members of the United Nations which have or assume responsibilities for the administration of territories whose peoples have not yet attained a full measure of self-government recognize the principle that the interests of the

inhabitants of these territories are paramount, and accept as a sacred trust the obligation to promote to the utmost, within the system of international peace and security established by the present Charter, the well-being of the inhabitants of these territories, and, to this end:

a. To ensure, with due respect for the culture of the peoples concerned, their political, economic, social, and educational advancement, their just treatment, and their protection against abuses;

b. To develop self-government, to take due account of the political aspirations of the peoples, and to assist them in the progressive development of their free political institutions, according to the particular circumstances of each territory and its peoples and their varying stages of advancement;

c. To further international peace and security;

d. To promote constructive measures of development, to encourage research, and to co-operate with one another and, when and where appropriate, with specialized international bodies with a view to the practical achievement of the social, economic, and scientific purposes set forth in this Article; and

e. To transmit regularly to the Secretary-General for information purposes, subject to such limitation as security and constitutional considerations may require, statistical and other information of a technical nature relating to economic, social, and educational conditions in the territories for which they are respectively responsible other than those territories to which Chapters XII and XIII apply.

Article 74 - Members of the United Nations also agree that their policy in respect of the territories to which this Chapter applies, no less than in respect of their metropolitan areas, must be based on the general principle of good-neighborliness, due account being taken of the interests and well-being of the rest of the world, in social, economic, and commercial matters.

See UN General Assembly Resolution 1514 (XV) of 1960 – Declaration on the Granting of Independence to Colonial Countries and Peoples,

1. The subjection of peoples to alien subjugation, domination and exploitation constitutes a denial of fundamental human rights, is contrary to the Charter of the United Nations and is an impediment to the promotion of world peace and co-operation.

2. All peoples have the right to self-determination; by virtue of that right they freely determine their political status and freely pursue their economic, social and cultural development.

3. Inadequacy of political, economic, social or educational preparedness

should never serve as a pretext for delaying independence.

4. All armed action or repressive measures of all kinds directed against dependent peoples shall cease in order to enable them to exercise peacefully and freely their right to complete independence, and the integrity of their national territory shall be respected.

See UN General Assembly Resolution 1541 (XV) of 1960 – Principles IV, V, VI, VII:

> Principle IV - *Prima facie* there is an obligation to transmit information in respect of a territory which is geographically separate and is distinct ethnically and/or culturally from the country administering it.
>
> Principle V - Once it has been established that such a *prima facie* case of geographical and ethnical or cultural distinctness of a territory exists, other elements may then be brought into consideration. These additional elements may be, *inter alia*, of an administrative, political, juridical, economic or historical nature. If they affect the relationship between the metropolitan State and the territory concerned in a manner which arbitrarily places the latter in a position or status of subordination, they support the presumption that there is an obligation to transmit information under Article 73 e of the Charter.
>
> Principle VI - A Non-Self-Governing Territory can be said to have reached a full measure of self-government by:
>
> (a) Emergence as a sovereign independent State;
>
> (b) Free association with an independent State; or
>
> (c) Integration with an independent State.
>
> Principle VII
>
> (a) Free association should be the result of a free and voluntary choice by the peoples of the territory concerned expressed through informed and democratic processes. It should be one which respects the individuality and the cultural characteristics of the territory and its peoples, and retains for the peoples of the territory which is associated with an independent State the freedom to modify the status of that territory through the expression of their will by democratic means and through constitutional processes.
>
> (b) The associated territory should have the right to determine its internal constitution without outside interference, in accordance with due constitutional processes and the freely expressed wishes of the people. This does not preclude consultations as appropriate or necessary under the terms of the free association agreed upon.

However, 60 years have passed by and the Raizals are still a hidden colony.

When is the Colombian state going to report on them? This is what they are struggling for, and they have the right to do so, since throughout the years requests for better treatment from the Raizal people have been deliberately ignored.

Moreover, there are several recommendations from UN Representatives to the Colombian state and other UN officials who have visited Colombia that have likewise been disregarded, such as those contained in the following excerpts from the Report of the United Nations High Commissioner for Human Rights on the Human rights situation in Colombia – E/CN.4/2002/17 – 28 February 2002 (ANNEX 26):

> Ethnic groups: During the period covered by this report ....Other groups particularly affected by different forms of discrimination and disregard of their specific rights are native islanders. (57) [namely the] Inhabitants of the San Andrés, Providencia and Santa Catalina islands, an English-speaking (Creole) people of Antillean origin. (85)
>
> [...]
>
> Despite constitutional recognition of their specific rights, ethnic minorities continue to suffer the consequences of racial discrimination and intolerance. This led the Committee on the Elimination of Racial Discrimination to express concern at the under-representation of these communities in State institutions, as well as at the racial segregation and conditions of extreme poverty and social exclusion that they have to endure. Some of them, as was pointed out last year, are in danger of losing their cultural identity and, in some cases, the ethnic groups themselves are in danger of extinction. (59)

In addition, in order to preserve the cultural identity of the native islander population of San Andrés and to protect the island's natural resources, the 1991 Colombian Constitution provided for the establishment of a special regime for immigration, population density, regulation of land use and the transfer of land ownership. Despite this, native islanders, who are currently said to make up only 37% of the population, continue to be faced with situations that threaten their ethnic diversity and harm the environment. This is addressed in the following sections:

> Page 76 – Recommendations No. 14
>
> 390. The High Commissioner urges the State to guarantee the human rights of ethnic groups, such as the indigenous communities, Afro-Colombians, native islanders and Roma people, and protect them from discrimination, exclusion and intolerance. She encourages the authorities to adopt the necessary preventive measures and to protect the life and physical integrity of the members of

these communities and their leaders by concluding agreements with them on programmes adapted to their specific needs. She equally urges the State to ensure the effectiveness of the forums and mechanisms for consensus-seeking with ethnic groups in order to develop effective policies for response, prevention and protection and guarantee cultural preservation. She asks the parties to the conflict to respect the communities' authorities and leaders, as well as the autonomy of their territories. The High Commissioner urges the following:

a) Priority should be given to compliance with the accords signed by the Government and the indigenous, Afro-Colombian and native islander communities, and the State should define and implement comprehensive policies to guarantee the enjoyment and exercise of the specific rights of these communities, including those of the Roma people; as laid down in the Colombian Constitution;

b) The State should provide timely follow-up and should implement the recommendations of the Committee on the Elimination of Racial Discrimination and those of other international bodies;

c) Racial discrimination should be categorized as a crime in the Penal Code.

Furthermore, excerpts from a letter of June 27, 2002 – Ref: INT/627/02 from the UN Commissioner for Human Rights Office in Colombia, subscribed by Carmen Rosa Villa, Director in charge, addressed to His Excellency, Mr. Guillermo Fernández De Soto, Minister of Exterior Relations, read as follows:

> The objective of this letter is to make reference to the situation which the population of the islands of San Andres and Providence are facing, particularly the Raizal People.
>
> During a visit to the region, the Office met with State authorities, religious leaders and representatives of the civil society. It could be verified that there exist high tensions between the Raizal People and the institutions of the Colombian State. A portion of the Raizal People feel themselves excluded and discriminated on the Island of San Andres where work opportunities for them are generally limited to labor that has to do with the informal economy. The supposed abandon of the Raizal People by the central part of the State has produced a condition where many of the Raizal People manifest their loss of affection towards being members of the Colombian population.
>
> Taking this situation into consideration the Office recommends that ethnoeducation in the schools be strengthened so that the Raizal People will obtain benefits by learning about their own culture and history. Likewise, the Office reminds the Colombian Government of its obligation to protect minorities and to guarantee the protection and promotion of their cultural

identity.

The Office was able to observe during its visit to the island, the tension that exists between the Raizal People and the Public Forces. Many Raizal People complained about the failure of having persons of their own ethnia among the police of San Andres and Providence and they blamed most of the confrontations between the police and the Raizal People on a lack of understanding and respect, from the police, for the language and customs of the Raizal People.

The mainland Colombians themselves also feel affected by the tense situation that is being experienced on the Island of San Andres and they expressed their fears that on the island their exists the possibility of an irruption of interethnic violence.

It is important to take notice that the suspension of Governor Ralph Newball Sotelo has provoked a lot of indignation and manifestations of rejection among the Raizal People. In order to minimize the possibility of new conflicts, the Office affirms the primary importance of assuring that any process against Dr. Newball Sotelo be managed with the guarantee of transparency and independence.

The Office urges the State to take measures that will help to diminish the tension under which the population is living on San Andres Island. In this sense, as a measure of recognizing the Raizal culture, it is important that the public functionaries, especially those who work in the administration of justice, speak the language of these communities, in accordance with the legal and constitutional rules that exist related to this.

During the visit to the island of San Andres, the Office was also able to obtain the following information on supposed violations of human rights, where the intervention of the Public Force in cases of the Raizal People is being questioned by them.

According to the information received, on April 9, 2002, at 3:30 AM, Irvin Howard and Lemos Lee Robinson Archbold, members of the Raizal People, were approaching the beach in their launch to land at Manchaneel Bay on Providence island, in order to pick up oxygen tanks for their fishing activities. At some 50 meters from the beach they heard a voice shouting, "Stop! Stop!" On stopping the launch they were met by a barrage of bullets aimed against them.

Mr. Robinson Archbold dropped dead, while Mr. Howard hid himself in the bottom of the launch to protect himself from the bullets. A few minutes later, the launch was boarded by a police lieutenant, a lieutenant of the Coastal Guard, an agent of the SIJIN and two soldiers, who took off from the launch Mr. Howard, along with the body of Mr. Robinson Archbold.

Clamor of the Islands

Clamor of the Islands

Mr. Howard was taken to the police station and the body of Mr. Robinson Archbold was taken to the hospital. The person arrested was charged with homicide, carrying illegal arms and drug-traffic. According to the initial version of the police, the one detained had murdered his friend meanwhile they were transporting drugs and the other had started shooting at the police, who responded likewise to same. As evidence, they had presented an empty 38 caliber revolver, which they supposedly found on the launch, along with 5 empty shells. The young man had been detained for 9 days at the police station handcuffed to a chair, until the Fiscal decided that no evidence existed to sustain a charge against him, and he was set free.

The Office urges the competent authorities to urgently examine the matters described and to ensure that exhaustive investigations about same will be carried out penally as well as disciplinarily. Likewise, they are urged to adopt all the necessary measures to protect the Raizal People from abuses on the part of the local authorities and, particularly, the Public Force, as well as to prevent the discrimination of those people. At the same time it is requested that the Office be informed about the measures that are taken in this respect.

I also invite the reader to examine the following excerpts from Mr. Doudou Dien's (UN Rapporteur) report on contemporary forms of racism, racial discrimination, xenophobia and related intolerance upon his mission to our territory in October 2003:

Afro-Colombians account for 17 per cent of the total number of displaced persons. The disastrous impact of the conflict on these populations reflects a cultural and social context marked by the persistence of attitudes that are the historical legacy of racial and ethnic discrimination against Afro-Colombians. The ethnic and racial dimension of the Colombian armed conflict is therefore a sad reality. For this reason, the Special Rapporteur's recommendations focus on the following issues: a political solution and human rights; a national programme to combat racism and discrimination; the situation of displaced persons; an intellectual strategy against discrimination; and the question of San Andrés island. (2)

The Special Rapporteur was able to visit 4 of the country's 32 departments, as well as the capital. He travelled to Bogotá; to Cartagena (Bolívar), a popular tourist destination on the Caribbean coast, where the shantytowns of displaced populations are a blot on the landscape; to San Andrés island, where the indigenous people, known as Raizales, informed him of their "double marginalization": demographic marginalization as a result of large-scale migration of Spanish-speaking Colombians from the mainland, and economic and social marginalization, owing to their low participation in the economic and tourist development of the island... (4)

The Raizales of the islands of San Andrés and Providencia, who number 24,444 according to official statistics, told the Special Rapporteur that they considered themselves to be victims of racial discrimination. As the product of a mixture of African, British and Amerindian populations, the Raizales claim an identity distinct from other Colombians. Their native languages are English and Creole, and they are predominantly Protestant. They also consider that they have been subjected to discrimination as a result of emigration from the mainland, which the Government has encouraged. (20)

Today, of the 80,000 to 100,000 people living on the island of San Andrés, which has a density of 3,000 inhabitants per square kilometre, the indigenous people are in the minority. They claim that they are victims of political discrimination that excludes them from decision-making processes concerning their department. They are confronted with the cultural domination of Colombians from the mainland in the educational and judicial systems; the exclusive language of instruction is Spanish, while the courts use only Spanish.

Although Colombia is a secular State, the Raizales believe that they are subjected to religious discrimination because they are not Catholic, the dominant religion. The State has given the Catholic Church control of educational institutions, and the Church has undertaken to convert the indigenous population to Catholicism, provoking opposition from that population. The economy of the islands, which is based on tourism and the import of manufactured products (San Andrés is a free port), is in the hands of the Colombians from the mainland, who employ very few indigenous people. The unemployment rate among the indigenous population is estimated at 70 per cent.

The Special Representative of the President of the Republic told the Special Rapporteur that the Government was aware of the special situation of San Andrés and was in the process of preparing a strategy to remedy the problems raised. This plan will make it possible to grant loans to persons who wish to create family inns for tourists or set up other types of enterprises. (12)

Conclusions and recommendations

The Special Rapporteur has found that, more than 10 years after Colombia's recognition of its ethnic and cultural diversity, and in spite of the adoption of laws and the establishment of promising institutions, the situation of the indigenous peoples, Afro-Colombian communities and the Roma remains precarious. The domestic conflict, which taps the largest part of the State's resources, poses a serious obstacle to the implementation of otherwise well-prepared policies. Aside from the relative progress in granting land titles to the Afro-Colombian communities, the economic and social conditions of these populations remain a cause for concern. Moreover, not all of the population has necessarily understood the meaning of Colombian's cultural diversity and holds on to prejudices against certain groups. For this reason, the Special Rapporteur has formulated the following recommendations:

The Government is invited to consider the possibility of granting special status to the island of San Andrés with a view to guaranteeing its cultural and linguistic identity and strengthening the participation of its indigenous population (the Raizales) in the management and economic development of the island;

In general, the Government should involve the communities concerned in the preparation of development projects and in decisions that concern them. It should also ensure their effective participation in institutions responsible for community affairs, such as the Advisory Commission on Afro-Colombian Populations and the Inter-Institutional Commission on the Human Rights of the Indigenous Populations. (16-17)

In our opinion, if Colombia has failed to comply with its national and international obligations towards us, must we just keep silent and wait? Is this what we want to do? The question that faces us today is: How long is too long to wait? Our conclusion is: We dare not sit and wait to see what the outcome will be. We must act now to prevent our extinction! (Please read carefully, analyze and come to your own conclusion.)

It is important to observe very carefully the concept, intervention and recommendations to the Colombian state for the solvency of the recognized conflict the indigenous islanders (Raizales) are going through. Notwithstanding, the recommendations suggested by the Special Rapporteur, the Colombian state has disregarded whatever was advised. But is this just an affair of a few years ago? No. Let's see:

THE CIVIC MOVEMENT

On different occasions islanders were prone to separation from Colombia for different reasons. Some of the older folks claimed to be of English origin and rejected Colombia as their mother nation, owing to the fact that they do not speak Spanish neither profess the Catholic religion. Moreover, most islanders still sense that they are of no importance to the Colombian nation, and they feel far closer to an Anglo-Caribbean culture that is more attractive to them than that of Spanish speaking Latin Americans. No matter how some of the people neglect things and show indifference to the multitude of problems, there is always someone who is seeing things from a different angle and feeling the pain in the most tender part. Owing to this fact, someone inspired a group of Saint Andrewans who were also downhearted by the undesired situation which they were facing, and organized the Civic Movement.

On the day of inauguration, May 17, 1980, with about 150 people, there was a motto written in English and displayed in the meeting hall which read: "The Islander Civic Movement Center, of the people, by the people, for the people of Saint Andrew and Old Providence Islands." As it is, in everything there is always criticism, notwithstanding the applauses. This movement was not supported with efficiency. Even a few within the movement felt it to be a response to inconformity for the nomination and possession of a continental to the intendancy of the Archipelago of Saint Andrew, Old Providence and Ketlena in 1979, Ana Garcia de Pechthalt. Others thought it to be of political interest, while a few Providencians were totally indifferent to the movement.

The lack of unity and comprehension did not permit a successful outcome since some of the Saint Andrewans and Providencians looked at it as a self-interest affair. Whether these critics were negative or not, it is to be believed that self-interest could have motivated many of the native administrators to assent to the radical transformation of both islands. Amidst the conflict and discomfort that brought about the Civic Movement, there was concern about the economic underdevelopment and displacement of the natives. From hence, the complaint that "Our rights are not considered by the national government" has been the daily cry. "Customs and traditions are not respected," say some; others say: "The island is gone." The anxiety for obtaining jobs was shown by demanding that, "At least half of all jobs in hotels, banks and stores, be held by natives." While a great number of islanders were grieved because of the situation at that time, others thought that it was just reasonable to promote color and hair mixing with the light skin and soft hair continentals. However, this mixture caused a more complicated situation since it bruised the neck of those involved in mixed marriages. The situation grew worse from day to day until it has reached the peak of inconformity among a considerable number of indigenous inhabitants.

The Civic Movement stated its objectives: "The Islanders Civic Movement has been founded for the purpose of doing whatever must be done to prevent such gross injustice (loss of land, negligible participation in the free port economy) from taking place. Its aim is to safeguard the culture and advance the social and economic interest of the native population. It stands ready to start a new course for San Andres and Providence and to help us to regain control over our destiny." Among the principles and objectives of the Islanders Civic Movement, objective #7 brings afloat the hidden yearning of the people, which reads: "To defend our rights to govern ourselves." It also states that: "There is no shortage of highly qualified native-born Islanders who are willing to assume the leadership of the intendency. Islanders are no longer going to accept any importation whatsoever of local government leaders who have no use for our language, no love for our people, and no appreciation for our way of life."

These islanders have been "beating about the bush" too long causing things to grow worse for themselves. What the author means by "beating about the bush," is precisely the personal and collective confusion whether they should or should not ask for a complete separation from Colombia. The author confesses that from his youth he would sometimes hear the older folks saying: "These islands were only given to Colombia under certain conditions;" others would say: "We are not even Colombians." As a matter of fact there were very few who pretended to be Colombians. The fact remains that there was always a division regarding what or who they really are. Before the free port, once there was a discussion among some older people in Ketlena, Old Providence, about whether they should ask the United States to take care of the islands since they were really abandoned by Colombia. A man who pretended to be a faithful member of the Conservative Party and an outstanding Colombian remarked: "Will never happen! Because the Gringos would put us in the back and they would stay in the front." While others replied: "Even so, we would be better off having the good things like those living on the Canal Zone, Panama."

There has been a constant yearning by some of the older and younger people for a better life that they presume they will never have from Colombia. This longing was made manifest in the 1960's when a group of people from Old Providence petitioned the United States Government and the United Nations to hear their case for withdrawing from Colombia. Their idea was to form a separate republic to be named "Federal Republic of Old Providence." These islanders were accused of disloyalty and lack of patriotism and were threatened with up to twenty-five years of imprisonment.

Subsequently, a U.N. Delegate was said to have come to the island of Saint Andrew to make discrete inquiries concerning the claims made in the petition. Providencians claimed that corrupted native politicians in Saint Andrew, who were directly responsible for the intolerable conditions cited in the petition, squashed all efforts at getting at the truth, even branding one of the leaders as a psychopath. Cabrera, writing in 1980, states that what really went wrong is that the discomforted ones, (Saint Andrewans) asserted that the petition made by the people of Old Providence was the work of a few malcontents residing outside the archipelago and that whatever resentment, if any, existed among the native population on the archipelago, was directed at the central government, due to the very limited participation given to islanders in the political as well as other spheres. But, "deep down what was uncovered, was the deep love for Colombia and the pride of the majority of the population in belonging to this nation." This so-called fact mentioned by politicians hustling to be enriched from government was shown to be absurd when in 1980 the Civic Movement stated: "As a small ethnic minority in Colombia, we must unite in order to maintain our cultural identity. If we remain divided we stand to lose everything we own and cherish. But in unity there is strength. The civic movement has come into being as the defender of a just cause around which all islanders, regardless of religion, political inclination, or station in life can and should unite to secure our rightful place in the future of this homeland."

As it is known, for political and personal interest, everyone's "loyalty" cannot be counted on. Jesus had twelve publicly known disciples and one was a traitor seeking financial interest only. He sold his Savior! In this civic movement undoubtedly something similar took place. The Civic Movement promoted a march proclaiming not to be Colombian. However, this impulse did not last long because of discomfort among others.

THE STRUGGLE

Please take a look at the past once more. Islanders have been attempting for many years to take steps toward freedom with lengthy, wavering movements as is seen in different occasions, which has caused a sort of discouragement among those who waited desperately for freedom. On February 1st 1912 a bilingual bi-monthly native publication named *The Searchlight* published the people's complaints against the Colombian state. In 1936 when a commission was sent to the island of Saint Andrew by the Chamber of Representatives supposedly to solve, or try to find a solution to the problems the people were complaining about constantly to the national government, some of the representatives of the islands attending the meeting expressed their discomfort.

Mr. Timothy Britton Newball, stated that: "The educational programs implemented in the schools were inadequate for the learning process, because of the unknown language (Spanish) used in the schools, forcing the students to memorize the subjects taught, placing the teachers in a difficult position."

Teacher Vernon May, emphasized and criticized the inhuman procedure of the Colombian state in signing an agreement with the Roman Catholic Church to "civilize the Saint Andrewans" as they pretended to do with the Guajiro (Wayuu) indigenous population in the mainland. This, he said, hurt islanders deep down because the Spanish language is unknown among them while the English language they consider to be their mother tongue is characterized as being a token of their supposed uncivilized state.

Dr. Bedel Duffis, rejected and rebuked the stigmatizing gesture of the Colombian government of placing the natives on a scenery of savages just because of the differences of customs between islanders and mainlanders.

Mr. Silvano May, (who was known as Teacher May), an active vice-president of the Municipal Council of Saint Andrew emphasized that the erroneous idea of colombianizing the islanders by catholicizing them with the belief that they will be drawn closer to the other sectors of the country, would never bring a positive result. Religious prejudice will have to be abandoned. The islanders are Protestants and they will continue to be. On the other hand, the constitution offers the same guarantees to Protestants as well as to Catholic citizens.

From that period of time until now, things have advanced a lot for the continentals, but not for Saint Andrewans. This can be proven as it will further ahead. Referring to Dr. Britons's comment above, it is worth noticing that after 78 years the instruction system has not changed much. What has changed is the method of forcing the children into the Spanish language for a more successful assimilation of the Spanish tongue and less love for the mother tongue. Teachers are still Spanish- speaking in the majority, except for those who are considered English teachers to teach English just as another subject, especially in high schools.

Given the fact that the Colombian state has refused time after time to recognize the rights of the indigenous to their land and to the surrounding sea of the archipelago, the people are in constant supplication before that state and before international organizations to hear their plea for justice. Because these people have been suffering loss of opportunities for jobs in their homeland and have been discriminated, they are eager for means of survival. This ardent desire can only lead them to a self-determination movement. There is a permanent question ringing in the ears when talking about self-determination or freedom: "How will they survive?" But the question that should be asked conscientiously is: Will they be able to continue living under a usurper pressure? There are many things that the people are concerned about even though they might not show it in their daily living, but it is there. At times it is really hard to say who is in favor of the movement and who is against. Whatever the situation might be, there are a few things that are worth-while mentioning. These movements began especially in Saint Andrew, due to the fact that that apparently has been of more interest to the national government.

The number of anticolonial organizations active in the archipelago along the 20th century speaks about the need for self-determination felt by islanders in general. Some of them are: The Wall Painters, the Ancestral Birth Rights Movement (ABRM), the Islanders Liberation Movement (ILM), the Sons of the Soil (S.O.S.), the Civic Movement, and the Archipelago Movement for Ethnic Native Self-Determination (AMEN-SD). The most mentioned in recent times are the S.O.S. and the AMEN-SD. The S.O.S. has summarized its achievements as follows: "Many marches on the streets of Saint Andrew island, contacts with many Caribbean Nations, the gain of access to many magazines and press concerning the Native problems, detention of the territorial expansion of the military base at the Cove Sea Side, then probably the most important, denouncing Colombia before the UN."

The AMEN-SD has expanded its activity with marches, protests and complaints reaching the outside world. This movement has established its basis on self-determination. It has not emerged as a special group of people different to former groups. It is something like a joining or combination of foregoing groups. This movement is building its hope on the Almighty God who does not tolerate injustice and with fervent prayers that with God's intervention the ancestral people, will be freed from the colonial bondage of the Colombian state.

Although this might sound silly to the readers of these pages, remember that it is not impossible to take the rights of a minority group to decolonization before the International Court of Justice. According to written and oral history, these islands have been going through different crises at different times. Tolerance has been going from one generation to another without positive changes; discouragement invading hearts more and more with increasing heartaches fill with depression, causing aversion against a plenipotentiary abusive nation (Colombia). If all colonized people have rights to decolonization, then, why should not these people of these islands be freed? Well, this is precisely what these people under oppression are striving for: Freedom!

In order to accomplish real action you have to be a living part of the situation of the Archipelago of Saint Andrew, Old Providence, and Saint Catherine, especially today when things are going from bad to worse. You would have to be an element or a living subject of that popular energy which has called for the freedom, progress, and happiness of the islands. The indigenous people of the archipelago are really in the great battle. For the past years, others that are now in eternity had pledged to seek the most important element in life which is known as freedom. As the people today understand more and more the seriousness of the present situation and are in the thick of the fight, they cannot risk minimizing the actions of the fathers, pretending incomprehension when considering their silence and passivity. Their forefathers fought with what elements they possessed then. If the echoes of their struggle did not resound in the international arena, the impact of their cry and supplication had reached the community in 1999.

Because it is time for a complete awakening of the natives, then if it is not known it must be understood that the islands' struggle for their release from colonialism has been distorted to the convenience of the national government. It takes the courage of a united people to stand and with great bravery and energy give the shout, "We have got enough." Then the downhearted spectators will understand the need to take part in the fight if simply they wish to continue to exist.

In 1969, Marco P. Archbold Britton, a native of Old Providence, residing in New York, supported by several natives, presented a memorial to the UN in which he promoted the creation of a mini-state with the name "Old Providence" or the annexation of the island to the United States if the first was not possible. During his stay in Colombia, he was accused of being antipatriotic and said to be a psychopath to whom no one should pay any attention, who was deceived by some Saint Andrewans (said the people from Old Providence). He returned to New York. Apparently there was not enough force and interest on part of the natives to support the movement. It is worth mentioning right here that a few people from Old Providence believed that there were a couple of low-minded traitors, islanders from Saint Andrew, who contributed to the failure of Mr. Archbold. These are the Pharisees who are always selling out to the Colombian colonialists. These never see any farther than the tip of their noses. Notwithstanding these speculations, it is known that at that time, and even before, there were Saint Andrewans who were really thinking of separating from Colombia.

On December 18, 1976 the vessel Betty Bee sank with about 62 people on board when traveling between Saint Andrew and Old Providence. It was estimated that approximately 42 people died. An accurate number is not possible since some stowaways were unaccounted for. It is said that while U.S. and Mexican Air Force planes, Nicaraguan and Honduran fishing and cargo boats were sent to aid the shipwrecked, the Saint Andrew naval station (belonging to the Colombian navy) did not take adequate measures to mobilize a rescue mission (*Cromos* 2/23/78:58). It was also rumored that the Captain of Port in Saint Andrew denied permission to boats to leave Saint Andrew's harbor and even defied anyone from going in search. A navigator from the island of Saint Andrew manifested that he was menaced with imprisonment if he were to leave Saint Andrew's port to rescue the shipwrecked. Mr. T. Wilson, residing in Panama, manifested that a radio broadcast from Colombia received in Panama claimed that there was only one Colombian on board the wrecked boat, the others being islanders. Is that to say islanders are not Colombians? Well, as a matter of fact, culturally they are not, but that certainly does not disengage Colombian authorities from the responsibility of coming to the rescue of the Betty Bee victims just like U.S., Mexican, Nicaraguan, and Honduran authorities did.

Because of this lamentable tragedy and the Colombian caprice of not responding to it adequately, the separatist groups declared that this occurrence was due mainly to Colombia's neglect with regard to the territory. On December 23rd an open letter was addressed by Old Providence citizens to the Colombian people censuring the national government and the local authorities for not giving immediate aid to the victims and, for the general abandonment of the region. Towards the end of December a flyer written in English circulated in Old Providence that said: "Down with the idea of being Colombians. People, it is time to declare our independence, let this colony separate and be freed from Colombia"(*El Espectador* 1976). This is the kind of occasion when natives demonstrate that they have no love lost for Colombia and let the world know that they are prone to think of separation. It is clear that instead of making Saint Andrew and Old Providence a center for the spreading of peace and love for the country, the national government has been creating more and more resentment in the hearts of the islanders.

What follows is a summary of some of the plans of the national government that have been lurching, slowly but unabated, since past years to present moment. The following are some of the asides taken from what we quoted at the beginning of this book as the "Secret Document" (1977/1978 - See addendum).

A-"The development of the Colombian communication media out of the islands is of utmost importance. It is convenient to study the technical possibilities whereby the radio stations can have sufficient power to be picked up in a large part of the Caribbean and Central America. Their transmission must be done in Spanish and under no circumstances authorized in English."

B-"The transmission of some live television programs from the Capital of the Republic will result in great influence, no matter the cost this means for the country. If it were technically possible, treaties might even be made with some Central American countries so they could be picked up there and this would increase Colombian influence in the zone."

C-"It is indispensable to spend whatever is needed in order that Colombian television get into Old Providence even if its operation is not profitable."

This plan also states: "The presence of the Military forces should be increased for the purpose of guaranteeing national sovereignty. It is considered indispensable to assign airborne elements for patrolling and controlling not only the airspace but also the territorial sea, plus some kind of naval means that make reaction possible when our rights are violated, to carry out patrols in the area and to relieve the personnel assigned to the cays. The influence of troops for fomenting patriotism and in all aspects that enhance national pride is of utmost importance, as is the admission of young Islander men to the Military schools of officers and National Police. The presence of planes and naval vessels is a security factor in case of emergency."

(See: "A Blow to Separatism," *Cromos*, March 2, 1977, No. 3085; "Separatist Movement Surfaces in San Andres," *El Tiempo*, March 23, 1977; "Saint Andrew will be Annexed to the United States," *Radar*, March 24, 1977.)

MILITARIZATION

In 1979 when militarization was taking over Saint Andrew, the excuse for such unnecessary event was that the islands were threatened by Nicaragua. This militarization process was supposedly petitioned by the then intendant ruling the archipelago in 1982. Saint Andrew was becoming something like a war zone. The Colombian daily *El Espectador*, reported: "Up to this moment several marine contingents, some war ships and combat planes of the Colombian Air Force (FAC) have been detailed to the island (San Andrés). These actions are being reinforced with the emplacement of anti-aircraft batteries and in the near future an installation of a modern military radar system; four Mirages have been assigned, an indeterminate number of duly armed T-33combat planes, and A-37 military reconnaissance airship. In the Caribbean sea, a small naval fleet patrols or lies at anchor, comprising two destroyers, four frigates equipped with anti-aircraft cannons and two submarines." (*El Espectador* 5/6/82.)

All of this ridiculous deployment happened just to cherish enmity toward a defenseless island people. A sham anticipation of invasion or loss of a part of the national territory was entertained in order to highlight the unlikely menace of the "separatists" to peace in the region.

In January 1999 the local radio station in Saint Andrew broadcast the voice of a Colombian admiral, inviting all the indigenous young men to integrate in the military and police force. This sounded very pleasant to some of the native people here in the island. However, the author will not applaud this action too vigorously, because it could have a different objective from what some of the native people believe. It is expected that this plan of getting young islanders involved in the Colombian police force could be a means of replacing those coming from the mainland, which would seem to be the best thing. Nevertheless, it could also happen to backfire on natives. The scenery here is worth studying and observing very carefully. It is quite clear that the Colombian government is in no way interested in helping the Saint Andrewans as a people in promoting their culture, as it was demonstrated in the foregoing pages.

The Colombian state's idea is to keep down the indigenous people of the archipelago, as much as possible while it conscientiously knows that all its negativism against the natives might cause a riot in the islands due to oppression or division between the indigenous and those from the mainland. Therefore, this could be another strategy of having native young people to fight against natives whenever such a situation arrives. Policemen have to receive and obey orders from their superiors and undoubtedly the national government is not going to allow a native Saint Andrewan to be in command.

PROTESTS

In a forum held on March 21st 1995 in Saint Andrew, with representatives of the indigenous people and government representatives from Bogotá, the native organization S.O.S. (Sons of the Soil), manifested clear discomfort with the oppressive abandonment by the national government of its obligations to the territory to which it claims sovereignty. The natives upheld their equal rights to jobs and housing and claimed to have been totally ignored by the former government. One of the greatest problems is urban development. The unplanned and irrational construction of buildings everywhere and anywhere is in no way beneficial to the natives, since they are not willing to work for an underpay. Besides the fact that this unheeded construction fever does not provide adequate jobs to islanders, the island is being deforested with great harm to the ecology and resources needed for survival. In the meeting it was said that living in San Andrés has become a headache. It was proposed that the money which is supposed to be used in housing for the non-employed illegal continentals must be used instead for relocating them to their homeland to reduce the population for a better living. In the meeting, the discontent of the representatives from Bogotá attending the forum was very notable touching the topic of relocation. This discomfort was expected since there were plans to get the natives off the island, which undoubtedly will be continued to be attempted in the near future.

On April 27, 1997 the natives held a manifestation to show their displeasure against the abuse of newcomers. The natives were claiming their rights and also control of the agency called Coralina, which is supposed to strive for ecologically sustainable development. The Saint Andrewan anthem was sung followed by the famous hymn "Onward Christian Soldiers." These manifestations showed the natives' pressing concern regarding the imposition of what they have no choice but to see as monstrous entities that are doing everything possible to get rid of the indigenous people.

There was a forum held at the Hotel Toné on the 10th of September

1999. Among the different things that were mentioned, pastor Alberto Gordon referred to the situation of the S.O.S. (Sons of the Soil) that are being displaced, forgotten, ill-treated morally, limited in their homeland; including the way the central government has been finishing away with the marine resources of the islands: "We do not have a space in Colombia as a people who are not even recognized by the Colombian government." He asked that there be laws which protect the natives and uplift them.

Professor Juan Ramirez spoke of the prejudice from the past century created by the central government until now: "More participation of the natives is of great importance and the menaces that endanger the islands should be diminished." He also pointed that these and other factors are what cause or bring violence, blood shedding and death. These threats to the islands and the indigenous people should be avoided. In the meeting held at the airport with the indigenous religious leaders, community leaders and the minister of interior from Bogotá on the 28th of July 1999, there were some petitions made by the leaders on behalf of the people. The leaders and the minister of interior signed such petitions by mutual agreement. One of the petitions was to relocate to continental Colombia the continental people living in Saint Andrew in chaotic situations.

It is known nationwide that Saint Andrew is one of the most populated islands of its size in the entire world. This overpopulated island occupied mostly by non-natives, in its majority Colombian continentals, has been suffering pollution of all sorts from the early sixties on. The cry of grief by the natives has ever since become supplicant before God and man with discouraging response. It seems as if though nature itself has rebelled against natives. The earthquake felt on the islands of Saint Andrew and Old Providence, on the 4th of February 1995 seemed to have been a simple reaction of the archipelago against the gigantic buildings going up to the heavens.

Some natives are very much concerned about such situation and in spite of injunctions made to control these buildings, nothing has been done to refrain constructions. As for relocation of continental Colombians, it was completely ignored, because until today no movement has been made whatsoever to relocate anyone. To the contrary, as usual, the national government rejected it in a very diplomatic way, by organizing a census in Saint Andrew on the 30th of May 1999 which resulted in 10,000 people less than in 1988. The result was not given until six months later to the natives by president Andrés Pastrana Borrero, in December 1999. The census gives a spurious number of just 57,000 people, of which 45% are natives, while most sources indicate that 125,000 or more people inhabit Saint Andrew today. This inconsistent census was made precisely because the central government does not want to relocate the people. Due to such nonsense deforestation is growing very fast and sooner or later the island of Saint Andrew will not even have where to plant flowers.

There is no doubt that the Saint Andrewans and Providencians have suffered the sickness of unconcern, ignorance and carelessness. After an epidemic decease of conformism has hit the islands it has spread throughout the generations as a dangerous cancer. If one should review a little of the natives' history it will be noticed that Saint Andrew and Old Providence have been persecuted fiercely by the Colombian government. Natives have been persecuted intellectually, physically, morally and religiously. It is also known that they have been persecuted economically. One does not have to be omniscient or a fortune-teller with a crystal ball to see the destruction that lies ahead of these islands and their population. The thing that really hurts and burns is to see the way how some people gave up their body, soul and mind to the adversary and gladly receive the imposed sufferings. The central government had a very thorough plan to get rid of the indigenous people; even when they knew it would take time, they have been working on it very hard and now they are not very far from achieving their goal. To get rid of the people does not mean to kill them. It simply means that among the nation's plans for the people one of them was to move them out of the island to Chocó and the Llanos Orientales —chiefly to Chocó, maybe because they wanted all the black people to be organized together in one area. From hence the Saint Andrewans became resented. Should there be any reason to doubt that this plan is forgotten? More on this further ahead.

Educated islanders with titles from outstanding universities seem not to be worried about the situation of the native. Paradoxically, those who would want to do, do not know when, or how, or what to do. The author of this book has not gotten clearly the meaning of "an educated dunce" (expression used by the ancestors of the islands), but probably it could be applied to some of these graduated people. No one could ever deny the fact that there are people from Saint Andrew and Old Providence that are well prepared intellectually, knowing the history of the islands, seeing the danger surrounding the people, knowing the laws, the nation's constitution and most of all the international laws which state the rights of an ethnic minority group. However, it is like those who know the Bible and scripture verses by heart and finally end up in hell, or like a rich man dying from starvation. The comment of the situation is the daily bread. Old and young, literate and illiterate lament the present situation; there is a vast preoccupation island-wise. The undesired situation is seen and felt in both islands. The AMEN-SD movement has been trying with great effort to make contacts nationally and internationally for a better living, promoting self-determination.

The few indigenous people who are much worried about the situation of the islands express their concern by marching the streets. The leaders of the Amen-SD group organized these marches and a series of them were carried out during the month of June 1999 in Saint Andrew, on the 4th, the 8th, the 10th and the 22nd. The largest of these was held on Tuesday the 8th. This was due to a death threat that was made to religious and civic leaders. A very big crowd, more than what anyone could have thought of, was there. Many thousands gathered as never before and maybe there will never be a big crowd like that again. Another march took place on the 27th of July 1999, a Tuesday afternoon. From 4:00 p.m. the entrance to the airport was closed. Even though plans of the group to close the airport were supposed to be secret, somehow the police knew about them, no doubt on account of a traitor. The police got to the airport ahead of the crowd and locked the entrance. Notwithstanding, the policemen said that the manifesting group closed the airport.

The protesting group demanded the presence of the President of the Republic Mr. Andrés Pastrana Borrero, but as usual he found some excuses and sent the minister of interior instead. The manifesting group remained all night at the airport and all flights were suspended until the following night. The leaders of the group held a very long meeting with the minister of interior in which many things were discussed and petitioned by the indigenous people. After agreeing on the petitions both the manifesting group and the minister of interior from Bogotá signed a document produced by the leaders. The manifestation was lifted on the 28th at 8:30 pm. The fact remains that whatever was agreed upon never went farther than the pages of the document.

On January 10th, 2000 there was a protest meeting at the Christian University in Saint Andrew from 9:00 a.m. to 5:20 p.m. Speeches were given by leaders of the self-determination project and the bottom line was "FREEDOM." All the attendees supported this claim.

On the 20th of July 2000, the indigenous people of Saint Andrews held a manifestation directed by AMEN-SD leaders. The manifesting group marched from the First Baptist Church on the Hill with the newly designed flag of the archipelago and a banner which read "Native people struggle for an Autonomous Self Governing Territory."

One of the big flags was displayed on a light pole facing the Coral Palace (Administration Building). Two smaller ones were placed on each of the two flagpoles in the Bolívar Park. The two placed in the park were removed by members of the DAS (secret police) hours after the marching group returned to their homes. The leader of the group removed the big flag hoisted on the light pole that same evening before leaving town since it was not high enough.

On Thursday, July 27th, there was another march from the First Baptist Church on the Hill to North End (the center of the city) through the 20th of July avenue, up to Hotel Isleño on the way to the airport and ended at the Bolívar Park where two of the flags of Saint Andrew were hoisted. The Saint Andrew anthem was also sung, led by Mr. Leno Duffis, its author. Reverend Marcelino Hudgson led a closing prayer. The flags hoisted on that day were not removed until a couple of weeks later by the AMEN-SD movement itself.

Public Employees

The natives of Saint Andrew, Old Providence, and Ketlena, apart from some important merchants, were farmers from ancient days. Increased depredation of land resources in the islands led by the central government has made people more dependent on public employment. But the fact remains that the evidence of central government pressure against employing islanders is mounting step by step. The public administration has never been a steady source of employment for the natives. Politicians elected to local administration employ many native supporters for the period of their tenure, who are then let go by incoming political leaders to be replaced by their own loyal supporters. This situation leads to discontent and conflicts between islanders. A person in danger will do anything to escape. It is said that a "drowning man grabs at a straw," and that "a hungry man is an angry man."

Some people educated away from the islands in the past 45 years have obtained government jobs and have been running around with politicians. Some have already been pensioned; and others are still going along with the daily shady task to sustain their families and their children that are studying in the Colombian mainland. Only a few can afford to send their children abroad to obtain higher education. A loan was given by the local government to a few aspirants trying to do professional studies in the mainland. Some have returned their loan after graduation while others have vanished, becoming completely invisible while the debt keeps floating in the air.

It is not surprising that some students graduating from college have also returned from the mainland of Colombia with the virus called "dishonesty," which has caused chaos in the islands. Those who get into the epidemical politics end up like a "tick" and finally behind the iron bars. These educated scamps have run the local government into bankruptcy leaving others in distress. These are called the "contaminated brain washed." It cannot be denied that there have been some hooligans called political leaders, who have been puppet directors, moving these dummies around, making them victims of a dark and dreary situation which has led them into the pit of disgrace and shame upon themselves and their nearest relatives and honest friends. Not knowing what would be the next step, others playing the role of Superman soon discover that their super gown is falling off, leaving them to land rapidly crashing and smashing against the edged stones of the comptroller or the boiling pot of the Attorney General's office. These two entities would soon be executing a fictitious justice to prosecute the demons, casting them into a mocking world. There is an old saying that goes like this: "You can do as much as you want, but not as long as you want." Precisely that was what took place with the disorder of the local government in the latter part of the nineties, causing a labor massacre of more than 800 public employees after a total strike. "After the kettle has accused the pot, there goes the worst!"

The Total Strike

Before the strike at the administration building (Gobernación) in July 1999, the critical situation was seen and felt everywhere in the island. Here is an excerpt taken from the journal *Cambio* (pages 61- 62, May 3, 1999) that serves as an introduction to the lamentable situation as follows:

> There is nothing to pay salaries with and many families are living from social welfare, from charity or from stolen food. To regain the prestige and tourism

of Saint Andrew, hotel managers have just initiated a campaign of promotion in Bogotá, Cali, Medellín and Bucaramanga with a program called "Caravan for San Andrés." It is a musical "show" in the principal cities where hotel managers and travel agencies meet to sell the image of the archipelago with prices from the year 1994. But there is an obstacle: the budget of the local tourism secretariat will go from 570 million pesos to 47 million.

Commerce in liquidation

The commercial crisis is more serious than that of the hotel industry. The massive closing of stores is evident. Signs of liquidation sales and promotions adorn shopping windows everywhere. Esteban calculates that half of the 60 stores of Saint Andrew are bankrupt and the other half is on the same path. Of the remaining business there are not even 40 that put their money in banks of the island. If individual business used to provide an average of three jobs, now only one is offered. Therefore there are 1,200 more jobless employees. Merchants attributed the economic crises to the increase in tax-free shopping centers and contraband in the Andean region. In the past most families traveled to Saint Andrew not just for tourism, but also to buy electrical household appliances because they were cheaper. The "san andresitos" (tax-free shopping malls established all over Colombia emulating Saint Andrews' free port conditions) devastated the island's commerce.

Referring to departmental finances, the suspended governor at that time, Mr. Leslie Bent, according to a local paper expressed: "If one wanted to rob now there is nothing to rob." The undermining of the local government's money was now about to bring to light what was hidden from the public, but would soon bring about an inevitable chaos.

In July 1999 a number of desperate, frustrated public employees decided to go on strike at the administration building (Gobernación). That afternoon whistles and shouts took place in the building, asking for solutions to the problem of the unpaid months. The acting governor Violeta Fakih said there was nothing she could do at the moment to solve the problem. After the uproar that afternoon, the Defending Counsel of the People from Bogotá, who was also present at the meeting, tried to give some consoling words that were not of much help to the protesters. Questions were asked by the people regarding a solution to their payment but there were no satisfactory answers given by the governor nor the People's Defending Counsel, so everyone returned to work the following morning. A few days later Mr. David Soto was sent from Bogotá to the archipelago as governor. After a couple of days the employees asked him for their unpaid money. He manifested to the outraged protestors that he would try to do whatever he could, but at the moment he could not give any guarantee of payment to anyone, because there was no money. What really caused dissatisfaction among the people was that they knew that the local government was still paying big money to contractors while the employees were starving.

Mr. Soto said he was doing some investigations concerning the money. Finally, he said that there was a big fraud, because he discovered that more than a hundred people on payroll were buried in the cemetery and another group on the payroll were living out of the island. So he said that they would have to solve that problem before doing anything else. Mr. Soto went back to Bogotá after staying for two months. During his stay in Saint Andrew employees were not paid. Mr. Felix Palacio, who tried as much as he could to keep the people's animus together, replaced him. The people were only talking about a strike, but seemingly they did not want to harass him because he promised he would pay some of the money. Being a personal friend of the president of the country, Mr. Andrés Pastrana Borrero, he managed to get some pesos from the national government and paid a month's salary. After a hard struggle for two months trying to uplift the people's courage, Mr. Silvio Casagrande replaced him.

It was not long after Mr. Casagrande took possession when the public employees asked him for payment. Nothing was done to release the money and the people decided to go on a total strike. Some 600 desperate, frustrated workers refused to continue laboring after being owed seven months of their salaries. The following week a syndicate was formed and on the 10th of September at 8:00 am the entire building was taken over by a great number of employees. No one was permitted to do any work. The doors to all the different offices were closed. The newly organized labor union SINTRADESAI supported this strike. The governor, Mr. Casagrande, upon the first shout and uproar of the people who had already taken over the building played the role of "deaf, dumb and blind."

That morning Mr. Casagrande was very early at the building, therefore, when the employees blocked the entrance to all the offices he was already at his desk. With the shouts and blowing of whistles of more than 200 people inside the building impeding the access to the offices that morning it did not take long for the police to arrive. Who called them? Apparently no one knew. Someone said it was the secretary of government, but others said it was the governor himself. Although the doors were closed there were four policemen inside the building on the second and third floors. One of the employees who was accused of letting in the colonel through her office window, explained that he poked himself through the half-opened window while she was receiving a receipt from someone. The presence of the police caused the people to become very furious and with great determination that no one would leave the building, and neither go up nor come down the stairs. There were many armed police with tear gas and shields. The colonel, who was already in the building, tried to go up the stairs because he wanted to talk with the governor. He was not allowed and neither was the governor allowed to come down to meet with him. The policemen were awaiting orders to attack the strikers.

Upon the insisting clamor of the people the colonel was asked by union leaders to leave the building. Marlene Bent, who was the spokeswoman using the microphone at the moment, insisted that the colonel withdraw his armed policemen since there was no intention of sabotage, riot or anything of the sort. By noon the police were back to where they belonged. Finally, after hours of discussion the governor was permitted to leave the building to attend a meeting in the afternoon at the Hotel Toné with the minister of interior and other delegates who had just arrived from Bogotá.

After the meeting with the delegates that afternoon the governor returned to the government building and nervously informed the people of his inability to respond to their claim, because, according to the minister of finance, there was no money for an immediate solution. However, the minister of interior guaranteed those present at the meeting that there were fifteen thousand million pesos standing right there awaiting a restructuring of eighty percent of the employees. This was contradicted by one of the representatives of the archipelago early next morning on Caracol Radio, who explained to the audience that there was no money to pay the strikers. Just think of it! One of these people was really telling a black lie. The unsatisfied employees decided to continue with the strike closing all the doors and denying access to all different offices including the governor's.

Of course, this was the first time anything like this had ever happened on the island. The strike kept on. The "Permanent Assembly" began and union members occupied the premises day and night. Some played dominoes, other played different games, others walked around; meanwhile a group of ladies did the daily cooking and brewed coffee and bush tea during the night watches. Why did a people who are known to be very peaceful since the time of their ancestors act like this? Because of an intolerable situation that was breathing the threat of starvation with an accumulated seven months of unpaid salary. With dissatisfaction darkening the working atmosphere, the meek and the mild could not avoid to raise up from the well of anguish to float on the surface of fury. The alms of a month's pay would not be the solution to a long standing debt that had even paralyzed shops which had gone bankrupt by selling on credit. Under the strain of such a complicated and perplexing situation, a few days later a group of seven people were allowed to enter the finance department to work on the budget for the year 2000.

Another group of five was also allowed in the personnel department to work on the payroll. The treasurer had his eleven assistants make up the lists. All these workers were allowed to labor after thirteen days of interruption. President Andrés Pastrana Borrero brought about the "solution" to this dire situation, recommending to: "Fire all the people to reduce the payroll to its minimum, so that the government can be relieved of financial worries." How long will it take to resurrect the deceased Department of Treasury?

The indefinite strike grew weaker and weaker each day after a month. The same faces were seen every evening coming for the night watch; meetings were held twice a week to inform the desperate strikers of the situation and of the determination of the local and central governments. Labor leaders held religious gatherings and prayers to strengthen the state of mind of the poor frustrated laborers. Out of 600 members who joined the union, there were only 150 to be seen around during the day and no more than 20 for the night watch, of which half would be home by midnight. This discouraging situation caused the president of the union, Mr. Olaya Herrera to call a general meeting to revive spirits, but there was not much of a positive response. Finally, most people were not attending daily meetings even when food was offered. It was very exhausting for just a few to maintain the strike. It became so boring and discouraging that on the 26th night of October 1999 a meeting was held at the assembly hall in which a majority voted to call off the strike.

Everyone went back to work downhearted, this time with eight and a half months pay owed to them. Christmas came and there was no money. Finally, by December 31st 830 employees were fired from government posts in Saint Andrew, but they were all paid off. The news spread around and some of the local stores and supermarkets raised prices. It was said that a few people were mugged coming from the bank on payday. The fact remains that there were 830 dismissed employees who, from then on have been looking up to yonder sky praying that the daily "manna" may descend from heaven to keep them from starving.

THE TURBULENT FUTURE

With a telescopic view from where one stands there is no clear perception of a safe port for the indigenous. The dark cloud is too thick so as to hope that an iceberg is not laying ahead. There is a voice giving an alert that is ignored by a confused and perplexed people who have lost their trust in all leaders. With this uncertain situation the people are called to diverge and point to a safer port where the harbor can be seen more clearly, where there are less surrounding reefs and dangerous shoals and rocks, a port where there is safety. The aboriginal are urged to take steps with unlimited determination. The situation is being analyzed year after year; things have been growing worse. Solutions have been put on roofs on a stormy day that were not there anymore at the end of a stormy night. The people cannot continue running barefoot on thorny roads; if they want to walk safely the road must be cleaned; they cannot swim among the piranhas unprotected. There might be a brighter and successful future for them, but they will have to look for it. The AMEN-SD movement has been trying with great efforts to make contacts nationally and internationally for a better living, promoting self-determination.

Saint Andrewans and Providencians will do anything to survive, because even when it is perceived that their greatest enemy is Colombia, they think: "When all your property is gone and life itself at stake, to save that life and property you gravel to a snake." (As in the story of "Handsome and Theodore", by Arthur W. Ryder.) After a man is put out of his house where will he live? The national government has studied the idiosyncrasy of the people for years and knows exactly how they think and act and where to touch them. Islanders are emigrating, seeking survival elsewhere and this is very pleasing to the government. Many of those who sold out and went away have never returned. Those who have not sold as yet are placing notices for sale. Now the idea of selling is not the worst, the worst is that natives are not selling to natives and all the purchasers are Colombian continentals or people from elsewhere. The Colombian Navy is also buying a great deal. To hint the reader as to where the author is going he will sum up the following: In 1926 there was a tremendous religious persecution against the non-Catholics; in 1930 with the disease that hit native coconut palms the farmers were denied aid from Colombia; in 1949 the national government was conducting ethnic cleansing by paying for the transportation of people from mainland Colombia to establish in the islands;

as early as 1982 Saint Andrew was being militarized *(El Espectador* 5/6/82).

Ever since, there has been a continuous piling–in of police, infantrymen, Air Force and Navy. There are just a few native policemen among the hundreds sent from the continent. Serving the government for an 18 months period is obligatory for young men to obtain a military document (libreta militar) to work in the country. Islanders are denied employment in the hotels and islander fishermen are persecuted by the coastguard; at times, natives' fisheries on the rocks are pestered by the police, the minimum means of living are harassed by the Colombian government. After the labor massacre of 1999, the only remaining institution where 90% of the employees were natives, the traffic department ("Tránsito"), was turned over to the police department.

Even the outlying maritime area that for centuries has been part of the livelihood of islanders was given away to Honduras in a treaty agreed upon in 1986 and ratified in 1999 that reads as follows:

> Maritime Delimitation Treaty between Colombia and Honduras, 2 August 1986
>
> The Government of the Republic of Colombia and the Government of the Republic of Honduras,
>
> Reaffirming the friendship bonds that rule the relationships between the two States and aware of the need to establish a marine frontier between the two States; Have decided to execute a Treaty and for such purpose have appointed their plenipotentiaries:
>
> His Excellency the President of the Republic of Colombia appoints Dr. August Ramírez Ocampo, Minister of Foreign Affairs; His Excellency the President of the Republic of Honduras appoints Mr. Carlos Lopez Contreras, Attorney, Secretary of Foreign Affairs,
>
> Who have entered the following agreement:
>
> Article 1
>
> The marine frontier between the Republic of Colombia and the Republic of Honduras is constituted by geodetic lines that connect the points located in the following co-ordinates:
>
> Point No. 1 Lat. 14° 59' 08" N Long. 82° 00' 00" W
> No. 2 Lat. 14° 59' 08" N Long. 79° 56' 00" W
> No. 3 Lat. 15° 30' 10" N Long. 79° 56' 00" W
> No. 4 Lat. 15° 46' 00" N Long. 80° 03' 55" W
> No. 5 Lat. 15° 58' 40" N Long. 79° 56' 40" W
>
> Between points 4 and 5, the marine frontier shall be constituted by a circular

line, the radius of which shall be measured from a point located in coordinates 15° 47' 50" N and 79° 51' 20" W.

No. 6 Lat. 16° 04' 15" N Long.   79° 50' 32" W

From the above point, the marine frontier shall continue towards the east by parallel 16° 04' 15" N, up to the point where a delimitation must be made with a third State. The marine frontier agreed upon is indicated only for illustration purposes in the nautical chart No. 28000, published by the Defense Mapping Agency Hydrographic/Topographic Center, Washington D.C., 74th edition, March 30, 1985, which, duly signed by the Plenipotentiaries, is attached to the foregoing Treaty, in the understanding that in all events, the contents of the same shall prevail.

Article 2

The delimitation stated in the above article shall not overrule the layout of the marine frontiers which have been established or can be established in the future between any of the Parties herein and third States, as long as said layout does not affect the jurisdiction acknowledged to the other Contracting Party by the foregoing instrument.

Article 3

The hydrocarbons or natural gas deposits or fields which are found on both sides of the line established shall be exploited in a manner such that the distribution of the volumes of the resource extracted from said deposit or field is proportional to the volume of the same which is correspondingly found on each side of the line.

Article 4

Any disagreement between the Contracting Parties regarding the interpretation and application of the foregoing Treaty shall be decided by the pacific means established in international law.

2 August 1986

(From: https://www.un.org/Depts/los/LEGISLATIONANDTREATIES/PDFFILES/TREATIES/COL-HND1986MD.PDF)

This treaty was approved in 1999 by the President of Colombia, Dr. Andrés Pastrana Borrero. The people of the Archipelago of Saint Andrew, Old Providence and Ketlena were not consulted because the national government ignores them as far as these matters are concerned. Notwithstanding, one of the community leaders, Bill Francis, from Saint Andrew, rushed off to the meeting held that day in Bogotá with thousands of signatures rejecting the approval of the treaty and requesting a consultation with the indigenous people of the islands. After his arrival, he was allowed a 3 minutes talk, which meant nothing to the magnates holding the meeting. The petition was completely despised showing that natives mean nothing to the national government.

Sooner or later the indigenous people of Saint Andrew and Old Providence will not have where to fish neither for food nor for business. Terrible situation!

The foregoing explains why today islanders are living a semi-disparate life and with very little hope of survival. With all the difficulties natives are going through, apparently they are divided among themselves and this division makes things worse.

OVERPOPULATION AND THE OCCRE

What is the OCCRE? It is an office established by the national government to control immigrants. After analyzing all the sufferings the natives have undergone is there anything to give Colombia thanks for, or to be proud of being a Colombian? The national government has been promising the natives to relocate some of the non-native people who are living in a very precarious state because of overpopulation in the island, but never complies with its promises. To the contrary, whenever the indigenous remind the government about it everyone is offended. To get rid of the idea, the national government in 1999 ordered a census on the island (as I already mentioned) trying to show that the island is not overpopulated but, surprisingly the result was not given until the president himself came in November of said year and gave the false number which was handed to him. According to the result there were 25,000 indigenous inhabitants and 27,000 aliens. What a big lie!

According to the data provided by the DANE, Departamento Administrativo Nacional de Estadística (National Administrative Department of Statistics): In 1951 the population of Saint Andrew and Old Providence was 5,675 and in 1997 65,000, while in 1997 the total population of Colombia was 39,694,185.[17] These figures of irrational growth that the islands suffer are dramatic, making the

---

[17] The official projection of the archipelago's population for 2019 is 79,000. The relative difference in population density between Saint Andrew and Old Providence stays constant. See: Resultado%20de%20 Gestión%20Territorial%20Departamento%20San%20Andres%202019%20().pdf. Website accessed 1-8-2020 (N.E.).

problem worse, while the rate of population growth of the country during the period of 1985-1993 was 2.8%, that of the islands was 6.66 %. Meanwhile, the mean density for the country in 1993 was 32 inhabitants per km^2. If we take into account the unequal distribution of the population within the principal islands, we would have that the density for Saint Andrew reaches 2,272 inhabitants per km^2, while the municipality of Old Providence and Ketlena has a mean density of 230 inhabitants per km^2.

In *The Caribbean Sun*, the editor wrote:

> Why is the census necessary for the island? [Referring to Saint Andrew]. If the census establishes that 100,000 of us are living on the island, then, they would design programs for water system, (aqueduct), sewage-system, housing, health and education for those 100.000 people. But if we do not collaborate, if we do not give the correct information, then, in reality the census gives that we are 70,000 people when really we are 120,000, those plans for public services, housing, health and education would have a deficit of 50.000 people.

Petitions have been always going to the national government without any result. We take the following from the *Archipelago Post* (September 1999):

Petition

The Indigenous AFRO-ANGLO COLOMBIAN people of Saint Andrew, Old Providence and Ketlena, to the Colombian Government, presented personally to the President of Colombia, Doctor Ernesto Samper Pizano, by the undersigned commissioner of said people, July 29, 1997.

To protect the Ethnic Identity and to guarantee the survival and economic, social, cultural and political development of the community of the Archipelago, we ask of the Colombian Government the following:

The over population in the island of Saint Andrew, is the cause of all the social-economic, political and cultural order of Saint Andrewans. We ask to reduce the actual population of one hundred thousand inhabitants under the program of resettlement in places of origin of the people with residence by the national government.

To guarantee the indigenous of the islands that their education will be imparted in their vernacular language (Standard English and Caribbean Creole). This according to the political Constitution of Colombia 1991, law 37 of 1993, law 70 of 1993, and international treaties, stating that Spanish is not only in the official language of the Country.

To respect the Presidential guidelines No. 15 of December 13, 1996.

To arrange that the national investment in the Archipelago begin in the indigenous communities of San Luis, Loma, Old Providence and Ketlena, especially in the area of public services, education, culture, housing, sports and recreational installations, etc.

To guarantee the sustainable development of the islands, for example, financing the natural reserves proposed by the indigenous community.

To guarantee the participation of indigenous people in the military control of the insular territory with a significant proportion.

To reduce the size of the military police force in the Archipelago, in honor of quality above quantity.

To conform a commission made up of civil servants of the national government on the one hand, and on the other, representatives of the indigenous community, to recommend thorough reformation of all the national and departmental institutes that function in the Archipelago, in all the branches of the government granting greater autonomy to the island people.

Juan Ramirez Dawkins

Native Rights Consultant Commission.

In one way or another natives are to be blamed for overpopulation in the island. A high percentage of them are only interested in money. So we go back to the question, in detail: What is the OCCRE for? What does it stand for? As its name explains it is supposed to be "The Office for Control of Residence and Circulation" (Oficina de Control de Circulación y Residencia). Its stated mission is to control and to hinder the entry of persons to the archipelago with the intention of residing on it without previous authorization and likewise to promote social development, through verification that jobs are held by native and resident persons, and that the rendering of public services allow for adequate living conditions for the population. Doctor Cesar Gaviria Trujillo, President of the Republic of Colombia issued this decree No. 2762 on December 3rd of 1991. The decree was declared totally adjusted to the national constitution by the Honorable Constitutional Court through SENTENCE C-530 of 1993, Substantiating Magistrate Alejandro Martinez Caballero.

I, the author of this book, will take from the Decree 2762 of 1991 some of its articles and add asides related to measures adopted to control the population density in the Department Archipelago of Saint Andrew, Providence and Santa Catalina exactly as they appear, as follows:

The President of the Republic of Colombia, in use of the faculties granted to him by the Transitory Article 42, of the Political Constitution, under previous consideration and non-disapproval by the special commission and considering:

That the Department Archipelago of Saint Andrew, Old Providence and Santa Catalina presents a high index of demographic density that has made difficult the development of the human communities on the islands.

That the natural and environmental resources of the Archipelago are endangered, making it necessary to take immediate measures to avoid irreversible damages to the ecosystem.

That the accelerated migration to the Department Archipelago of San Andrés, Providence and Santa Catalina, is the principal cause of its population growth, making it necessary to adopt measures to regulate the right of circulation and residency in the insular territory.

Decrees:

Article 1. The present decree has as its objective to limit and regulate the rights of circulation and residency in the Department Archipelago of San Andrés, Providence and Santa Catalina, in procuring the purposes expressed in Article 310 of the Political Constitution.

Article 2. Whomsoever is within the following situations will have the right to establish his residency in the Department Archipelago:

a) To have been born in the territory Department Archipelago of San Andres, Providence and Santa Catalina, provided that one of the parents has, for such time, been dwelling in the Archipelago.

b) Not having born on the territory of the Department, have native parents of the Archipelago.

c) To have been residing on the islands, proved through documental proofs, for more than three continuous years and immediately previous to the issuing of this decree.

d) To have contracted valid matrimony, or lived permanently and continuously with a person resident in the island, providing that they have established relation for more than three years previous to the issuing of this decree, and common dwelling in the territory of the Department of the Archipelago.

Article 5. Only the residents of the Department Archipelago of San Andres, Providence and Santa Catalina, can exercise within the territory of the Department, the following rights:

1. To work permanently.

2. To study in an educational establishment of the Archipelago.

3. To be inscribed in the mercantile registry and exercise permanent commercial activities.

4. To exercise the right to vote in the Departmental and Municipal elections.

PARAGRAPH. In no case will lose their qualities of residents the persons who have been born in the Department of the Archipelago of San Andrés, Old Providence and Santa Catalina, neither the persons that, not having born on the island, have native parents of the Archipelago.

The party interested in obtaining provisional residence must prove that adequate housing and economic capacity for self-support are obtained in the Archipelago.

Article 10. Provisional Residents can remain in the territory of the Department of the Archipelago during the time they have been authorized for the development of the activity that motivated the conferring of this right and should be used only for the fulfillment of such purpose.

In all cases the Provisional Residence will be granted for the same time, without summing to exceed three years.

Article 12. For contracting of workers not residing in the Department of the Archipelago of San Andrés, Providence and Santa Catalina, the employer should fulfill the following requirement:

a) Obtain an insurance policy through which he guarantees compliance on his part and on the worker's of the dispositions of the present decree.

b) Prove the working capacity of whomsoever pretends to work on the Archipelago without being a resident.

c) Make a one-time payment, corresponding to a legal minimum monthly salary, to each non-resident employee, which will be used for the creation of a special fund for work capacitation of the residents of The Department of the Archipelago.

d) Obtain the provisional residency for the duration of time for the contract.

Article 13. Employers that employ non-residents without the fulfillment of the previous requirements will be sanctioned with successive fines of up to one hundred legal minimum legal monthly salaries.

Article 17. Persons who travel as tourists to the Department of the Archipelago of San Andrés, Providence and Santa Catalina, can remain in the territory only for a lapse of time of four months a year, continuous or discontinuous.

Article 19. Persons that are found in irregular situations will be returned to their place of origin and should pay a fine of up to twenty legal minimum monthly salaries.

Article 22. The office for control of circulation and residence is created as an organ of the Archipelago of San Andrés, Providence and Santa Catalina for the fulfillment and compliance of the dispositions of the present decree.

Article 36. From May 30th, 1992, the competent authorities should require from persons in the Department Archipelago, the carrying of the card that identifies the legal situation they retain.

Transitory Dispositions

1st. Transitory Article

Persons residing in the department Archipelago that do not fulfill the three years dealt in letters c) and d) of the second article of this decree will have the quality of Provisional Residents and will be subject to the dispositions that for such a situation the present decree determines.

2nd. Transitory Article

While the Office for Control of Circulation and Residency is in the course of beginning its functions, the Governor of the Department of San Andrés, Providence and Santa Catalina is authorized to carry a record of the persons that enter the department. These persons will have the rights to the resident card only if they fulfill the requirements established in the 2nd article of this decree.

For Publication And Fulfillment
Given in Santa Fe de Bogotá, D.C. on 13 December 1991.
President of the Republic
César Gaviria Trujillo
Minister of Government
Humberto de la Calle Lombana

Extract of the Sentence C.30/93 From the Honorable Constitutional Court
Substantiating Magistrate:
Alejandro Martinez Caballero.

The Honorable Constitutional Court through Sentence c.530/93 dated November 11, 1993, declared attainable in its totality the Decree 2762 through which measures are adopted to control the population density in the Department of the Archipelago of San Andrés, Providence and Santa Catalina. In the following some of its asides of Capital importance are transcribed because of their legal and conceptual profundity of great transcendence for the regulation not only of the relations the inhabitants of the Archipelago with the majority of the Colombian Nation, but also of all of the other minority groups with the majority of the Nation, wherein the concepts of equality among equals and the differentiation between different, the survival, and this survival within a framework of dignity, the protection of the culture and the environment requires a real and tangible dimension under the command of our 1991 Constitution.

In the public audience celebrated within the frame of this process it was asserted that San Andrés is the most densely populated island not only in the Caribbean but also in the world, even above Japan.

Therefore Dr. Julio Gallardo Archbold, Representative to the Chamber of Congress of the Department of the Archipelago of San Andrés, Providencia and Santa Catalina, and member of the Commission for Constitutional affairs, affirmed that "the implementation and application of the dispositions on control of the population density are of essential priority to guard the possibilities of conservation of the natural riches of our Islands and the survival of a community whose culture and ethnicity enriches the patrimony of the Colombian Nation."

As it is then seen, the real purpose of the OCCRE is to control the overflowing of immigrants into the archipelago. However, this agency finally ended in the hands of unscrupulous politicians and with a few employees who made it a business. With people who only think of money the islands will never prosper. There is an article that states that no person who does not speak English can hold a government job in Saint Andrew and Old Providence, law 47 of 1993. Notwithstanding, there is a great number of people in government jobs who cannot even give the time of the day in English. On the other hand, they refuse to learn the language and bluntly tell customers to speak to them in Spanish. Public employees are supposed to be bilingual, but in practice this rule is applied only to the indigenous.

In spite of decree 2762 of 1991, one can see people piling in day after day. Some even come from afar with their OCCRE card. The author knows the case of two young lawyers whose friendship was at stake because of negotiating an OCCRE card for the value of 300,000 pesos. One of them ended up with the money, which was causing a big affair. The author of this book being a friend of both, served as a mediator for reconciliation. Don't you think that there are many more cases like this? The daily talk is that most of the OCCRE cards are sold instead of being given to the residents after fulfilling the requirements demanded by the law. Whether the rumors are false or true, anything can be expected from anyone who does not love his/her land and ignores the damage one can do by legalizing the illegal, endangering others along with themselves.

If the employees working with the OCCRE office do not come to the conclusion that the islands cannot take more people and buildings, corruption will continue to lead them to destruction. It seems as if there are natives who care not about their own people, neither themselves, and are ready to do anything and everything possible to get some pesos regardless of the consequences it might bring. Sacrifices ought to be made and at times they are ineludible, but they should always be for the better and in no way cause oneself and others to disappear. Sometimes it is said by the Paña that the indigenous are "anti-Paña" (Paña = Spanish-speaking person). Some of the shortsighted ones go along with them. This is really not the case. To the contrary, Pañas are the ones that look on the natives as a lower class of people who are characterized as lazy.

If the OCCRE office were functioning the right way, carrying out its laws step by step with sincere and serious workers, we would not have to witness all the problems that the office is going through today. According to the OCCRE law only those who have been residing on the islands before 1991 can hold a residence card. How many thousands have not come in since that year and are now residents?

Once the author of this book was told by a lady from Bogotá that islanders are stupid people, because, she added, "I know of Islanders who lend witness in favor of people unrelated to the island to get a resident card, saying that they have lived here for years, just because these people pay them a few pesos." From a different point of view it can be seen that the OCCRE could be a beneficial instrument for the islanders, but unfortunately it is not being used for the purpose it was created.

For the OCCRE to be successful, it will have to be an entity that operates independently from the environment of politics and its corrupt circles, with a director who is willing to bluntly say no to bribery and apply the decrees; working with people who care for the Islands and also themselves.

Precisely, because of politicians the OCCRE is where it is today. It is not self-governed and that is why the levy collected from the tourist cards is being spent for any purpose other than equipping the office for a better service. Another problem is that the OCCRE is not really commanded by the head of the office, but rather by the governor of Saint Andrew and the national government. The money for the tourist cards goes to the "Gobernación" and there it is used for everything besides what is needed to strengthen the control of unsustainable immigration.

Unless the OCCRE can exist with the aforementioned characteristics, there should be no reason for it to exist. Nevertheless, it will continue to exist, because of the big money accrued to those playing the game. If the indigenous are to survive, they must do so with dignity, moral, pride and love. They must love themselves before loving others; they ought not to give away their beds and go on the floor; swim to save others and drown themselves. If they do not work against these dangerous elements, they will all disappear very soon and be read about in the future as an ethnic group which existed until the year 2050 or so.

IMBALANCED POPULATION

The indisputable factor that has caused social fragmentation is high population density (1,170 persons per sq. km).[18] The population of the archipelago has increased by more than 7,000 between 1993 and 1999, going from 50,094 to 57,324 people (for Saint Andrew). It has reached an annual average growth close to 24 per thousand. Density is above the national 244.91 inhabitants per sq. km, and higher than that of Aruba and Curaçao (315 and 337 inhabitants per sq. km. respectively). Population growth in Saint Andrew and Old Providence is bound directly to migratory processes stemming from the Colombian Caribbean coast. Up to 42 percent were born elsewhere.

The migratory flow is due to the search for adequate living wages. The radical increase in population density has placed unbearable pressure on natural resources and has heightened tensions among settlers and natives related to land use, access to social programs and jobs. To this we should add that the average income is very low, with 32 percent of the population of working age receiving no income, 67 percent receiving less than four minimum wages, and the 32 percent earning less than a minimum wage. Extreme population growth is seen as one of the principal factors against sustainability. The diminishing carrying capacity in ecological and cultural terms is one of the conditions that

---

[18] As of 2018 officials reported a population density of 2,000 per square kilometer specifically on the island of Saint Andrew. See https://www.rcnradio.com/recomendado-del-editor/por-sobrepoblacion-casi-la-mitad-de-habitantes-tendra-que-salir-de-san. Website accessed 1-8-2020.

is being studied globally in order to avoid situations in which the excessive growth of population might impede any further development. The archipelago is not far from reaching a situation like that of Haiti, which is presented by international aid organizations as an example of critical deterioration due to the uncontrolled growth of its population.

Official data put out by the Colombian government based on the census pilot of 1999 registered that 12.01% of the population of Saint Andrews live in a state of misery, 37.42% live in poverty, 27.69% live in an intermediate state, and only 2.86% can be classified outright as non-poor. (Source: SISBEN of Saint Andrew, last date: 2000-05-04; total information corresponds to 86% of the total population of Saint Andrew according to census pilot of 1999.)

The evident conditions of crisis approached by the archipelago have exerted a negative effect on the quality of life of the population comprising mainly children, young people, women and people above 65 years, by putting them as a social group of high vulnerability.

After all the things that have been said by the SISBEN and the OCCRE, what seems to be an enigma is where does article 309 of the 1991 Colombian constitution fit in. Because, in addition, article 310 specifically grants the Islands rights to determine who is allowed to live on the islands, to restrict the sale of lands and to protect the physical and cultural environment. Essentially, Saint Andrew enjoys the rights of special constitutional status not extended to other regions of Colombia. Article 310 reads that...

> in addition to the norms provided by the constitution and laws for the other departments, the department of the Archipelago of Saint Andrew, Old Providence and Ketlena shall be governed by special norms established by legislation relative to administrative, immigration, fiscal, foreign trade, foreign exchange, financial and economic development. The laws approved by majority of each house of congress, make it possible for Saint Andrew and Old Providence to limit the exercise of the rights of circulation and residency, establish control over the density of the population, regulate the use of the soil and subject to special conditions the sale of lands for the purpose of protecting the cultural identity of the native communities and of preserving the environment and the natural resources of the Archipelago.

In keeping with these special privileges, injunctions were made against the construction of big buildings, but as usual, there have been a couple of natives toadying around and, unscrupulously favoring strangers and new-comers, thus eroding the islanders' rights. This means that part of the real problem is due to the low-minded unscrupulous native scamps. The fact cannot be denied that among these particular mischief-makers we find some of the few brainwashed individuals who made their studies in the Andean region or even on the Colombian coast. It is a wishful hope that it will not be long before the stupid mania of giving first place to continentals and other outsiders will be corrected and others join in with the few who are struggling for a better future for the coming generations. Unless a positive change of mind is developed in these quislings, the opportunity for native survival will never come through.

On the other hand, due to the uncontrollable violence in Colombia, the daily massacre of innocent people committed by the guerilla, thousands and hundreds of thousands are moving out from the rural areas and into the cities. Some of these displaced people are also coming to the island of Saint Andrew, one by one, but consistently, and no control is executed to avoid these disorders. Pregnant ladies drop by to have their babies on the island for their children to have the rights to residency, which they believe will also give them equal rights as mothers. Girls between 14 and 17 years of age are having more babies than adult women. Continental women are procreating uncontrollably. Thereby the population growth is terrifying and of great preoccupation. Unless a law for birth control be created or imposed, the survival of the island and its future generations is nothing more than a mirage!

PARABLE OF THE ALLIGATORS

Facing the aforementioned facts, I, as the author put it this way: The indigenous people are on the brink of the river with tigers behind them and alligators in front of them. Therefore, it is a very serious and confusing situation, because in the middle of the river there are the piranhas awaiting them. Which is more risky? To face the tigers, or to swim among the alligators and the piranhas? The little river was once freed from alligators, but one day Saint Andrewans saw a pair escape and seek refuge in the little river. They thought of no harm having them there, so they paid no attention to them. In time they grew and reproduced. When there were just a few everyone played with them in quiet water and even provided for them to eat as they harmlessly took the food from their hands and ate peacefully.

As time went by, they became numerous, self-providing, independent and ferocious. Whose fault is it? The tigers', the alligators', or the peoples'? All this could have been avoided, couldn't it? Why did they permit them to grow in the little river? Why didn't they take out the first few? Why did they feed them? Why couldn't they see and know that they were not like them? Is there any solution to this enormous problem today? What I, the author, am saying is that the central government of Colombia and its henchmen are the tigers; the adult foreigners are the alligators, their offspring are the piranhas, while the indigenous people are the victims that are now confused, against the wall and their lives at stake, crying in despair seeking defense from on high through God's mercies while trusting that he sends another "Moses" to lead them to a port of freedom where they will be able to regain strength morally, spiritually and economically. The difference between Israel of old and the Saint Andrewans, is that the Israelites were slaves in a foreign country and the Saint Andrewans are slaves in their own homeland. On their way to liberation, the Israelites were confused and somewhat faithless. Discomforted whenever any little difficulties aroused and would always think of the food their slave masters would give them, forgetting their sufferings and oppression would seem to be attached to endurance even when they were offered a better life promised by God himself.

The struggle of the indigenous people today is for the recuperation of a land that was given to them two centuries ago and they have lost almost all of it because of ignorance and stupidity. The desire for freedom is rooted deep down, but to face the tigers is as dangerous as to swim among the alligators and the piranhas. Notwithstanding, a move is on its way. As the proverbs say. "God helps those who help themselves."

It is believed by some Saint Andrewans that things are in better condition in Old Providence, but given the speed at which Old Providence is deteriorating spiritually, economically and demographically, there will be a worse situation within 20 more years or so than anywhere else in the world. There are no sources of regular income in Old Providence, no jobs, nothing to live from. Nevertheless, continentals are arriving day after day and are accepted no matter if they are drug addicts, thieves, prostitutes or whatever. It is like a competitive affair between the two islands to see which can resist a more disastrous way of living.

After seeing all the different problems the people have been going through and amidst the division among the indigenous people themselves there are still a few that cannot take the pressure and for such reasons they have still been complaining and demanding justice from the national government. The following section directly quotes a petition with self-explanatory claims and demands made since 2001 that are still outstanding.

Demands of the Indigenous People of Saint Andrew Island - June 13, 2001

The indigenous people of Saint Andrew, Old Providence and Ketlena, make public our energetic protest for neglecting the fulfillment on the part of the national government on the agreement with our spiritual and community leaders at the airport in San Andres, on the 20th of July 1999, and especially for not complying their own decrees, 2547 and 2548 of said year. We reiterate the same demands in the following terms:

1. The transference of the necessary resources for the efficient functioning of the office for control and residency and circulation, OCCRE. Specifically, we demand 2,600 million pesos for the current year and 1,000 million yearly beginning on the year 2002 in order to systemize the office and to staff it with technical and professional personnel and the equipment that are required for, among other things, to hinder the arrival of more people illegally.

2. Deportation of all the people that are found to be staying illegally in the Archipelago according to decree 2762 of 1991. The National Government must carry out reconnaissance raids weekly, inclusive in stores, hotels and pirate districts, guaranteeing the mean and necessary resources to deport all the illegals within a maximum period of six months. We demand moreover, the revocation of all appointments to public posts still in force obtained by non-resident personnel of the Archipelago.

3. The relocation of Colombians and foreign residents of Saint Andrew to their lands of origin in order to reduce the population density of the island to a maximum of 1,200 inhabitants per km^2. To this end we demand the appointment of a special commissioner of the national government to lead the program of relocation under the supervision of the Indigenous people.

4. The creation of the institute of lands, at the latest the 30th of September of the present year, with the purpose of acquiring land in the Archipelago for the environmental conservation or to transfer it to Indigenous islanders individually or collectively for housing, agriculture and other uses.

5. The destination of resources for the amount of 15,000 million pesos yearly

beginning on fiscal year of 2001, contributed by the national government for the next 20 years for the acquisition of land on the part of the Institute of Lands.

6. Award to the Institute of Lands the following lands: all those confiscated from persons that have obtained them with illegal money and some that are properties of official entities such as those of Telecom in Sarie Bay, the Hotel Isleño, the old cemetery of Sprat Bight, the properties where the factory of grease functioned at the Cove Seaside and the land of the Armed Forces bordering the sea and beach section of Rocky Cay.

7. Cancelation of all concessions given by the national government for construction in beach and sea areas of the Archipelago.

8. All Magistrates, Judges, Prosecutors, Professors, Notaries, Police, Military Officers, directors of official entities and other civil servants in places of public duties in the Archipelago must be able to speak Creole, in other words, "the English commonly spoken in the Archipelago" which the law 47 of 1991 stands for. This requirement must be fulfilled at least in 50% at the latest December 31st 2001 and in its entirety at the latest the 30th of June 2002. It must be guaranteed that at least 80 percent of said posts be occupied by the Indigenous.

9. The termination of discrimination practiced against the Indigenous people in the private sector of the Archipelago, guaranteeing that at the latest the 31st of December 2001 at least the 80 percent of the employees in all hotels, airlines and other commercial enterprises be Natives.

10. The non-approval by the national government of macro projects in the Archipelago such as the international tourist dock and the base for the Coast Guard without previous consultation of the Indigenous people by means of representatives elected exclusively by the people in accord with their own procedures.

11. The cancellation at the latest September 30th 2001, the debt of the "Gobernación" (Government Entity of the Department Archipelago) with the national government and the assumption by the national government of the debts that the Territory Entity has with private entities, so as to permit greater Departmental investment in social projects in benefit of the Indigenous people. Remembering that, it is more important to invest in the conservation of peace than in the recovery of peace.

12. Complete support to the administration of Governor Dr. Ralph Newball.

13. Recognition of the complete Archipelago, including the Sea, the Coastal areas, the Cays and Banks as the territory of the Indigenous people.

14. Respect and recognition of the proper Authorities of the Indigenous people under a new system of Government for the Archipelago based on the

right of the indigenous people to free-determination.

After the proclamation of the above quoted petition, to the surprise of the indigenous people, the DAS (Departamento Administrativo de Seguridad—the secret police that acted at the time like a Colombian FBI) issued requests to the non-Catholic churches asking for the names of their members, and the means of their income, to which an answer was given by one of the Baptist Pastors, German McNish which reads thus:

> San Andres, Island, 23 August, 2001
> Doctor
> JOSE ANTONIO TRIVINIO ABRIL
> ANTICORRUPTION GROUP
> DIRECTOR DAS
> SAN ANDRES, ISLAND,
> GREETINGS.
>
> I, German McNish, of age and citizen of this city and identified as it appears at the end of my signature, acting Pastor and legal representative of the Lynval and Cove Baptist Church, a non-profit entity, with due respect address your office with the purpose of exercising the rights of petition treated by article 23 of the political Constitution to seek and obtain access to information about the object and forms that I will indicate in this petition.
>
> ### ACTS
>
> Through official letter No. 387229-0/ Das. SSAI. GOPPJ. GA: 122 of August 16th of current year, I was asked for information with regards to the members of the Church that I am pastoring.
>
> ### PETITION
>
> For the foregoing I refer to your office for information about:
>
> a) What reasons does that entity have to solicit said information, if we keep in mind that we are protected by article 19 of the Political Constitution.
>
> b) Whether the present person or the Entity as such, or any member of the Church that I minister is being investigated.
>
> In case of answering affirmatively to point b), please indicate the establishment of the record, such as day and hour to be heard in acquittal on discharge in presence of a Proxy, according with subsection 2 of article 325 of the new C.P.P.
>
> Notify if the petitions contained in your official letter were made to other

religious and civic organizations or only to those pertaining to the Baptist Faith, made up of the Indigenous people?

NOTIFICATIONS

I will receive notifications in the secretary's office or in the office of the Linval and Cove Baptist Church.

Sincerely
German McNish
Pastor

Another claim was made before the Governor-In-Charge which reads:

SAN ANDRES, ISLAND
13 June, 2001.

DOCTOR
EDBURN NEWBALL
GOVERNOR (IN CHARGE) OF SAN ANDRES, OLD PROVIDENCE AND KETLINA

Mr. GOVERNOR:

The undersigned are pleased to convey to you in the name of the Indigenous people that starting from today there will be a general protest initiated against the policies and actions of the State of Colombia, that menace our survival and have displaced and laid us aside territorial, financial, political and culturally, that until now the Native Government has not complied with the commitments agreed upon in 1999.

We appreciate that our Constitutional rights of protest are to be guaranteed.

Cordially,

Members of the Delegate Commission

The few people who are concerned about the situation of the islands and have been working so hard with expectation of something positive from the Colombian government are becoming disappointed with the indifference of that nation with regard to these demands and petitions. On the other hand the antinomy of the very natives causing division is enough for anyone to drop off. However, very small groups are still hanging on. Unless these two or three little groups be combined as a whole and get in the same boat and sail for the same port, there will never be a better land, a satisfactory answer from the Colombian government and in the end both the fighting groups and the indigenous spectators will all end up totally crushed and destroyed in their own homeland, (if it can still be called their homeland). This shameful situation observed in Saint Andrew is heart breaking. And what can be said about Old Providence and Ketlena? Even when the situation there is not so tense demographically it is very difficult to gauge the people's feelings because of their apparent indifference or cold feet.

Coralina

What is Coralina? It is the Corporation for the Sustainable Development of The Archipelago of Saint Andrew, Old Providence and Ketlena. The general office of this Corporation is in Saint Andrew. Coralina has been working on some very good projects to conserve the little that is left of the Islands' biosphere. It´s not an easy thing to educate and influence a population that does not see the destruction ahead, which needs to be controlled. These islands have lost a lot of their natural resources since the free port in 1953, especially in Saint Andrew. Because of uncontrolled growth and preposterous changes that have taken place from the fifties until today, including extreme population growth and irregular distribution of people and lots, demand for services has increased to the point of desperation.

Law 99 of 1993 declared the archipelago a Biosphere Reserve. The Biosphere Reserves promote conservation and sustainable human use of the ecosystem. The ecosystem is the complex network of a community and its environment functioning as an ecological unit in nature. The law also stated that Coralina is the agency directly responsible to take the necessary steps to accomplish this decision locally and internationally. Among the different concepts of biosphere it is worthwhile mentioning three of the greatest importance for the archipelago, which say:

> 1. Biosphere Reserves preserve natural and cultural values through management that is scientifically accurate, culturally appropriate and operationally sustainable.

2. Biosphere Reserves include lands and sea areas in which people live and work and which are managed for multiple objectives ranging from complete protection to intensive yet sustainable production.

3. Biosphere Reserves are examples of human dependence on the natural environment of voluntary cooperation to conserve and use resources for the well-being of people everywhere.

- Conservation strategy makes clear that the economy and the environment have to be managed together to stop excessive deforestation, control soil loss, prevent atmospheric pollution and limit urban expansion into irreplaceable agricultural land. These benefits include protection of basic land and water resources, improved land management skills, a productive and diverse economic base, alternative for land-use, rejuvenation and protection of farming and fishing, additional employment, enhanced educational opportunities, opportunities to express and fulfill local needs, increased local autonomy and participation in land use decisions, a clear and healthy environment, protection and recuperation of local traditions, and improved quality of life. Because the principles of Biosphere Reserves ensure that local values are a fundamental part of the reason for establishing protected areas, Biosphere Reserves are of considerable value to native people in protecting their traditional culture and lifestyle.

The Archipelago of Saint Andrew, Old Providence and Ketlena was selected as a Biosphere Reserve and the ceremony of inauguration took place at the First Baptist Church in Saint Andrew on the 16th of January 2001 at 7 p.m. For this special occasion there were special guests from UNESCO, The United States, Colombia and of course the Director and Staff of Coralina. There was special emphasis made on conservation of the ecosystem. Natives are very much pleased to have the archipelago selected by the UNESCO MAB program as the Seaflower Biosphere Reserve. This means that efforts will have to be made to organize, promote and maintain specific programs for sustainability. With Coralina as the "watchtower" everyone trusts that good things will be done for the benefit of the archipelago and its people. It will not be an easy task since the islands have suffered great deterioration due especially to overpopulation causing deforestation and other factors, being the protagonist the national government.

With an overpopulated island with the threat of more slums and deforestation, serious decisions will have to be made to avoid a total chaos. Even when Old

Providence apparently is not going through the same process of decadence as Saint Andrew, there is a dread of future deterioration, because of the peoples' negligence. Even when there are not so many vehicles contributing to air contamination, motorcycles are piling in day after day. underground water is not extracted as it is done in Saint Andrew since there is not so much of a great demand as it is in Saint Andrew. However, the beaches need more protection and the disposition of garbage that is now becoming a serious problem with the burning of the waste materials. McBean Lagoon, Iron-wood Hill, Crab Cay and the Brothers Cay are considered part of the core area that needs special attention for preservation since it is qualified as a natural park. The few that are concerned about this affair trust that more care will be exercised to protect and preserve these important areas.

TOURISM

Everyone talks about tourism and promoting tourism for Saint Andrew and Old Providence, but is it growing? Tourism means much more than just talking. Apart from promotion or encouragement of touring there must be accommodation for tourists. If a city, a country or an island wants to become a tourist center, then that city, country or island has to be prepared for such environment. There must be something of interest to attract the travelers. To make money one needs to invest money. There should be something to motivate tourism, something people will find and be satisfied with as they make their visit. You would not be interested visiting a place that is worse off than your own. Would you? Everyone knows that Saint Andrew has beautiful beaches with clear crystal water. The cays also offer very good beaches and clear crystal waters to entice anyone who visits them. No one can resist delighting himself/herself with caresses of the harmless waves that obligingly always reserve a space for their visitors. As he/she dips in, the irresistible water experiences the unforgettable caresses of its warmness.

These cays, Johnny cay and Rose cay, are just ten minutes away from the Saint Andrew seashore. There are also a few hotels trying to give an acceptable service to their guests. But you might want to know how well have these tourists been attended. For shopping, if they are Spanish speakers, very fine. Any other language, they just have a hard time. Then you might ask, don't the indigenous people speak English? Of course they do! But the fact is that they are not employed in stores or hotels. Why are they not? Two reasons among many: they do not welcome blacks, considering them as a lower class; the other, because they never consider them as competent. The stores are playing the same role, although most of them are owned by Syrio-Lebanese and they attend their own business, employing mostly relatives.

A lady from Bogotá once said to me: "I was in the store of one of my friends (who is also from Bogotá) one day and an island (Raizal/indigenous) girl came in and asked her for a job, because she wanted to work. My friend told the girl that she did not need anyone at the moment. The girl went away. Just after that a Spanish girl came in and asked for a job and the lady, my friend, told the girl to "come back tomorrow." I asked her "why did you tell the first girl there was no job and now you told this last one to come back tomorrow?" She said: "I do not want any of those blacks in my store." Then it is not really because they are lazy as some might put it, but because they are black.

Another factor is the abuse that is seen day after day perpetrated by store owners against the tourists. The author refers to experiences during his time working at the Price Control Office at the Administrating Building (Gobernación) as a technical assistant. Many times, people would go to the office complaining about the way they were insulted by store owners, especially the Syrians (generally called Turks) after being fooled with the merchandise they purchased. A lady once bought a microwave oven from one of these stores in the city (North End). She was shown a good one, she bought it and had the store send it to the hotel where she was lodging. After receiving it, she opened it to see if it was ok. Unfortunately, it was not the same one. It was a used one packed into a dirty discarded carton box. After returning to the store to speak with the owner about it, she was told that it could not be changed, neither the money refunded. Finally, she was chased out of the store. The tourist took the microwave oven to the office along with the receipt. The merchant was summoned to the office. The box was opened and the microwave was found to have rust and bread crumbs. The owner of the store was forced to return the money to the lady. There have been many other cases worse than the one mentioned.

How prepared is Saint Andrew to receive tourists from different parts of the world? Once a small tourist ship came to the island and was moored to the dock in North End. The passengers, upon leaving the ship, noticed that the dock was infested with soldiers armed with machine guns and searching the taxicabs. This was enough to scare anyone, especially those coming from afar hearing about the problems with the guerrillas! There are always accounts about one incident or another. So as not to cite all of them, just one from the Regal Cruises will be mentioned. Apart from the abnormalities people may find upon their arrival to this wonderful island, they may also find typical things. What about the food offered on the beaches or near the beaches especially in the city? Many have heard about the famous "rundown" fish stew (pronounced "run-done"), which is the typical food of the islands of Saint Andrew, Old Providence and Ketlena. This stew is made up of cassava, yam, plantain, pumpkin, sweet potatoes, flour or corn meal dumpling, and fresh or salted fish all cooked together in coconut milk. There is also the fried fish served with fried breadfruit and steamed rice. However, most of the times you might find dishes from continental Colombia such as the "arepas" (fried corn flour dough), "chuzos," (roasted meat slices strung on a stick), and other niceties. It might sound absurd, but more permissions are granted to the Spanish for selling on the beach than to natives. Therefore, our typical food is not displayed as it should.

Another factor that is very noticeable is that in the urban hub there are no good streets to walk by and enjoy, even to go window shopping, and with just a little shower, the streets become rivers or lagoons. Filthy overflow is present most of the time due to insufficient drainage. However, using the bypass going around the land end to the south end of the land, the north west end, and San Luis the road is very much more accommodating for a bicycle tour and sightseeing. The Blowing Hole in the South End is very attractive and everyone goes there to see the water going up to ten feet or more when it is windy.

Tourism is in the hands of non-natives. Most of the taxi drivers are non-English speakers from the continent. There is a train-like wagon touring around the land for sightseeing owned by a non-native and operated by Spanish-speaking employees. The question is: can Saint Andrew survive positively, healthily, economically, based on tourism? Well, maybe, but not the way it is going. Probably no one is really prepared to enhance tourism. If the islands need to survive from tourism, there will have to be a change on a structural basis in tourism. A more presentable environment, honesty, pride and unity to uplift the islands, especially Saint Andrew which is characterized for its commerce and beaches, which the island of Old Providence does not have. Except the leading group and the secretary, the ship of tourism does not fill these and other requirements, a dependable and beneficial tourism industry will only be a daydream or a sort of science fiction. It was said that thousands of millions of pesos were given by the national government to Saint Andrew for different purposes, including tourism. Most of it was badly spent and the rest of it no one can give account of. Somehow, it was reported that it got lost in the gangsters' pockets. It seems as if no one really cares about the progress of these islands and their inhabitants. The indigenous people need to be more serious and concerned about the islands, and if they have to survive from tourism, a better program of development for progress will have to be made. Old Providence, for instance, receives tourist ships now and then, but there is not even a restroom/ washroom anywhere in the town to satisfy the physiological needs of anyone at any time.

The former Governor of the Archipelago of San Andrés, Old Providence and Ketlena, Mr. Simón González, welcoming the people from the Caribbean to the Green Moon Festival in 1992, praised the great things about the island of Saint Andrew as follows:

> Today's tourists though they still marvel at the sea and its seven shades of blue and the beaches with the whitest sand to be found anywhere, have started delving a little deeper in the island's architectural styles, native dishes, music, dance and other common expressions of local culture. It has become commonplace to see tourists at one of the lectures defending the Archipelago's ecological balance, or to hear them exchanging opinions with the islanders during one of the reggae concerts. The San Luis and the Loma *barrios* are the traditional neighborhoods for the natives of the island and a big tourist attraction. San Luis offers brilliant white sand beaches that contrast magnificently with the blues and greens of the ocean. La Loma is interesting because of its architecture, full of thousands of anecdotes and an equal number of colors.
>
> The Baptist Church is the most representative monument on the island and the oldest Baptist Temple in America. It was built with pine lumber, brought all the way from Alabama. Inside the Church you feel a spiritual magic that invites you to meditate, and it has been a site where many of the world's Baptists have come to pay homage.
>
> Spratt Bight, the bay surrounding the island's principal hotels and tourists zone, is the busiest beach in the urban area. With white sand beaches and calm water, shaded by palm trees, this beach is the perfect place for a safe relaxing swim, directly in front of the hotels.

This beach, Spray Bight mentioned by Mr. Gonzalez, is now losing a lot of its sand and the people working with the tourists in the area are now worried about the reduction of space and complaining about the muggers. If Mr. Gonzalez could be here today, he would be amazed to see the changes that the island has undergone. Changes for the worse! In San Andrés, because of its disastrous economic crisis it is understood that to repair damaged streets, beaches and public locales is not an easy task even if the good will existed. People talk about the high seasons when tourists are piling in and low seasons when they are off. However, how much money circulates during the high seasons? There are complaints all over: taxi drivers, bus drivers, launches etc., most of the tourists coming from Colombia during the high seasons are students. They come with an everything-included package, therefore, no money is spent on shopping; these hotels that have these plans use their own buses to go around the island for sightseeing and their launches to go to the cays and so forth.

Most tourists coming from foreign countries (other than Colombia) come with these everything-included plans and the big hotels absorb everything. This means that there are only a couple of hotels and agencies that have everything monopolized. The others outside the monopolizing circle grab at the leftovers. Lately, natives have been dedicated to running guesthouses for low budget travelers. Passenger buses for natives are always crammed with tourists, thus forcing the natives to use motorbikes and moto-taxis, because of the limited space available to them in bus services. Saint Andrew may have what it needs to become a tourist attraction, but what it doesn't have is the necessary programs to make it what it ought to be.

What about tourism in Old Providence? Old Providence is an island of tranquility and peace at present. Even though it does not offer flashy beaches and commerce as Saint Andrew does, there are beautiful and unique experiences to be lived in the island. Most tourists, whether Colombians or from other countries, usually stay in Fresh Water Bay where most hotels and log cabins are found very near the beach. The best and largest beach in the island, Southwest Beach, is not far from there. Some travel by speed launch to visit Morgan's Head in Ketlena and Crab Cay where the water is crystal clear. There is no beach at Morgan's Head neither at Crab Cay but they are great for swimming and snorkeling undisturbed. There is a very small and quaint beach about half a mile from Morgan's head called The Fort. Some choose to hike along a steep trail for 50-70 minutes up to the Peak, which is the highest mountain in the island (more than 1,000 feet) from where one can observe the entire island. Most tourists do their shopping in Saint Andrew, because there are no real shopping centers on Old Providence. Because of the smallness of the island and the warmness of its people touring is especially pleasurable and relaxing. There are a few restaurants where typical food and whatever else one wishes to eat or drink are served. However, as was mentioned before, there is a pressing need for public restrooms not only in town, but also in all other tourist spots.

RACISM

To get a clearer idea of the racial problem in the islands especially on the island of Old Providence, one would have to go back to the 17th and 18th centuries, and get an outline of the first population on the islands. It is known that the first colonizers were English Puritans that after overcoming brief religious scruples eventually turned into slaveholders and maintained a cruel dominant reign over their slaves, who were probably all blacks. This distinct and animal-like treatment held the slaves in a very low inferior level while they were forced to look at their white masters and even some black ones as superior beings to whom their greatest respect and honor were due. This ideology lived among them through the ages and has taken roots in islanders as far back as one can recall.

The practice of slavery was not necessarily continuous and uninterrupted. Upon their initial occupation and settlement of Old Providence in 1629 the Puritans did not bring slaves, but they shortly introduced them. According to Newton (1985), at the beginning of 1635, the population of the island of Old Providence was of approximately 500 white men, a few of whom were Dutch, 40 white women, a few children and 90 blacks, presumably slaves. By 1641 the Puritans were ousted by the Spanish and very few people remained in the island, most of them Afrodescendant, but it is not clear if slavery was practiced during the scarcely documented years following the ouster of the Puritans. However, it is recorded that by 1666 one Captain Hatsell was in charge of the island with 35 free men and 50 slaves, no doubt these slaves were blacks. There are other relatively undocumented lapses of depopulation extending along what some call the "lost century," of Old Providence, from 1688 to 1786, during which it is not clear to what extent slavery was practiced. Given that population estimates retrieved from historical documents fail to take into account the marginal maroon settlements that are consistently mentioned in historical accounts of different periods, there should be no doubt that descendants of African slaves have constituted the bulk of the population and a permanent presence in this island since the seventeenth century. With the unstable comings and goings of Spanish, Dutch, French and English adventurers in the area at the time, it seems that inhabitation levels only surged noticeably after 1786, when Captain Francis Archbold, a Scottish captain of a slave ship and his little daughter Mary arrived from Jamaica, accompanied by several settlers and black slaves. He brought with him slaves from Africa to establish his plantation in Bottom House, on the fertile southern end of the island, and was granted permission by the Spanish government in Cartagena to settle as a planter.

It is assumed that in those days slaveholders were whites. Then it is to be assumed that Archbold and his men were white. It is also said that the majority of whites were English, but there were also Scottish (like captain Archbold), Irish, Dutch and Portuguese. Miskitu Indians from the coast of what is now Nicaragua, who foraged and fished occasionally in Old Providence, mixed with whites and blacks since the early days of Puritan occupation. Since those days, the dominant ideology was to treat people as superior or inferior according to the degree in which they could or could not be identified with or related to the elite of big land owners, traders and bearers of powerful arms and ships who were almost without exception white Europeans and their descendants.

This caused a harsh racial and social segregation that limited social mixing and upward mobility, creating partially separate communities, although considerable mixing really occurred all the time without being explicitly recognized. From those days until now, one can see and feel the trace. In Bottom House the blacks developed more and lived a sociable life among themselves, and "by themselves," given that in spite of their courtesy they were always ignored by the other classes or societies because of the color of their skin. Some of the lighter-skinned folks settled in other areas like Fresh Water Bay, Salt Creek and Town. People in possession of significant landholdings or other important sources of income, who were generally of lighter complexion, were considered to be "white" regardless of their specific family history or racial ascendancy. In addition to property and lighter skin there were other aspects that "whitened" people socially, such as: "respectability," which was a standard of behavior and style; maintaining a monogamous marriage; church going and schooling children. All this defined an "upper class." The "lower class," was presumably made up of the descendants of slaves, was supposed to be dark skinned, with little education and unconcerned with maintaining the standards of respectability. This was, of course, an ideology that did not necessarily apply to real individual people. It was mostly a generalization that unfortunately was used to prejudge persons irrespective of their real personal qualities. The middle class, those that just fit in between the two extremes of high and low were supposed to be the small shopkeepers, captains of vessels, school teachers, preachers and some skilled artisans and professionals. I, the author, use the past tense (*was, were*) because this problem has a history, but it is also a present reality in many respects.

However, in spite of all these standards, and also because of them, men from the "upper and middle class" secretly and frequently engaged in sexual relationships with women of the "lower class." These happenings caused a mixture of race as can be seen at present. Notwithstanding, the "lower class" was always pushed aside. Promiscuity was not publicly seen, but was practiced very scrupulously. The blacks were somewhat despised by the lighter skin folks who thought themselves to be superior and pretended to be of white lineage. A sort of male chauvinism among the "upper class men" and even the "middle class" caused children to carry surnames that are spurious. At times, certain ladies who considered themselves inferior would willingly fornicate with these "upper class" men for economical means or to bear children who would be accepted in middle class society and have a father who would seek the child's welfare whether done secretly or publicly. Sometimes some of these ladies would simply seek to have children with clearer skin and other "European" features.

People in Old Providence from olden times would talk about their color, hair and descent. Some would emphasize that their grandparents were of white origin, especially if they were not accepted in the so-called "white" or "half-white" groups. One would often hear from parents or grandparents expressions like, "I can't believe that A is going to marry B's black boy, she *mossah* mad" (she must be crazy). Other times it might come up this: "You can't permit that, *becaze deh dah breda ah sista*" (they are brother and sister). Of course this would happen with a married couple one of whose partner's infidelity would cause such a frustration between lovers. At other times, a child would seem to be the living picture of a man who was not the lady's husband, and there goes the comment! Sometimes the case is not that the child resembles the father, but someone among the relatives who could be the grandmother, grandfather, or maybe an uncle or aunt. But there was always a sort of promiscuity in Old Providence. This kind of behavior has continued over the years and even when it might not seem to be as radical as in the 19th and 20th centuries, it is still going on.

The author of this book remembers going through this kind of discrimination because of color and hair. Once, a young girl said to him: "I have to raise my head." Meaning that she would have to look for a boy with lighter color and straight or curly hair. A young man once used a sort of metaphor referring to the "superiority" of his sister who the author pretended: "That water is too deep for you to fish." A man who was a foreigner, but married an indigenous woman in Old Providence, once said about a young man who pretended one of his granddaughters: "His parents are decent, well-off economically, respectful and he is a nice guy in our society, but he is black." Owing to these problems the people have developed a complex of inferiority that has been very much noticeable. This situation has led some of the young ladies to incline to the idea of clinging to the Spanish-speaking policemen that have worked there on the island for their yellow skin and curly hair. These policemen, after falling in love with these girls, would be so jealous that no one could talk with her except a very close relative of hers even if the man was just pretending the girl and she was not corresponding to him, but rather someone else. It was very dangerous for any young man to approach that girl.

Which has been the most important? The texture of the hair or the color of the skin? Well, this has been the dilemma! Some go for the hair, others for the color. Actually, most of the young people prefer the hair, therefore, in Old Providence Pañas with this hair type are very much welcome whether they are male or female regardless of their background. Racism, referring to hair and color, has been more noticeable in Old Providence than in Saint Andrew. The people in Saint Andrew probably might not have paid so much attention to these affairs and have shown to be less complicated, so maybe that was one of the reasons why in Old Providence there were more light-skinned individuals than in Saint Andrew. However, notwithstanding the level of mixed marriage in these islands, if the indigenous should be sorted, there would still be fewer Blacks in Old Providence. This problem has caused a rapid increase of Pañas (Colombian mainlanders) in Old Providence. Today, because of the corruption of so-called control of immigrants (OCCRE) many unmarried Paña men or women that arrive in Old Providence very quickly find a partner who they marry or live with. This is done especially for the purpose of obtaining residence in the island. Given these distinctions guided by consideration of phenotype, people will always tell you how black you are and how knotty your hair is. It might sound crude, but racism has hit Old Providence so hard that not even the "Christians" have shown any exception.

VIOLENCE IN OLD PROVIDENCE

Early in the 20th century there was persecution and pressure against the indigenous people of both islands, Saint Andrew and Old Providence. These irregularities were caused by soldiers and policemen sent to both islands from mainland Colombia. Therefore, it has been a long time since islanders have been going through oppression. In different occasions young men were harassed by policemen, just because the Paña felt themselves to be superior and looked on the people as Negroes without human values. There were times when young men were chased and hunted in their homes and farms as if they were wild animals to be caught and penned for shipment to mainland Colombia for an obligatory military service. Many conscripted young men were sent away to Cartagena, Colombia, during the decades of the nineteen thirties. Some of these remained in the continent and others returned to their homeland. A couple of them became policemen in the islands and established a peaceful relationship with their fellowmen. Of course, they worked along with Colombian policemen from the mainland. One of the problems, among others, was the language, since they never spoke English; much less the English based Creole that is the vernacular. In those days the few people in both islands who knew a little Spanish could be counted on the fingers, especially in Old Providence. Even though the majority of those Colombian policemen were violent, there were always two or three at the most that were kind and easygoing. Among many incidents, four will be mentioned as follows:

1- In the year 1951 when the surge of extreme unrest known as "The Violence" was hitting Colombia, the Central Baptist Church in Old Providence was attacked and many glass windows broken by a drunken policeman from the continent. Mr. Hurvis Davis lived that experience and relates the following:

> I was in charge of the electricity plant in Old Providence, but there was a little problem with me and the cabo (police corporal), because there was an order from the mayor to shutdown the plant at 11:00 p.m., but the cabo, because of a grudge held against me, wanted me to continue running the plant well after the stated time, which I did not. A few nights later, after closing down the plant I went home and was just about to lie down when I heard glasses smashing in the Baptist Church building next to where I lived, so I went to see what it was all about. My mother in law had also gone before me and, unbeknown to me, she peeped in through one of the windows and the policeman being in the building and seeing her, fired a shot at her but missed her. I went to

the police station and complained, with no positive result. On my way back home, I saw the policeman in the park in front of the Church loading his gun. As soon as he saw me he rushed at me and asked: "Protestant or Catholic?" He stood in front of me, and as I continued to walk he saw a machete I had on my waist, took it from me and started swinging it and cut me in my head with it. So then I wrestled with him and recovered my machete and also took his gun. Finally he was arrested because of Mr. Ronald Taylor's intervention with the other policemen. The following day this policeman publicly said that he was going to wreck both the Adventist and Baptist Church buildings. A telegram was sent to the police chief in San Andrés and the Lieutenant personally came to Old Providence and took him to San Andrés before he could do anything else.

2- A young lady, the daughter of a respectable, humble preacher, while walking on a district near her home in Old Providence, was attacked by a policeman, who intended to rape her. Her younger brother came to her rescue, but the attacker scared him by firing his gun to the air and he ran away seeking help. Upon reporting the incident, he came back to his sister's rescue accompanied by young fearless men. Sensing their coming, the policeman started firing without hitting his blank. When they managed to rescue the girl, they found she was very exhausted and half naked. The policeman was caught and well beaten. A man came by and begged for him, taking him to his abode. The young men were all put in prison, but not long after were freed with the intervention of Mr. Silvanus May, who was known as teacher May and was pastor of the Central Baptist Church in St. Isabel. The superior in rank was very upset about the beating of the policeman and said that the young men should have been shot. This superior officer went one evening on a visit to his fiancé somewhere in Rocky Point. He was taken off his horse and well beaten and returned to his station. Soon after, he got married and left the island. As for the other policeman who attempted the rape, he was sent away to the hospital in Saint Andrew and from there to Bogotá. It was rumored that he didn't survive. No one knows how true that was.

3- On October 3rd, 1965 the young man Nimroy Archbold was shot to death by a policeman in front of the police station in the district of "Guerrat," because of jealousy.

4- In 2003 a young man whose name was Lamos Lee Robinson was shot to death by a coastal guard in the island of Old Providence. The felon justified his action by saying that the young man was loading his launch with gasoline containers in order to transport drugs. This young man was first shot in the launch but was still alive when he was immediately pulled to the beach and finally murdered. There was no proof that the dead boy was transporting drugs, but that could not bring him back to life. As usual, nothing was done about it and these murderers will continue to be thorns in the flesh as long as these islands remain as colonies under the Colombian flag. There are many more cases that the author will not mention, but the fact remains that from those days until the present time, there have always been abuses. Incidents like these are what have caused most of the people on the islands to keep certain resentment deep down where policemen and soldiers are concerned. Saint Andrew, which was known more to the visitors than Old Providence and has been more appreciated because of its wonderful beaches, today has turned out to be a red zone. Killing, robbing and drug trafficking have become its daily bread. Because of these late incidents policemen have been piling in from the Colombian mainland with the pretext to control the situation. Unfortunately, things are going from bad to worse.

IS THERE REALLY ANY HOPE FOR BETTERMENT?

Analyze the following situation:

Environmental Information (2006-2007)

The rural area of the island of Saint Andrew consisting of portions of San Luis, The Hill, Cove, South End, all with a majority Raizal (indigenous) population, have no drainage system. Therefore, latrines, septic tanks or holes are used to dispose of residual water. These are usually located and constructed in such a way that subterranean water is not contaminated. Some of the families in these areas provide themselves with cisterns for potable water to be obtained during the rainy seasons. Nevertheless, rainy seasons affect drainage of used waters in areas such as Sound Bay, Pepper Hill and North End. These sectors are usually overflowed. The problem in the North End section is due to filling of the land at the time when the harbor was being dredged. The filling remained lower than road construction on Newball Avenue, making it difficult for water to drain to the sea. Therefore, most areas in this part of the island where septic tanks are located have contamination problems with wells.

There is an average of 70 tons daily of solid waste produced just during the low season in Saint Andrew, which breaks down as follows: organics 19 tons, glass 8 tons, textiles 5 tons, plastics 9 tons, carton 9 tons, metals 2 tons, cardboard paper 11 tons, board 2 tons and dirt 5 tons. Readers might not want to even imagine how the high season goes. This massive production of waste is a permanent life threat to those who live in the area immediately surrounding the rubbish dump, which is an open-air affair. Recent studies made by the local government recommend the establishment of a perimeter of 200 meters to be considered as buffer zone where farming and other environment-sensitive activities will be prohibited because of the presence of lixiviation. We don't know if and when this will happen.

One of the problems with the different services offered to the people in the island of Saint Andrew is the systematic underestimation of population density. Due to the false census taken by the government, there is always and will forever be less people living on the island than the real existing population. For example, according to government projections the mean demand of potable water for 2010 was estimated for 62,588 inhabitants with a maximum consumption of 271.6 liters per second daily. The estimate for 2018 is a population of 68,774 with a maximum consumption of 312 liters per second daily. But everybody in the island knows that these estimates are wildly below mark.

The population is increasing extremely rapidly. In the year of 2007 a total of 487 births were reported by the secretary of health in both islands, Saint Andrew and Old Providence, of which 20% corresponded to Old Providence. One of the situations that call our attention in the report given by the secretary of health is that 18% of the total childbirths were by adolescents. Is there any possible betterment for these islands? May the mercy of God rest and abide upon them.

THE COLOMBIA-NICARAGUA DISPUTE AND THE DEMANDS OF THE RAIZAL PEOPLE OF THE ARCHIPELAGO

In light of the aforementioned situations and their historical causes, and upon consideration of the international border dispute between Colombia and Nicaragua regarding outlying maritime areas belonging to Saint Andrew, Old Providence, and Ketlena, the Raizal people of the archipelago continue to manifest their needs by articulating the following petition, which is self-explanatory and I quote at length.

Considering that, in seeking solutions throughout the years we have exhausted every internal effort to bring our problems to the attention of the Colombian State, without any positive results, the Raizal People of the Archipelago of Saint Andrew, Providence and Saint Catherine, vehemently demand:

a) That nationally and internationally, we must have a voice over our own fate, and as the autochthonous people of the territory in question, the Raizal Archipelago of San Andrés (Saint Andrew), Providencia (Providence) and Santa Catalina (Saint Catherine), being its true owners, it is our right to intervene and to be heard in all disputes, and, at this present moment, to intervene and to be heard independently of both the Republic of Colombia and the Republic of Nicaragua in the present dispute over our territory between the two referred countries;

b) That our right is to have our own designated representative, and as the interested party most affected, to intervene in the suit Nicaragua filed against Colombia on December 6, 2001 as part of the dispute said countries are engaged in for sovereignty over a territory which does not belong to any of the mentioned States;

c) That we be allowed to intervene in the dispute independently of both Colombia and Nicaragua over our territory, and that no person(s) named or appointed by the Republic of Colombia or the Republic of Nicaragua, whether such person(s) be *Raizal* or not, may represent us or speak for us in this case, inasmuch as such representative(s) or spokesperson(s) must be chosen by us exclusively and directly;

d) That: 1- the Colombian State recognizes our indigenous status as descendants of the first settlers of the Raizal Territory of San Andrés, Providence and Saint Catherine; 2- that we be exempted from paying taxes over our own lands, and 3- that our youth is not recruited for military service, without consultation and agreement with the Raizal People;

e) That it be internationally declared that the States of Colombia and Nicaragua are violating the obligations to international law by not recognizing the Raizal People's ownership of our territory, the Raizal Archipelago of San Andrés, Providence and Saint Catherine, as well as our human rights.

f) That Colombia and Nicaragua immediately cease and desist from advancing their dispute at the International Court of Justices (ICJ) over the maritime boundary that involves the territory of the Raizal People, the Raizal Archipelago of San Andrés, Providence and Saint Catherine, with whom none of the aforementioned States has made any previous consultations, which therefore violates international laws and their rights, as a people, to participate in the process;

g) That Colombia and Nicaragua immediately cease and desist from promoting incursions into the territorial waters of the Raizal People of the Raizal Archipelago of San Andres, Providence and Saint Catherine, and from granting concessions to foreign countries, parties and individuals for oil and gas exploration as well as the exploitation of our other natural resources (fish, turtle, etc.) as well as their infringing on our freedom of action within our ancestral territory, which involves harassment and causes interruptions of the Raizal People's traditional peaceful maritime activities;

h) That the Colombian State immediately demilitarize the territory of the Raizal People, the Raizal Archipelago of San Andrés, Providence and Saint Catherine, and implement positive and adequate humanized measures to repatriate the excessive number of Colombian mainland individuals and other citizens who the Colombian government, by its permissive attitude, unconcerned procedures, erroneous policies and uncontrolled measures, has deliberately permitted to overpopulate our territory;

i) That the Colombian State recognize the Raizal Peoples' right to full autonomy over our territory, including traditional maritime area, airspace and natural resources, in accordance with UN Resolutions on The Granting of Independence to Colonial Countries and Peoples No. 1514 (XV) of December 14, 1960 and 1541 (XV) of December 15, 1960;

j) That a similar process be authorized as that contained in the UN General Assembly's Decision 2299 (XXI) of December 20, 1966, on the Question of Ifni and Spanish Sahara;

k) To consolidate with the Raizal Peoples' full participation an organization that shall represent all the Raizal People;

l) To draft, with the full participation of the Raizal People, a Plan of Action to carry out the mandates of such organization;

m) To constitute, with the full participation of the Raizal People the necessary institutions of Raizal self-government;

n) To devise, with full participation of the Raizal People, a comprehensive plan that will enable us to reassume control and administration of our own affairs;

o) To seek ways and means, with full participation of the Raizal People whereby we may secure and recover possession of our lands and territories and restore our culture to its position of preeminence in our own environment and cosmovision;

p) To reaffirm our Raizal' sovereignty over our territory, and to create, institutes and establish our own national symbols, including holidays, a flag and an anthem. To give a proper name to our island territories, and to their people and language as well. Furthermore, to restore the traditional names of their cays, towns, urban areas, neighborhoods, districts, streets, roads, sections and other public places and surroundings that have been changed;

q) To propose, if possible, a new treaty between our Islands and the Colombian State, if so desired by the Raizal People, with the following objectives, among others, previously leaving adequate space to include those that may appear at a later date:

r) Reduction of the population density of their islands, especially San Andres, through a process of adequate and humanitarian relocation of non-indigenous residents;

s) Conditions for the full exercise of our right to full autonomy and self-government with guarantees that our right to prior consultation and consent will always be honored in cases, activities, actions, procedures and processes that will affect us;

t) Declaring that all rights pertaining to us, particularly our right to full sovereignty over our territory and the right to self-determination shall be paramount in all decisions to be taken.

As it was discussed throughout this book, the damage done to the archipelago has been exercised by the Colombian state. The previous pages have reiterated that the indigenous people of the archipelago have lead a struggle for survival ever since they possessed the territory. Finally, let us be reminded of some highly symbolic incidents that define a struggle for self-determination.

In 1806, March 27 the English Captain, John Bligh with about five ships took by force the island of Saint Andrew in the name of His Majesty, with such an insuperable force that Lieutenant Tomás O'Neill, who was the official in command of the Spanish military, surrendered, lowered the Spanish flag, and hoisted the English flag. Tomás O'Neill and his small troop were carried near to the coast of Cartagena by order of Captain John Bligh.

On the 10th of April 1806, John Bligh freed the indigenous people (Raizales), who established their new capital in a locality of Free Town (Saint Andrew), for which reason the sector carries his name. This is the true independence of San Andrew, Old Providence, Ketlena, and the Mosquito Coast.

From 1806 to 1822 the Raizal people of the Archipelago of Saint Andrew, Old Providence Ketlena and the Mosquito Coast (which did not effectively belong to the territory of Nicaragua at the time) were completely freed. The

Elders and Pastors administrated them with the traditional self-government principles of the Puritans and Anglo-Saxon communities embodied in the famous covenant of the Mayflower in 1620.

The archipelago, exercising its sovereignty and the privilege of choosing freely an institution or nation to protect its rights, voluntarily and with free will adhered to the Constitution of Cúcuta and Gran Colombia in June 23rd, 1822.

In 1903, once Panama had obtained its independence from Colombia, loyal Colombian troops that had been in Panama "exercising national sovereignty," arrived in Saint Andrew. From 1903-1905 these troops were abandoned in Saint Andrew. The merchants helped them with food. The military began to buy on credit. Finally, hunger and desperation as a result of abandonment by their government led them to ransack the merchants, which brought blood shedding and humiliation. The islanders defeated this aggression by poisoning the drinking water of the attackers.

In 1912 the Raizal people, faced with discontent and with justified reasons were prone to separate from Colombia. The first Raizal lawyer and journalist Francisco Newball, in his grief had become the mediator of reconciliation between the surviving Colombian troops still living in the islands and the Raizal people. He spoke with the President of the Republic, Carlos E. Restrepo. The administrative category of the archipelago was raised to the status of National Intendancy of Saint Andrew and Old Providence, but this act was accompanied with a perverse decree conferring the massive immigration of continentals. By 1984 the continentals and their descendants duplicated the number of the indigenous people displacing them. This constituted an act of ethnic cleansing and displacement of indigenous populations that is contrary to human rights.

In 1953 Lieutenant General, Gustavo Rojas Pinilla, is the first Colombian President to visit the archipelago and declare it free port.

In 1972, on the 23rd of June the President of Colombia, Misael Pastrana Borrero visited the island of Saint Andrew to inscribe in the annals of the history of Colombia the presumed 150 years of adhesion of the indigenous islanders to the territory of Gran Colombia and changed the name of the airport to "Aeropuerto Sesquicentenario." It was first named "Aeropuerto Rojas Pinilla." So much for the president's concern for the islands.

In 2001, Nicaragua sued Colombia in the International Court of Justice (ICJ), claiming all the Raizal territories without any consideration or participation of the Raizal people. Colombia went to the ICJ to defend its sovereignty over the claimed areas, but both countries systematically neglected to consult the Raizal people of the archipelago. Through this systematic exclusion of the Raizal people, Colombia, as well as Nicaragua and the International Tribunal reveal their low esteem and total unconcern for the inhabitants who have historically settled and dwelled on the territory. This intentional exclusion means that they do not consider the human rights of the islanders, that they consider them as only inhuman dumb creatures. We already quoted above the petition of the people of the archipelago and its lateral "g" section, which reads: *That Colombia and Nicaragua immediately cease and desist from promoting incursions into the territorial waters of the Raizal people of the Raizal Archipelago of Saint Andrew, Providence and St. Catherine, and from granting concessions to foreign Countries, parties and individual for oil and gas exploration as well as the exploration of our other natural resources (fish, turtle etc.) as well as their infringing on our freedom of action within our ancestral territory, which involves harassment and causes interruptions of the Raizal people's traditional peaceful maritime activities.* Just ignoring this specific section suffices to bring total chaos in the not so distant future.

All efforts to conserve the Raizal (indigenous) territory have turned into a nightmare. *The awakening of a dreadful morning came. The unforgettable day of the 19th of November 2012 when the verdict from the Hague was broadcast worldwide:* The Islands of Saint Andrew, Old Providence and Ketlena belong to Colombia, but not the seas. These pertain to Nicaragua, and, absurdly, the cays are declared to be properties of Colombia, but with no sea access to them.

The eldest to the youngest, the educated and the illiterate Colombian from every corner of the country boastfully proclaim: "The Archipelago is Colombia." Notwithstanding, no one was able to rescue it from the clutches of Nicaragua. Would it had been better to go back to the past and exchange the archipelago for the Mosquito Coast? On the Mosquito Coast the people are much better off simply because they have better options for survival: a) there is a great extension of land for farming with inexhaustible sources of water and a territory expanse with less than 8 inhabitants per km^2; b) a sea that is rich in fish on account of the shallowness of its coastal continental platform; c) possibility of subsoil resources and d) the possibility of an interoceanic canal.

The island of Saint Andrew is known to have 24 km^2. Of which at the present moment there is no land for farming, neither for industry or anything to create jobs. Old Providence has an extension of 17 km^2, and the soil is very poor for farming and on the other hand the low average rainfall does not help. Ketlena is only 1 km^2. And has the same water and soil limitations of Old Providence, even when there is space for farming. Saint Andrew, the most populated of the three, is mostly occupied by Colombian continentals making it almost impossible for the Raizal/indigenous people to survive. The only possibility of life in the archipelago is fishing and tourism that depend on the protection of its biosphere.

The islands may possess heavenly beauty as some may proclaim, but what is all that to do with a people who apparently Colombia, Nicaragua and the International Tribunal Court of Justice assume that the Islanders or Raizal people have glorious bodies that do not need to eat, neither think, feel and not even sleep. The ecosystem of the archipelago is so fragile it cannot resist the shout of an enemy.

The fact remains that the Archipelago of Saint Andrew, Old Providence and Ketlena are worse off today than before the free port was established 60 years ago. With the loss of its seas the Colombian government, "moved with compassion," has decided to give monthly alms to the frustrated fishermen until they can find other means of survival. This unexpected monthly donation has caused an uncontrollable and dissatisfactory situation owing to the fact that many people have inscribed who had never even been to the bayside to cast a hook into the sea and are now enjoying the best of it, while others who have been authentic fishermen are deprived of it. The aid/ alms lasted only 18 months and the beneficiaries are now worse off today than what they were before, because they neither have the alms, nor the sea where to fish.

In 1912 the Intendant of the archipelago, Jorge Tadeo Lozano thought that the island of San Andrés was overpopulated, the people were without jobs and needed to emigrate to the Colombian mainland, while he was bringing people from the mainland to occupy their spaces in the island. The question is: now that the Raizales / indigenous are displaced, that there are no jobs for them, that they are despised by the merchants and hotel industries, will they have to go in supplication before the Nicaraguan government to admit them in their country, placing them somewhere on the Mosquito Coast and becoming Nicaraguan so as to escape starvation and a possible riot-massacre among Raizales and continentals? Will these people be able to continue resisting the inexplicable pressure they are undergoing at the present time? It might seem as if there is nothing wrong and the Raizal people are relaxed and happy, but it is all to the contrary. At present, thousands of Venezuelans are seeking refuge in Colombia, Ecuador and Peru due to the oppression of the Venezuelan government; the quest for the Raizals is a very serious one: where are they going to seek refuge, given that they are trapped between the intolerable situation in the Colombian mainland and the oppressive aliens in the archipelago?

It is a wishful thought that one day the Almighty God will remember the Raizal people of this archipelago and with mercy rescue them from the clutches of Colombia's hegemony.

CUSTOMS ON THE ISLANDS

The Archipelago of San Andrés (Saint Andrew), Old Providence and Saint Catherine (Ketlena), has a history, tradition and customs somewhat similar to those of the rest of the Caribbean islands that developed under an Afro-British system. The life of the communities before, during, and after slavery was not that of the new settlers from the mainland (Colombia), but followed the tradition of their ancestors who inhabited the islands during the greater part of their colonial history. Therefore, when the native people were freed from slavery, their culture and customs were deep-rooted. That is to say that it was difficult for them to make the sudden change from one culture to another that was virtually enforced by a new dominating nation in the twentieth century, that is, Colombia. The methods used to teach and learn subjects and languages were worse than those of the previous policy of buying and selling slaves. The folklore handed down from their ancestors is totally different from the national (Colombian) language and culture. The efforts made by that nation to enforce language, religion, and culture on the people have led to numerous changes, although not as many as the government anticipated. The Colombian central government decided to impose their culture and language upon the islanders.

Before the free port, life for the native islanders was completely different from that of today. As there was not much contact with the Colombian culture previous to the early twentieth century, it had little or no influence on day-to-day life even in the 1920's. During conflicts with different nations over these islands from the 17th century up to the 19th century, they were not as populated as they are today. Apparently there were no specific reasons for any of the different nations claiming the islands to make immediate changes that would offer a more comfortable way of life for the few who inhabited the territory. There was no electricity, the roads were just tracks, and life was somewhat primitive. Nonetheless, the people were happy, relaxed, and lived in harmony with nature and Almighty God.

The Social Level

Each family had a small house, hut or ranch, with a cistern, barrel, or tanks made from wood. These recipients provided the family with rainwater caught from the roof. Those who did not own land and wished to farm could either borrow or lease a piece from someone who had a lot, for a period of 5, 10 or more years. No one was really wealthy, but those with a better standard of living would build a two-story house with a shop downstairs. The sale of land was almost non-existent and, when there was a sale, it would be purchased by a native islander. A few were seafarers, but the majority of the people made their living from farming. Even though the islands did not produce enough income for anyone to be rich, no one was in a state of impoverishment.

As commerce was not abundant the natives were not equipped to live from the few stores or shops that existed in those days. Nonetheless, living on the islands was like living in paradise. This means that everyone respected each other, living as one family. Fishing, whether for food or business, was almost a daily affair.

Farming

The native islanders were known to be farmers rather than merchants. However, this does not mean that there were no merchants on the islands. Everyone could not dedicate themselves to the same thing so it was necessary to develop different commercial activities. During the era of slavery, slave masters on these islands carried out cotton growing, and the product was shipped to England or the United States. Grueling labor under the burning sun made it necessary to have people who were able to resist the heat, therefore the work was done by slaves. After some years the production began to decrease and coconut palms replaced cotton. When the planting of coconuts began on the island of Saint Andrew, the people on Old Providence decided to grow

Clamor of the Islands

oranges instead. Some coconuts were also planted on Old Providence, but not as many as on Saint Andrew. Although these trees would take a longer period of time to produce, they were more productive and the labor less strenuous than was the cotton. Waiting a few years for production would finally give a better financial result, while the cotton would produce during the same year it was sown. However, cultivating coconuts was less laborious and production was more profitable than cotton.

From the late 1870's food for the islanders was never lacking at any time. Natives used to cultivate many crops: cassava, plantain, sweet potatoes, yam, pumpkin, cocoa, bananas, breadfruit, as well as grains such as beans, gungu, and corn, which was the most abundant of the latter three. Fruits like oranges, sweet-sap, sour-sap, guava, avocado, grapefruit, tangerine, bittersweet, lime, plum, coco plum, cocoa, papaya, and different types of mangoes were also cultivated. Lots of sugar cane was also grown. Specific information will be given on the cultivation of sugar cane further ahead.

There were some slight differences between the islands of Old Providence and Saint Andrew, but not so as to divide an historical culture. Santiago Guerrero, a commissioner from Bogota, Colombia, who visited the islands in 1911, commented that the people from Old Providence were somewhat more obliging. *'They were more sea faring than those on Saint Andrew, but more racist and quiet. There is also a little difference in their speech or pronunciation of words. But the fact is that they are all identified as native islanders suffering the same consequences of misunderstanding with the Colombian state. Whatever happens to one island, the other suffers as well. Both have been abused with detestable injustice from the 19th century onward. Their customs and culture are unique. Religiousness has its differences in creeds and dogmas, but it does not serve for division among its people.'*

The island of Saint Andrew produced a greater quantity of the following: sweet potatoes (more than the inhabitants could consume); avocado, which also brought some income from exportation, as well as breadfruit, cocoa, mami and coco-plum. Cocoa, or cocoa bean, was never grown on Old Providence, and breadfruit plants never survived there either, whereas they usually do on Saint Andrew. However, jack-fruit has been more productive on Old Providence. Cocoa was a tropical fruit encased in a husk. The seed was covered with a very sour white pulp. This fruit was husked and the seeds placed on sheets of zinc in the sun for 2 or 3 days and, after drying, would be parched and beaten in a wooden mortar or ground in a hand mill, then made into balls. These would be stored in special bottles or other recipients, and whenever one or two were needed for a beverage, they were grated and boiled with milk for a delicious breakfast or supper.

The customary breakfast in the 1900's was *'bush tea'* or cocoa, with bread or fritters; lunch was substantial, and the food eaten at breakfast repeated for supper. Breadfruit and other products that were cultivated in those days were not so easy to sell since almost everyone grew the same thing. However, those who had shops and weren't able to cultivate because of their duties, or other reasons, would sometimes trade rice, flour or other goods for produce such as pumpkin, sweet potatoes, plantains, cassava, beans, yam and cocoa. Cloth and shoes were never exchanged or swapped.

It can be concluded then that, due to farming in those days, the islands were self-sufficient regarding food and fruits, and had even achieved a capacity for exportation. We have learned that our ancestors were active and highly productive in cultivating the land on which they lived or possessed. This was a healthy tradition that was passed on from one generation to another.

COCONUTS ON THE ISLANDS

Although coconuts were not as abundant on Old Providence as they were on Saint Andrew, they were also exported. At times they would be sent to Cartagena either directly or via Saint Andrew. Coconuts were also shipped to the United States. In the 1870's coconut exportation was very prosperous and was increasing, and records, show that in 1873 exportation exceeded two million nuts a year and, ten years later, rose to four million a year. However, hurricanes and droughts hampered the crop in later days. The palms were afflicted by a sickness in the 1930's —the worst year being 1931— reducing production to a minimum. With such crisis, the Colombian government was asked by the natives to help in controlling the situation, but none was forthcoming. The excuse, according to the chief of the Department of Agriculture, Carlos Duran Castro, was that there was no money to transport the entomophagous insects called '*criptognatha nodiceps*' to Cartagena from Trinidad. This was the answer to a petition made by Arthur May, referring to the sickness and refusal of aid from the Colombian government. In later years, after controlling part of the sickness, the coconut palms began to flourish once more and the business continued, but not as before. In the 1940's exporting both the copra and the nuts to Cartagena was profitable, and even when exportation to the U.S. was discontinued the islanders used to make a living from the nuts gathered on the islands. In the 1950's and early 60's there was an oil factory at the Cove Sea Side, where the soldiers' barracks are located today. Nowadays, owing to so much deforestation, the export of oranges and coconuts has come to an end. Ironically enough, oranges are imported on both islands, and very soon coconuts will also be imported. With regard to cultivating food at the present time, there is not much to say about it, except that it's almost out of the question, and what used to be in abundance is now being brought from Costa Rica and the Colombian mainland. It is not that the earth refuses to produce, but rather that there is hardly any land available on Saint Andrew for farming and, besides that, the younger generation is given to consuming drugs, and laziness.

SUGAR CANE

Cultivating sugar cane was most profitable on the islands, especially on Old Providence, and in the 1900's became very important. Harvest was during the months of January, February, March and part of April, before the rainy season began. Cane grinding was done by mills turned by two horses going around in a circle, and was also a means of producing jobs during the season. Cane juice was used to stew coconuts that were either cut in very small pieces or shredded. After having been boiled for a few hours, small balls were made. Papaya, oranges and other fruits were also stewed. Cane juice was boiled down to syrup in very large cauldrons of 60, 90 and 120 gallons and would yield about two thirds of clear honey-like syrup. Many people used this precious syrup in place of sugar, to sweeten lemonade, tamarind cordial, tea, and sometimes coffee. Syrup was also used to make an alcoholic beverage called '*bush rum*' or '*cumphia*'. This often tasted like whiskey, depending on how many times it was distilled. Sugarcane grinding was always done in the cool of the evening hours when the sun was about to set, and continued until the last cauldron was full. At times three cauldrons were used for boiling the liquid.

At nights in the early hours, people would gather at the mill to drink fresh cane juice, which was given out to the natives free of charge. This was especially popular during the moonlit nights, when young men would visit the mill yard to sing, play their guitars and exchange jokes while the cane grinding was going on. (This was always done, especially in Old Providence.) The entertainment would revive the workers and make their labor more enjoyable, not to mention the presence of the young girls and young women who would gather at the same place to get a taste of the delicious cane juice and also to take some home. These girls, of course, were delighted by the singing of the artists. It must be remembered that cane juice was not sold to the visitors at the mill yard, either to drink there or to take home. It was only sold for stewing purposes, because of the great amount needed for that. At times though, if the mill yard were located at a distance, the young people would not visit it.

Usually, a hut was built at the mill yard to protect the workers from the rain and sun during the day, and as a place to take a short rest. Sugarcane was so abundant that at times cane grinding would continue up to the month of April. Sugarcane grinding produced a few jobs for as long as it lasted. There was what was known on the islands as the *mill feeder*, who fed the cane into the mill; the *trash man*, who received the trash on the other side of the mill after the cane was mashed; the *horse boys*, who drove the horses around the mill; *the boiler*, who took care of boiling the sugar cane juice until it became syrup. Some planters used to grind at one spot for three weeks.

Very few songs were sung in Spanish. The English songs were picked up by overseas radio stations or obtained from records by those who had a record player in those days. Country music from the United States was very popular with the islanders. Other songs were made up on the islands, especially those for dancing. At that time there was no radio station on Old Providence. Cane grinding still exists on a smaller scale on Old Providence but it will never be like it used to be in those good old days.

Nowadays farming is very scarce on both islands. First of all, because there is not much land available, especially on Saint Andrew, and even though a few people from both islands are trying to return to farming, it is not really very encouraging. Secondly, the government does not stimulate it much; thirdly, the ground is becoming dryer and dryer every day, because of the many wells where water is being drawn out from the earth without control (on Saint Andrew); and lastly, the government does not pay any attention to theft, therefore the thieves do whatever they like, scandalously outnumbering the few farmers. These rogues roam the bush stealing whatever they can and also destroying the plantation to sell what they did not plant just to satisfy their hunger for drugs. As for Old Providence, it does not rain much, which causes the earth to be extra dry.

Customary Food

The islanders were seafood consumers. Fishing was almost a daily affair whether for business or food. Fish was a basic for domestic consumption, on both islands. Because there were just a few refrigerators, most people used to salt, fry, or roast it. However, at times there would be changes on Sundays in most homes. I can always remember in my youth on Old Providence, when people would eat conch, lobster, turtle, crab, and sometimes chicken. Conch and lobster were very abundant. Lobster was plentiful in the extensive mangrove area in Ketlena (Santa Catalina), Town and wherever there were mangroves there were always lobsters by the hundreds even when these were not full grown. In Saint Andrew prawn would be added to this list. The famous '*run down*' (a stew) was made from salted fish and produce from the land (known as *bread kind*). Pigtail was never used in cooking *run down*. Rice was not consumed much, especially by the poorer class of people.

Because most of the people were farmers they would eat produce from the land as well as from the sea. Cassava, for example, was not only used for food but also to make starch. This was done by grating it, then, wringing it in a piece of cloth, and the liquid obtained would be set in a basin or another container until it dried. This was used to starch clothes since most of the clothes had to be ironed. It was also used to stick papers and other materials used in handcrafts. The flour from the cassava was used for making cakes, dumpling and also '*baamy,*' a flat cake made from the flour pressed in a pot, baked on one side, turned over, and baked on the other side until thoroughly cooked.

Corn was abundant on both islands and was a versatile foodstuff. It was used for making cakes and porridge; it was roasted; and also used in soup. Some people used to parch it and then boil it as coffee. As some farmers had so much of it, they would dry the cobs, peel off the husk, then tie them together and hang them from their kitchen beams. Whenever they were needed they would be soaked in hot water overnight then grated into flour, which would be used for making cakes, corn bread, or whatever the cook wished to use it for. Those who had a surplus would feed their chickens with it.

EDUCATION ON THE ISLANDS

The islands were never without a school before the Capuchins took over the education system, action that was promoted by the Colombian state. On San Andrés for example, there was a school in each district, whether maintained by the community or by the parents of the students, except for the Catholic school. The islanders knew how to read, write, and carry out the four mathematical operations in their own native language, in other words English. Those parents who could afford it would send their children to the United States of America or to Jamaica for higher education.

There were many young people who could never go away to school though. These young men and women would stay home, and their basic means for subsistence would be a canoe to fish in and a piece of land to farm. Even though for many, many years Old Providence did not have a high school, the people who attended primary school learned enough to take care of their own business. There were teachers who had never been to the U.S. or Jamaica, or even to Colombia for a college education, but were excellent teachers, such as Rafael Archbold, Ulysses Dawkins, Alfredo Taylor and a few ladies, among others. Reverend Alpheus graduated from high school away from the island, and used to teach while pastoring the Baptist Church in Smooth Water Bay. (The above mentioned were teachers on Old Providence.) Today there are lots of high schools on Saint Andrew while there is only one on Old Providence. There was no high school on that island until the 1960's. Some parents sent their children to high schools out of the islands, even though many could not afford private education. As in the past, many are able to finish high school today, but cannot afford university studies, so they do special intermediate programs at the SENA (Servicio Nacional de Aprendizaje or National Training Service). This Institute functions on both islands and all training is affordable.

What is the difference then, between education 60 years ago and today's home training? The children of today and those of the 20th century cannot be compared, specifically, students in the 1920's through 1980, in comparison to those from 1981 up to the present day. Parents had had a hard struggle from the 1920's on, and even before. They were always concerned about the way their children were taught and brought up. The parents' concern was that the children grew up with respect for others, especially for older folks. Children were rebuked, scolded, or lashed, if necessary, by their elders, whether relatives or non-relatives, with the consent of their parents, so as to observe and carryout the rules of obedience, respect and proper moral conduct.

In those days school children were taught to respect and obey their teachers. Whenever they were disobedient or disrespectful, students would be punished by being locked up in a dark-room, made to kneel on the ground for hours, or the palms of their hands lashed with a leather belt, a ruler, or a tamarind whip. These methods of punishment were carried out with the consent of the parents, and were observed up to the late 1950's. It was a general custom for all minors to be at home by 9:00 pm, since bedtime coincided with that hour. Exceptions would be the usual holidays such as the 20th of July, 7th of August, the 24th and/or the 25th and 31st of December.

Whenever there were special events in the community, they would end at 9 or 10 pm at the latest. Because there were no vehicles for transportation available, nor paved streets, people would either walk or use horses for transportation. On account of the lack of electricity, entertainment was always carried out on moonlit nights.

Since the 1970's things have gone from bad to worse. Parents have become unconcerned and excessively liberal. Children are not even taught obedience, respect and moral behavior. They behave wantonly and have become characters of self-determination and do as they wish, supported by their own parents. Today's parents are mainly vulgar and are a negative example for their own children. At times it is difficult to tell who are the parents and who are the children in the homes. Obscenity is used by both parents and children alike; in the home and also on the street. Once upon a time parents used to tell minors until what time they were allowed to be on the street at night. Nowadays the children under age, supported by their parents, are the ones telling the parents when they are leaving and what time they are returning from a party. Sometimes they don't even know where their kids are going, or when they will see them again. In fact they often challenge their parents and/or teachers.

The youth of today are on the road to nowhere. Schoolteachers are looked upon as being equal to their students, and respect for these teachers is out of the question. At times teachers are defied by both students and parents, and often insulted with vulgar expressions. In fact, the latter frequently defy them. Everything has undergone a complete change, and a distorted mentality is leading to a complete moral and spiritual breakdown. All this has caused certain aversion to education and moral virtue. Because of the general concept of this modern age, older folks with their customary life-style are considered by the young generation as old fashioned, awkward, and ignorant of modern technology, which is an attractive distraction and leads, in some cases, to corruption. This does not mean that everything that is newly invented is for moral and spiritual destruction. However, it is mostly used to lead others to immorality. An example is the internet, which is used by many for corrupt purposes.

In our forefathers' days, students were forced to think and be active in reading, writing and more skillful in mathematical operations. Nowadays, because of adding machines, computers and other electronic aids, students cannot do any mathematical operations without using one of these devices. What about handwriting? This important skill has lost its essence in our modern world. In our childhood days it was very important to practice clear handwriting that could be read by everyone. Orthography was the key subject in language classes in school. Nowadays it is of less importance, since handwriting is not used as before, neither is it accepted in offices now that everything is done by computer and also corrected by the computer itself. So then, this means that comprehensive handwriting apparently does not have the importance it used to have in the past 70 years or so. As for the cell-phones, their use and misuse is causing most primary and high school students to be totally distracted, whether in their classrooms or elsewhere. In many churches these cell phones are called '*worship service interrupters*'. Those who are not talking on them are concentrated on '*pinning*', and most students during their class hours are more devoted to sending and receiving messages than paying attention to their lessons. Therefore, on account of the misuse of this device, many students graduate each year from high school knowing little less than nothing; and without the appropriate academic preparation they become half-prepared professionals who, in the end, are nothing but a failure.

To whom are these disasters attributed? Is it the system, the parents, the people in general, the internet and cell phones, or the students themselves? It takes more than one ingredient to make a pie, therefore all of the aforementioned could be guilty. One good example of part of a lost culture on these islands of Old Providence and Saint Andrews is the funerals.

So-Called 'Modernism'

Before these islands were what they are today, when a person died, regardless of who it was, each one would be extending his/her sympathy to those who mourned their lost ones. The unity of the people was shown, and there was respect for the dead. If a party was planned to be held on the day or night a person died, then it would be suspended and, at times, postponed even until after the ninth night.

Once there was a party at the Town Hall in Town, Old Providence, and during the party about 9:00 pm, the *'circle'* was heard announcing the death of someone who had passed away on the other side of the island and, although the dance was not in the same area, it was suspended by order of the Mayor himself, Mr. Ronald Taylor Senior, who was present at the party. Nowadays, the dance would continue just the same, even if the dead person were next door. I have attended ninth nights in Old Providence where the hi-fi 50 meters away from the meeting sounded loud enough so as to interrupt the religious service that was being held.

An incident took place during the carnival week on Old Providence just a few years ago. A man died in the district of Old Town and had to be buried during the morning hours (which is not the custom), in order to avoid the disorder and excessive noise during the afternoon. However, in-spite of the precautions taken by the deceased's family, motorcycles without silencers, horns blowing full blast, were disturbing the funeral procession, weaving in front and behind the vehicle taking the casket. That's the way it happens nowadays, when respect and consideration for others have become obsolete.

Easter

The custom of celebrating Easter was something sacred. The general custom was to abstain from eating meat during the entire week, especially on Good Friday. Ninety percent of fishermen stayed at home resting from fishing activities. Lots of beans, crab, lobster and conch were consumed during that period. Going to swim at the beach on Holy Thursday and Good Friday was not done by anyone except those who were indifferent. Perhaps two families would go to Crab Cay (Old Providence) in search of birds known as *'shaywater'* that used to live on the cay. In those days when there were no tourists visiting Old Providence, Crab Cay was not much frequented by the Natives. Lots of coco-plum trees grew there and at times people would go to pick the fruit to stew during the cane-grinding season. There have always been coconut palms there, but many more than what there are today.

At twelve noon, on Good Friday some people would chop a physic-nut tree to see it bleed. Some declare to have done it and swear it is true. It was believed that bathing in the sea on Good Friday would cause the person to become a mermaid but, in fact, this has never happened. Nowadays many disregard Holy Week, and Holy Thursday and Good Friday are just ordinary days without any special meaning. Nonetheless, many churches celebrate Good Friday with services held generally in the afternoon. Those who are indifferent to this celebration or observation of the day continue with their usual activities, and some even use it as a week for vacation, traveling from one island to the next or to other places, and also for partying and drinking rum. Christians think of it as a time when Jesus began his suffering and finally died on that day to save humanity from their sins and to have access to the throne of Grace. Things change; nothing ever stays the same and everyone expects that, even when it is not always for the better.

Changes made on these islands have influenced us negatively in some way or another. For example, when Old Providence was still without electricity there was only one little canteen in the town. Today, there are two billiard places in Town and a discotheque which does not have much activity. There are billiards and discotheques in other districts of the island where many men go to squander their money. These distractions often lead them to gain money illegally so as to keep up with the *'good time'*. Old Providence is not as corrupted as Saint Andrew, but corruption is active. At present there is no brothel on Old Providence and, hopefully, there never will be. Good customs should be cherished everywhere and even though new things appear that are tempting, they should be sorted to keep the best.

The youth of today are always saying: *'that was in your day'*. The fact remains that everyone looks at things from their own point of view. The senior citizens remember the way they used to do things, and their way of life. They recall islands of quietness, peace, love, freedom, Christianity, and respect in every sense. Events in the past vibrated in their very being, and they long for all that have been lost to so-called modernization. In a changing world things refuse to stay the same, and the youth cannot compare the past of the older ones with the present, because they did not live it; the youth are living in the environment in which they were born and grew up. Therefore, Christmas, Holy Week and Good Friday are just the way they see it, with the changes these have undergone in the past few years.

Some of the few outsiders living on Old Providence, especially mainlanders, would sometimes comment on the inhabitants, and their life-style 30 or 40 years ago when they first arrived. One lady said: *'When I came here there was no electricity and at night there was only darkness; the people I met were wonderful, kind and cooperative; there were no supermarkets, but I loved it very much and I wish it had never changed.'*

What the outsiders are analyzing and comparing is precisely the loss of what they had found on their arrival and the new worthless things of today. For example, rum drinking, cursing and partying were always present, but only by very few, and it was done moderately and on special occasions. Now it's out of control and growing worse each passing day. Even though things at present are not as tense and critical as they are on the sister island of Saint Andrew, everyone is concerned and wonder *'how long is it going to be before it's the same way here?'* On Saint Andrew, mainlanders, especially those from the Andean region, and foreigners who have lived on that island for over 40 years, are saying the same thing as those in Old Providence. The radical and dreadful change is overwhelming. It's unsafe to walk some of the streets on Saint Andrew; the scandalous sounds of Hi-Fis are deafening; robbery and killing happen daily; people are not only robbed in the streets, but also their houses are burgled. Burglary occurs at times in Old Providence as well. All these despicable changes are what the older people, whether native islanders or outsiders, are worried about. Crop theft was a common thing ever since people began farming, but it has increased scandalously over the years. Undoubtedly, former customs and culture will never be what they used to be many years ago, since the new generation will continue making changes, and it may happen that, in the future, neither Sundays nor Good Fridays will represent what they used to, and what they meant to us, in olden days.

Fishing

More than a hundred years ago the islanders used to fish for a living, and farmed to maintain their families. Fishermen from both islands used to fish at the cays for fish, turtles and hawksbills. They would go to East-Southeast Cay, or South-Southwest Cay for a week or so in big catboats. Because they had no ice, they would salt the fish for preservation. They would not only catch fish but also trap turtles and hawksbills. Fishermen would build huts on the Cays where they could be comfortable during the time they intended to be there. These catboats never traveled to the other faraway Cays like Roncador, Serrana, Queena and the others.

Bigger boats were used to go to those Cays. One of them, owned by Captain Sam May, named *Sea Star* had a built-in cistern to keep the fish alive so that there was no need for salting. Years later another boat, the *Meritwell* owned by Captain Antonio Bryan (*John Bull*), used to operate the same way with a cistern. These boats were big enough to travel to all the fishing areas. Apart from these boats and catboats, there were others that used to come to fish at the Cays, competing with the natives. For that reason, in 1911, Santiago Guerrero, a commissioner sent from Bogotá to the islands, complained to the Colombian Government concerning the abnormalities and abuse of the Cays and entire fishing area, and suggested that the government take control of this situation. Guerrero's complaint was about the fishing boats from the USA, Jamaica and Grand Cayman, and he expressed that the Government should control the fishing of those cays, because the foreign boats were extracting an excessive amount of fish, turtles and hawksbills. This abuse, he said, should be stopped, since the natives were not equipped with the fishing gear possessed by the foreigners.

In 1891, Mr. Eduard B. Bailey, who lived in Washington and was chief of the Colombian Manure and Phosphate Company, went to Roncador and extracted 950 tons of guano, which he sent to the USA and earned $148,500 in gold. Mr. Guerrero suggested that the national government, via the Ministry of Foreign Affairs, pass a circular to the English and American ministers residing in the country's capital concerning the Government's rights on these Cays and, therefore, the prohibition to use them for fishing without previous permission.

Regardless of the abuses committed by those foreigners, and although

Mr. Guerrero talked about the absolute rights that the islanders had in those days regarding fishing activities and the preservation of the species, there were not that many fishing boats from the islands equipped for big catches and modern preservation. Nowadays the North Americans and Caymanians are not present as before, but neither are the natives as numerous as they used to be. The privileges the islanders should have with these Cays for fishing are now restricted by the Colombian soldiers who inhabit them, plus the fact that some of the waters have been ceded to the Hondurans.

Because of drug trafficking there is such harassment by the Colombian Coastguard that the *serious* fishermen don't feel free to carryout their activities. Fishing for a living is becoming a precarious affair. The Coastguard plagues fishing on the banks; fishing near the shores means a problem with the islands' environmental regulatory agency, Coralina. In the past 60 years, apart from the fish, turtles and hawksbills, eggs from the birds living on the Cays also played an important role. Fishermen used to collect these eggs, especially during the month of March. If the birds were sitting when the fishermen arrived at the Cays, the men would break the eggs or pile them in heaps so that the birds would lay again. Eggs were taken to the islands by the thousands. Nowadays, although the birds are still there, no one bothers about the eggs.

One of the reasons why fish is not so abundant in Old Providence is due to the role played by launches. When only canoes and catboats were used for fishing, fish were always found in shallow waters, as were the turtles. When launches began to replace canoes and catboats, the fish started to move away. This phenomenon was due to the noise of the outboard engines, which was affecting their habitat, and causing disturbance, so they traveled to a more comfortable zone. Diving and the use of fishing rods have also caused the fish to retreat from shallow waters. The Coastguard, with heavy noisy engines has also contributed to this problem. Fish pots, which have been used for many, many years, were not as harassing then as they have been in the few past years. Today, fishing in the shallow waters of either island just for a day's meal is not fruitful. As well, most of the conch has disappeared from the areas where they were once found, and young ones around Serrana and Serrania are being extracted by fishing boats from other countries. Even though the islands' environmental regulatory agency, Coralina tries to ensure the conch's growth by securing the young ones in pens in very shallow waters, they are taken out by unscrupulous people and sold to their accomplices.

Entertainment

Another custom on the islands long before the free port were the different games and activities carried out by children on moonlit evenings: hide and seek, ring play, flag, merrily, three blind mice, brown girl in the ring, moon shine dolly, and others. These were performed when there was moonlight, because in those days no one had electricity except for a very small group of people in Town, in Mountain, and in Old Town, a district close to Town. On Saint Andrew at that time there was only light in the commercial district of North End. On Old Providence the electricity was on only from 6:00 pm. to 10:00 pm, so the inhabitants would make much more use of the moonlight. There used to be entertainment 5 or 6 times a year on the island. Drama, reciting, singing, and other games were usual, and these were held in different districts.

Those well versed in these activities would prepare selected actors for certain dramas and recitations. These actors, both young and adults, would study and rehearse their parts until well memorized before the presentation. It was a way of cultivating their knowledge and culture. At the end of each school year, or during school breaks, each school would have its own presentation, which was attended by all the students and parents. Apart from this, there would always be entertaining activities during other periods of the year. There was no discrimination in these activities, regardless of religion or class. Sometimes there would be a queen contest to raise funds for a specific program, school, church, or for other purposes. When these activities were held at public schools either during the school year or during breaks, they would be performed in Spanish even though the actors didn't know or understand it. All that was done or said was memorized. The majority of the audience didn't understand much either. However, when the activities were performed on other occasions and not at the public schools, they would be in English or Creole, which was understood by everyone. There were no bars, discotheques, or movie theaters where people could go for distraction; so the youth were not led astray. There were only activities that were of cultural and folkloric interest. These entertainments were always held during the early evening after everyone had finished their day's work (farming and fishing), and when there was moonlight, since transportation around the island was either by horse or on foot. The people were very cooperative and united in all these cultural activities.

There were no motor vehicles, so horses were used for transportation.

However, many people used to walk to the different districts where these events were held. It was very pleasant to walk in the moonlight, especially for lovers. These events were not held when there was no moonlight. None of these programs were performed in Ketlena (Saint Catherine) because of the difficulty of transport from one island to the other and, besides, there was no place suitable for that purpose. There was no bridge, and so canoes and catboats were used to get from one island to the other. There was just a little track in Ketlena that was very difficult to use when it rained because of the mud. No one rode horses on the little island. Because the environment was so different from what it is today, the native islanders used to enjoy themselves in various ways, but very decently.

THE QUEEN CONTEST

The queen contest was a fund-raising program that was held at any time of the year considered appropriate. It was a one-night affair. The organizers of the event would select two or three young girls to be the candidates and then begin to work on the program. On the day of the contest there would be singing and recitation, and sometimes a drama. Because it was a fund-raising activity, the winner would not be the most beautiful, but the one who had gathered the most money. Each candidate had a group of people who worked very hard holding fairs and other activities during her campaign, and on the night when the candidates were presented, after several additional performances, each representative would go round with the offering plate. The money was counted and the amount each candidate had received was announced. Following this there would be further presentations, whether poems, songs, or drama. The offering plate, or basket, would go around for the second and last time, and whoever got the most money after the second collection was added would be the winner. She would be crowned, and would 'reign' until the next contest was held.

Nowadays, this is done in a completely different way. Because of the so-called '*carnival*' the queens are elected based on their beauty, culture and speech. Actually, it is an imitation of a real carnival, with disorder and excessive sensual indulgence as in any big city in other countries. It is not for fund-raising, but only brings disturbance and orgy. This *'carnival'* is supposed to celebrate the regretful adherence of the island to Nueva Granada (in the early nineteenth century), which is now Colombia.

STORYTELLING AND RIDDLES

Storytelling was another pastime that everyone enjoyed. These tales and riddles, in part, were brought from Jamaica and other West Indians living on the islands in the 19th century, some of whom were teachers. This and other similar customs were also practiced in Corn Island, Bluefields, Bocas Del Toro and all over the Caribbean. Storytelling and riddles were a source of amusement in the Saint Andrew, Old Providence and Ketlena archipelago. On Old Providence, entire families, neighbors and friends, would gather to tell stories about 'Brother Nancy,' 'Brother Monkey' and 'Brother Tiger.' These stories would be very creative and full of humor, but some of them were also sad, depending on the way they were presented by the storyteller. As children, we would take these stories very seriously and they would make us either happy or sad, depending on their narration. Riddles were somewhat more amusing since one had to solve or guess the answer. A person would feel very proud if he/she got the most points by guessing correctly. All entertainment or amusement was mostly carried out during the moonlight, from 7:00 p.m. to 9:00 p.m. since, in those days, 9:00 p.m. was generally bedtime, especially for minors.

Our people on both islands believed in *duppies* (ghosts) and obeah. On Old Providence the older folks would get together at night to share their experiences of *duppies* they had seen, while the young people and children listened to them. Among the most famous *duppies* were the *'long tongue dog'*, the *'cut off head man'* and the *'long teeth man'*. Apparently there were people who had the privilege to see more ghosts than others. These were the ones who were said to be born with *'call'* and they were serious enough to convince us of what they said. There were people who would swear that they were slapped or hit by evil spirits *(duppies)*. Our ancestors, who were known to be very serious people, would do everything to convince the truth of these stories, and the young people wouldn't dare to say they were telling lies. That is to say, the spirits of the buccaneers who died during the intermittent conflicts with the French, Spanish, English and Dutch pirates, were the evil spirits that still restlessly roamed the islands night after night, in the form of humans or animals, scaring whoever they could on the islands of Old Providence and Ketlena. These stories frightened the younger people as they listened to them. Some people guaranteed to have seen the spirit of the recent dead and, out of respect for the older adults, no one would attempt to refute such testimonies. It was said that because there was no electric light on the islands, the ghosts used to take advantage of the situation during the dark nights. The island of Saint Andrew was not an exception concerning the riddles, storytelling and *duppies*. In those days Saint Andrew, like Old Providence, was without electricity, and shared similar experiences with the ghosts or evil spirits. In fact, the people from both islands practiced and believed the same things.

WHAT ABOUT OBEAH?

This is known all over the world. It was said that once upon a time there were sorcerers on the islands of Old Providence and Saint Andrew. Whether this is true or false, the fact remains that the islanders do believe in obeah (West Indian denomination for witchcraft). Many years ago (maybe more than 60 or even 70), people from both islands believed that most sickness was caused by obeah. Because of such belief people would travel to Jamaica, Puerto Limón, Colón, Panama, and Bluefields, Nicaragua, in search of an obeah man whether to cure, to kill, or to harm someone in one way or another. On both islands people would say that Mr. or Mrs. So-and-So died because of obeah. Or, you know, someone would say, '*That poor lady died in childbirth because Joe Bloggs put her so.*' At other times it would be, that, '*Mr. J. B. was tricked by drowning*'. His enemy went to Nicaragua or Port Limón and that was it. Even when some people, if not all, might say, '*duppy is out of style*,' they would never say '*obeah is out of style.*'

There have been many people from both islands who actually have or had indulged in witchcraft, or what is commonly known as obeah. For example, not too many years ago at a funeral on Saint Andrew, there was a sort of rag doll found placed in a grave at a funeral, supposedly prepared to hurt or kill a certain person after the body is buried and decayed. However, it was removed by the pastor conducting the ceremony. This proves that, regardless of the many religions and churches on the islands, people nowadays are still dealing with obeah or witchcraft. Some still believe in getting a '*guard*' (protection) from the obeah-man to shield them from bullets, knives etc. They are sometimes involved in crime, and try to protect themselves from others who they fear will attempt to kill them.

WOMEN'S ROLE IN THE HOME

It was the custom for married women to look after their children and tend to their homes as proper housewives. They would wash, cook and attend to their children. Most families had more than four children, and the man of the house had to work hard on his farm to feed them. At times some of them would work on ships to better their financial situation whilst the women took care of the farm, doing the little they could. If the farms were far from their homes, they would just have a small garden in their yard. Most families had a very big yard.

Apart from growing fruits and tubers (sweet potato, cassava, yam etc.), they would also raise chickens which, as well as serving as food for the family, would be exchanged along with eggs, for sugar, flour, salt and so forth that were sold at the shops. After the 1930's a few ladies emigrated to Colón, Panama, the Colombian mainland, and the Andean region, in search of work. Those who went to Barrancabermeja, Colombia, worked for the North Americans at the petroleum company there. The company preferred islanders because they understood English. After working for a few years some returned to their homeland whilst others remained in Colombia. Many did not work long enough to qualify for a pension, but others enjoyed theirs after a long period of loyal service. Those who went to Colón lived there for the rest of their lives, marrying Panamanians, Colombians, even North Americans and others. Some, though, never married at all. However, the truth is that most married women living on the islands never left their homes to go away in search of jobs, because their husbands would never agree to it. The men preferred to leave their homes to go to the end of the world to maintain their homes and have a better standard of living, but would never allow their wives go out seeking jobs; contrary to today's *modern* system, where some women are forced to work in order to take care of their homes.

The 'Sterics'

The *'sterics'* as it is known on the islands, is a derivation of hysteria; a sort of trance in which the person would faint or pass out. This generally happened at a funeral or at a *'set up'* where the people would stay awake all night at the deceased's home singing hymns until daylight, before the burial. On the ninth night they would gather again at the same home to have a religious service, a consolation message from the Bible, and sing until daylight. The singing would arouse the emotions of some of the relatives who would get *'sterics'*. This would always occur in women, almost never in men. This custom came from our ancestors and still continues today. The behavior of some of these women was said to be fictitious. At times some of these ladies would *'faint'* conscientiously, in the hope that a man she loved would come to comfort her. At times it worked, but at others it really didn't. Occasionally, when these ladies pretended to be *'knocked out'*, some mischievous men would take the opportunity to carry them to a dark place and touch them, only to discover that the supposedly unconscious lady would react indignantly to their intentions. Apparently in these *'modern'* days things have changed a little.

Although these *'set-ups'* aren't like they used to be in the past, the mourners still sing and the women still faint, but no one stays up all night as they used to, neither on the first night of the death, nor the ninth; they still sing, but only until midnight. When a person died on the islands during the years when there were no paved streets, the news used to be carried around the land by someone riding a horse, shouting the person's name, dwelling, and the hour of the funeral. This method of spreading news was called carrying around the *'circular'*. On Saint Andrew this is not done any more, due to the fact that it is mentioned on the radio or printed by a funeral parlor and placed in public places where it can be read. Caskets are also sold at funeral parlors, which also have facilities for the vigil of the dead body. From there it is taken to a church where the funeral service is held before going to the cemetery.

Unlike Saint Andrew, Old Providence conserves almost the same customs as those from the past. The *'circular'* still exists, but nowadays the news is given by someone in a vehicle instead of on horseback. There is no funeral parlor on the island; however, there is a branch office of one from Saint Andrew, where caskets are sold for funeral services. Despite this, on some occasions when a person dies carpenters from the deceased's district or from a neighboring one make the casket with wood provided by the family, just as in days gone by, or at times by the municipality, depending on the person's financial situation. Those who make the caskets on Old Providence never charge for them.

The Seasons of the Year

There have always been two seasons - summer and winter, or the rainy season. It used to rain much more before than it does nowadays. The older folks used to say that *'April showers bring May flowers.'* This meant that April would be the month for farmers to begin planting. The rainy season never lasted long. September, October, and November were months of heavy rain. It was the custom in those days to prepare for the season when the Northwest wind blew very hard, accompanied by intense rain. People would gather wood, coconut husks and coconut shells for fuel, as very few had kerosene stoves or coal for cooking, and fish, pork, conch, etc., would be salted and stored for those days. On the island of Old Providence, whenever the Northwest wind blew, heavy waves would roll into the harbor of Town and Old Town leaving heaps of seaweed on the shore. This wind usually lasted from nine to twelve days.

No one could fish during this period, but after the wind was ceased, fish could be easily caught close to the shores. Fish was very cheap in those days, and if for one reason or another someone did not have the money to buy some, any fisherman would give that person enough for a day's meal. This kind of human charity also showed the solidarity among the people, who would willingly share whatever they had with their neighbors. The coming of the wind was usually predicted by very experienced seamen and it was the signal for storing food for the season. Most of the houses were set on posts above the ground, therefore it was easy to store the wood, husks and shells underneath to protect them from the rain. All the houses in those days were built from lumber and roofed with zinc. The kitchen was built away from the house to avoid total loss should the kitchen catch fire. As time went by lumber was becoming more and more difficult to obtain from the USA and bricks replaced the wooden ones. Today, almost all the houses are made from bricks.

Sports on the Islands

There were special activities during the celebration of the Colombian festivities; on the 20th July and 7th August, and held every year as a custom. I will mention the most popular ones that were practiced on both islands. There was horse racing, which always drew a crowd; cat boat and canoe racing was more popular on Old Providence than Saint Andrew; but of all the sports mentioned horse racing was the most popular on Saint Andrew, and more common than it was on Old Providence. Jockeys had lost their lives from horse racing on Saint Andrew. People would gamble on the horse races more than anything else and sometimes lost their very last penny. There were special trainers for the big races where a lot of money was involved. It has been said that in those days some trainers dealt with spirits and used certain drugs to control the horses to win big races.

There were times when horses would be seen in a cemetery with their trainers late at night. Naturally this was done secretly, and only by those who dealt with evil spirits or obeah (witchcraft.) Furthermore, the racetrack would also be *'rigged'* for winning or losing a race. Things were buried at a certain place on the racetrack to cause a horse to run off, take a different course, and lose the race. As I remember, it was said that on two different occasions jockeys were killed due to obeah. One was struck dead on a coconut palm, and the other was killed in a similar way. These two deaths happened on the island of Saint Andrew.

Once, in South West Bay, Old Providence, where the big races used to be held, a horse ran off the track during the race, took to the sea, and swam out with the little jockey still mounted, and had to be rescued by some men in a canoe. The Old Providence racetrack was the beach itself, so it was easy for the horse to run off into the sea. There was also another long beach in Old Town, which is not far from Town. This beach was called Old Town Bay and continued on to what is known as Black Sand Bay. This was approximately one mile long and minor races used to be held there. At present, this beach has almost completely disappeared, so it is not used anymore for such purposes. Part of what is left is occupied by the Coast Guard.

On the 20th of July the children from all the schools on Old Providence would meet in Town for gymnastics after parading down to the Catholic Church in

Free Town for Mass. Attending Mass was obligatory for all the schools. However, sometime in the early 50's, Mr. Silvanus May, known as 'Teacher May', who was the pastor of the Town Baptist Church and also director of the Baptist School, stopped the Baptist School from participating in the Catholic Mass. A religious service was then held at the Baptist Church for the Baptist school, at the same time as the Catholic Mass. Following the religious services, gymnastics would be performed in a big open space that belonged to Mr. Victor Ray Howard, in front of the Town Hall. Later this place was bought by Mr. Felix Newball, known as '*Pindanga,*' and now belongs to his children. Each school would wait their turn for gymnastics while observing the performing school. The school that performed the best would win a prize. Everyone cheered the schools and the teachers. It was a day of merrymaking and joy; there was dancing, catboat and canoe racing, skittle alley, dog racing, climbing the greased pole, and plait poles. People would shout, *'Long live Colombia.'* All this was carried out to honor the Independence of Colombia.

On the 7th August there was another festivity, but not as ostentatious as that of the 20th July. If for some reason the 20th July celebration could not be held it would be postponed until the 7th August, and if the Colombian Independence Day fell on a Sunday, the parade and gymnastics would be held, but not the other activities. Everyone respected Sundays, so dancing and other activities would mean a dishonor to the day; for this reason, after the parade and drilling, everyone would go home. Today, the 7th August is celebrated on Saint Andrew as it has been since the 20th century. Nonetheless, the celebrations may be carried out on Saturday if the 7th falls on Sunday, so as not to interrupt religious services. There are different activities performed by all the schools.

Baseball was never played during these festivities, but a very amusing activity that was practiced on those festivities was the greased pole. A pole, covered with grease, was well secured in the ground and the one who managed to climb it would win the prize that was tied to the very top. It was a very difficult task, but not impossible for those who wanted to show their skills in climbing such poles.

There were some experienced captains who took part in the canoe races, such as Mr. Cetnah Williams, Mr. Hector Hoy, Mr. Ernest Taylor, and others. The canoes were very fast and the enthusiasts would always bet on them. Catboats were not included in races until long after canoe races were considered as a sport. Nowadays the canoes are not in existence and only catboats are used for racing.

An incident that took place on one 20th July on Old Providence is worthwhile mentioning here. In 1958 that day there was a great competition with several canoes racing from Fresh Water Bay to the bridge in Town where a flag pole was placed as the finishing point. Mr. Cetnah captained one of the fastest canoes, the Sea Queen, which had everyone´s attention. Just as the race started the canoe swamped, and this setback caused the others to take advantage and race ahead. By this time the *Exita* had the lead. After baling out the *Sea Queen* the challenge was to catch up with the others that were now a good distance ahead. Upon entering the harbor in Town, the *Sea Queen* was rapidly approaching, and the *Exita*, which was supposed to be the fastest among the rest, was now being threatened by the *Sea Queen*. The situation looked bad for the *Exita's* crewmembers, and tension was mounting. At that moment Mr. Ernest Taylor, the captain of the *Exita*, after uttering some panicked words, suffered a brain hemorrhage (stroke), and was rendered speechless, his hands gripping the rudder. Pandemonium broke out; the canoe was out of control; then Mr. Testley Archbold, one of the crewmembers nearest to the captain, managed to control the situation and won the race by a canoe length. Captain Taylor never recovered from the stroke and died a few days later.

Other famous canoes were: the *Lesbia*, owned by Mr. Winston Jay and captained by Mr. Lansuel Hoy; the *Beverly*, owned by Mr. Gimston Jay and captained by Mr. Hector Hoy; the *Sea Queen*, owned by Mr. Lynzie Bush; and the *Exita*, owned by Mr. Rudolf Newball and captained by Mr. Ernest Taylor. Catboat racing was also important, but not as fascinating as the canoe races were in those days. Then, the fastest catboat was owned by Mr. Vicente Webster. These sports are not as common as they were in the past, although catboat racing is very popular on Old Providence today, but it is much less important on Saint Andrew than it used to be. How great it would be to go back to those good old days! How wonderful it would be to have the young people engaged in these pastimes instead of ruining their lives with drugs and other things that are destroying their very souls.

Even though people enjoy the parade and the other things involved in the festivities, what seems out of tune is that the islanders celebrate Colombian holidays with more pomp than the Colombians themselves!

BASEBALL

Baseball was a very popular sport that was played on both islands. Over 40 years ago it was played at the schools in different districts on Old Providence. For example, at the Junín primary school, where Maestro Rafael Archbold worked for most of his days, there would be two groups selected by the teacher that would go to Mountain Swamp (part of the National Park today) to play on weekends during school months. There were other teams that would play in other parts of the island. Women used to play in the big space in front of the Town Hall, next to Mr. Harmon's and Mr. Victor (Ray's), and ladies from Town and Old Town would meet to play softball. It was very enjoyable and pleasant. Football was not played by anyone on either island at that time. Although the games were very popular, no one played on Sundays until Mr. Ogden Pomare and Mr. Sonno Duffis started it in Old Providence sometime in the 1950's. Baseball was organized with bigger leagues on Saint Andrew and was sometimes played in Nicaragua. There was a famous baseball player in Cartagena, Colombia who was known as '*Chita Miranda,*' who could never be punched out by any pitcher. However, this invincible batter was finally punched out by Mr. Burton (also known as Mr. Sledge) in one of the professional games in Cartagena. Today baseball is still played on Saint Andrew in stadiums, but on Old Providence it has been replaced by basketball and football. All of these sports are practiced on Saint Andrew nowadays.

CHRISTMAS AND NEW YEAR

Once upon a time the Christmas and New Year season was one of the most remarkable and enjoyable affairs. During my childhood, and even as a young man, I can remember that Christmas and New Year were celebrated in a very special way. It was a season when everyone put seafood aside. These holidays were celebrated in the same way on both Saint Andrew and Old Providence. At that time of the year everyone consumed beef or pork. It was the custom for most families to raise a pig or cow for that special occasion. One family would kill a pig on the morning of 24th December, and another, on the morning of the 31st.. The latter family would borrow a quarter of the pig from the farmer who killed his on the 24th and repay him on the 31st. In the case of a cow being killed, pounds were borrowed in the same manner. There were a few families who did not raise a pig or cow for such a purpose, so they would buy a few pounds, having ordered them beforehand. Meat was roasted during the morning of the 24th so that, by the evening, it was ready. Cakes, bread, pumpkin pies, plantain tart, and such like, were baked on that same day.

During the night of the 24th a few men would go serenading, saying as they went, '*Baked meat, cake, wine or a pretty girl.*' Of course they would always get anything they requested, except for the pretty girl. They would go from house to house with a sock, singing happily, playing the mouthorgan, accordion, guitar and mandolin until daylight. Undoubtedly some of the boys would take along a bottle of booze or what was called '*cumphia*', but all this was carried out in a very enjoyable and decent manner.

No violence, no riots. On the 25th there were no activities except for Church services, as this was the day on which the birth of Jesus Christ, the Saviour of the world was celebrated. Social activities such as skittle alley, greased pole, dog racing, canoes racing, horse racing, and sometimes catboat racing, would be held on the 24th or 26th, and repeated on the 31st. Whenever the 24th or 31st fell on a Sunday, there would be no activities apart from worship service, as that day was respected as The Lord's day. In those days Sunday was highly celebrated and respected. People would go to church services in the morning and also in the evening; it was a day of worship and visiting, especially to the sick and those who weren't able to go out. Some people would even prepare their meals the evening before so as not to have to cook on Sundays before or after returning from their worship service. For Christmas and New Year a special drink was made from sorrel to accompany the cakes, pies etc. Children also had their own activities, the most important of which was writing to Santa Claus, and preparing their stockings for the Christmas and New Year eves. On those nights they would go to bed earlier than usual so as to give Santa a chance to sneak in and slip something into their stockings. However, if, in some houses the stockings were too small, he would just leave the gift on the table, or under the Christmas tree if there were one.

In the case of a family who could not afford a cake or a piece of meat, the neighbor would give them something as a present so that they wouldn't feel forgotten. On the night of the 31st there was always, and still is, a religious service held at midnight at different churches, called the Watch Night Service. In those days there were no sirens, so at midnight the church bells rang while the hymn '*What a happy New Year*' was sung. On leaving the church people hugged and greeted each other and those they met on their way home. Folk music was heard in different sections. Some people would go dancing until daylight, and everyone seemed to be happy. Watch Night Services and greetings are still the custom, although not as they used to be, but the rest of it has gone down the drain, or gone with the wind. We have lost some very good things: our customs, culture and identity. To children in those days it appeared as if the time from one Christmas to another was a whole century. Everyone enjoyed this holiday season according to their own belief or criteria, but the great majority did it the Christian way. People lived in unity, harmony and love in spite of religion or belief. In Town, in the little park right in front of the Central Baptist Church, a little band would wait for the Watch Night to finish, then sing and play their music while Mr. John Bryan Senior performed the '*juba*'. He was very good at it and it was also his favorite dance. On the 31st December there used to be *plait poles* and also *skittle alley*.

Something else that used to be practiced on the islands on different holiday seasons was the '*bull fight*' or '*crazy cow*'. This was very entertaining. It was held at night and consisted of a person carrying a bull's head and other disguise to make him/her look like a bull. Fire was attached to the horns and the '*bull*' would rush through the crowd scaring everyone.

It was said that in the 1880's ladies used to buy eight yards of cloth to make a dress that was double flared from the waist down. It would reach down to the ankles and was extremely wide. For this special occasion the ladies would start dancing from Bottom House, a district in Old Providence (inhabited mostly by the darker skinned people). These ladies used to dance around the land, and it would take them three days, because the dancers would stop in a district and stay until the following morning. On the night before leaving they would dance with the people they met from that district. Some districts were far apart and it would take about an hour to reach them. For example, Salt Creek, which is also known as Lazy Hill, was a good distance from Old Town. There has always been a road around the island although it was in a much worse condition in those days, rocky and very narrow in parts. One could set out from any part of the land and go round, returning to the place of departure.

Old Providence is approximately 5 miles long, so it would take a good while to walk around the land. The ladies began walking and dancing around the land at sunset and there was no danger or fear of thieves or evildoers. If anyone was afraid of walking at night it was because of the '*duppies*' (evil spirits.) There were about ten districts where the ladies would stop. There was no problem of having to go to work the next day, as there were no public or commercial jobs. Women were mainly dedicated to their domestic affairs, and would sometimes help their husbands on the farm. It is said that *'when the rum is in the wit is out.'* and there used to be brawling among the drunken men, and at times they would break a guitar or banjo on someone's head or other parts of the body. However, no one was ever seriously injured. After the incident everyone embraced as if nothing had happened, and then they would rest until the following day. During the 19th century, people used to dance all night on the 31st December and *'send home old Christmas'*. Afterwards, everything would return to normal.

ADDENDUM

Secret Plan for San Andres and Old Providence[19]

INTRODUCTION

This document is the Secret Plan of the Government of Colombia for San Andrés, Providence, Ketlina and the entire island territory.

Islanders have always been loyal to Colombia, trusting that for its part the Colombian Government always had their best interests at heart, even when it seemed incapable of doing anything right.

However, it turns out that this trust has been a house built upon sand. This Colombian Government document marked "Secret," a photocopy of which we were [unreadable] to obtain, is proof of the betrayal of the native people by the Colombian Government. It is a written record of Colombia's official decision to eliminate the "diversity" of the native people (page 32), root out their language, religion, and culture (pages 12 and 35) and even break up their racial unity (page 30). On page 12 it explicitly states that the Protestantism and English language of the islanders hinder "the complete integration of the Archipelago into Colombian nationality." The document also confirms that the immigration of Colombians into San Andrés is not accidental but is the result of deliberate colonialist policy (see pages 18, 21, and 33).

The document carries no date, but its content indicates it was prepared in 1977 or 1978. Of its authenticity there can be no doubt, for all major decisions regarding the islands since 1978 conform exactly to the Plan. For example, the total militarization, ordained on pages 39 and 40, is well under way. The justification given for it is that it "would not only ensure sovereignty before foreigners, but would also serve to deter any separatist movement that might be attempted." Likewise, as prescribed on page 37, steps have been taken lately to make San Andrés and Providence into "a center for spreading Colombian culture (but not for spreading native culture!).

The reader of this Plan will understand why efforts to persuade Colombian authorities —by appealing only to their good faith and

---

[19] This part is a direct transcription of the facsimile copy of a typewritten document titled "Secret Plan for San Andrés and Old Providence," kept by the author of this book. (N.E.)

sense of justice toward the native people— to take steps to stem the immigration tide and restore English to the classroom, have always been doomed to failure: they are totally contrary to the Plan and the anti-native purposes of the Colombian government.

Immigration, of course, is ruining San Andrés. An estimated 40,000 immigrants, the vast majority of them Colombians, are crowded with the natives into the island's scant ten square miles of territory. And they continue to pour in every day, lured by the Free Port and the tourist business, only to end up as they inevitably do, in the shantytowns which for this reason are spreading all over San Andrés. The only group benefiting from this situation are the so-called "investors," in other words the relatively small number of foreigners and Colombians who own the hotels and shops, [who] rake in more than 90% of the total island income, and misuse the island's resources for their own personal profit and hire no islanders in their business because in the immigrants they find an inexhaustible supply of cheap labor to exploit.

On the other hand, and as an example of the cultural ethnocide which is reducing islanders intellectually —as well as in other ways —the government has completely imposed Spanish in island schools and on television and radio.
And now we know the truth: that it all takes place according to this monstrous Plan.

The following pages in English are a translation of the photocopy we obtained of the secret Colombian government document on the Intendancy of San Andrés and Providence, consisting of a plan to dispossess the native people of their culture, identity and territory.
—The Sons of the Soil (S.O.S.) Movement
[cover page]

PRESIDENCY OF THE REPUBLIC
HIGH NATIONAL DEFENSE COUNCIL
PREMANENT EXECUTIVE SECRETARY

THE SPECIAL
INTENDANCY OF SAN ANDRÉS AND
PROVIDENCE
[page 1]

THE SPECIAL INTENDANCY OF SAN ANDRES AND PROVIDENCE

DEFINITION OF THE PROBLEM

In recent years different expressions of separatism have arisen in the Archipelago of San Andres and Providence, as well as manifestations by some Caribbean countries on the illegitimacy of the sovereignty Colombia wields in this sector.

The present study attempts to analyze the factors that bear upon the problem for the purpose of determining if a separatist movement really exists, its bases, its possibilities, what its actions and achievements have been so far, and what can be foreseen for the future.

And in the event said movement exists, what are the immediate and future measures to be adopted to counteract its effects.

CHARACTERISTICS OF THE AREA

a. Geographical aspects

　1) The existing situation

　　a) Location

　　The Special Intendancy of San Andres and Providence, formed by the Archipelago of its name, is located in the Caribbean Sea to the northeast of the continental territory of the country. The island of San Andres, which is the principal one, is located between 12°29' and 12°36' north latitude and 81°41' and 81°43' longitude west of Greenwich: and Providence is between 13°19' and 13°23' north latitude and 81°21' and 81°23' longitude west of Greenwich. The Archipelago is formed by the islands of San Andres, Providence and Catalina; the cays Blowing Rock, Crab Cay, Bottom House, Cotton Cay, South South West Cay, Roncador, East South East Cay, Bailey, Brothers Cays, Rocky Cay, Rose Cay, Hines Cay, Johnny Cay, the Alice Banks, Quitasueño, Serrana and Serranilla, and Bajo Nuevo. The intendancy has an area of about 44 square kilometers. It is 720 kilometers from Cartagena, 230 kilometers from the coasts of the republics of Nicaragua and Costa Rica.
　　　　　　　　　　[page 2]

　　b) The physiographic aspect

The two main islands are made of different rocks:

San Andres is the product of recent limestone sediments and Providence is the result of an andesite volcano, extinguished during the Miocene period. The first of them features a small mountainous system with maximum heights of 85 meters that spans the island from south to north.

Providence island has a mountainous aspect with elevations of up to 550 meters above sea level at the top of Peak, in the central part of the island. Catalina Island, separated from Providence by a 150-meter wide channel, is relatively uneven, with elevations of up to 133 meters above sea level; the cays have small coral reefs formed from sand, and some have hills of low elevation. The climate of the entire Archipelago is characterized by high temperatures and is subject to the influence of trade winds from the northeast, which determine the rainy seasons from August to December. It has an average temperature of 29°C and 1,800 mm of average yearly rainfall. The island of San Andres lacks freshwater currents, so the inhabitants store the water they catch in the rainy seasons in large cisterns. Providence has some streams, the main one is Gallinas, which satisfies the water needs of the population. The vegetation of the Archipelago is of a transitional type between a dry forest and a tropical rain forest.

c) The administrative division

See ANNEX "A" - Law 1 of 1972. The Special Statute of San Andres and Providence.

d) Means of communication

The principal means of communication between the Archipelago and the Continent is by air, made possible by good airports on the two main islands. Next in importance is sea transportation, for it has large and secure bays that allows all kinds of ships to anchor, such as San Andres Bay in the island of the same name, and Catalina Bay, formed between the islands of

[page 3]

Providence and Catalina: communications among the islands of the Archipelago is effected mainly by this means. San

Andres has a highway that goes around the island and another that starting in the North End forks at the Hill police station to go to Cove and San Luis. Providence also has a highway that goes around the territory connecting all the coastal hamlets such as Fresh Water Bay, Smooth Water Bay, Bottom House and Town.

2) Effects on the problem

The insular situation of San Andres and Providence, as wella as their relative great distance from the Colombian coast and from the capital of the Republic and their proximity to other Caribbean countries, facilitate the activity of separatist groups making it difficult to react rapidly to ward off any de facto action. The rapid transportation of control forces requires the use of air routes, so the area's airfields are important critical points.

The insular situation itself and the small size of the islands facilitate their control.

A greater danger lies in the constant influence of interested international forces on the inhabitants of the Archipelago. This influence can only be counteracted be an equally permanent action.

b. The social aspect

1) The existing situation

a) Social groups

   1) Demographic statistics

Data from the 1973 census, furnished by the National Department of Statistics (DANE) show for San Andres a population of 20,000 inhabitants and for Providence 2,615. The current population of San Andres is estimated, by projection, to be 35,500 inhabitants. There is no projected estimate for Providence available.

[page 4]

The above gives a density of 900 persons per squqre kilometer, one of the highest in Colombia with a tendency to keep rising.

(2) Ethnic groups

There is no official data on social groups in San Andres and Providence. Using data from other sources, the following is estimated to be the ethnic make-up of the Archipelago:

(a) The immigrants from the British Caribbean possessions, particularly Jamaica and the remnants of the first English colonists are called "natives." The name "native" then, is applied to the ethnic group which has been the longest in the islands, which remained uninhabited for a long time. In the absence of official figures from the DANE as to what percentage of the total resident population of the islands corresponds to the "native" group, from other sources they are estimated to be about 50%.

This group has very special characteristics since they are of the black race, speak English or "Patois" —even though almost all of them understand Spanish —and the majority are Protestant.

It is to be noted that the natives of Providence have in their background more mixture with the white race and it is not unusual to find tall blacks endowed with perfectly blue eyes.

(b) The group of recent immigrants is comprised of the national workers and the national foreign investors. This group is called "Spaniards" or commonly, "pañaman."

The workers for the booming construction industry have been brought mainly from the Atlantic coast. They arrive with high expectations and convinced that they will earn better wages, but soon realize that the high cost of living does not enable them to live with it,

[page 5]

so they ask for raises and are fired to be replaced by newcomers brought from the interior. In his way the numbers of those unemployed of having disguised jobs increase. This group is estimated currently to be 30% of the population.

The group of investors is comprised of businessmen from the interior of the country and of foreigners generally of Arab origin, commonly called "Turks." It is estimated that of the residents in the islands, 10% are foreigners and 10% are nationals from the interior of the country.

(3) Integration

The ethnic groups have not been able to integrate completely, especially in San Andrés, where the native groups have been moving to the south of the island. It is noted, for example, the non-acceptance of blacks from the Atlantic Coast because of differences in customs, language, religion, etc.

Among the native group an elite is emerging comprised of young islanders, professionals from different universities of the country and abroad, who increasingly challenge the dominant economic class which basically consists of Colombian and foreign store and hotel owners.

It is noted that Continental storeowners or investors generally bring workers from the interior while the "Turk" minds his own store himself or uses his relatives.

This has given rise to a special situation, for given the unemployment of natives and their poor training to comply with the different requirements of business and the tourist industry, the Intendential Government has tried to provide paying jobs to a good number of islanders who in fact are persons that have swelled the ranks of the bureaucracy. The hiring of islanders only by the Intendential Government almost led to a confrontation with the merchants, who threatened to fire all their islander workers. However, the threat was not carried out.

[page 6]

b) Housing

The social organization has determined the kind of housing groups. While at the North of San Andres there are modern homes where investors live and where the needs of the expanding tourism are catered to, the "native" group is scattered over the rest of the island where they have housing concentrations such as San Luis, the Hill and Cove. Around North End shanty towns such as El Cocal, Cartagena Alegre, John Well, Rock Hole, Buenos Aires and Modelo are home to the immigrant population of the north coast of Colombia.

The housing occupied by investors and important island personalities, in North End, are modern buildings with all necessary services.

"Natives" build their homes mainly of wood, with a characteristic style set on posts, and with their kitchens and latrines outside of the house. The land they build on is generally inherited from their ancestors, which is an economic advantage, since they can build in accord with their tastes and needs. The native population uses their living space adequately even if the area is small.

The Continental sector has no land, so they have to pay a monthly rent and are subject to conditions of the owners as regards the type of construction, which is usually improvised, and the materials used, which are often box boards, crates, sheets of zinc and similar things. Such living quarters lack minimal sanitation, ventilation and protection from the elements. Eighty percent of them are one room units where all family activities are concentrated, so there is a high degree of overcrowding and promiscuity.

[page 7]

As to property, it is necessary to mention the problem of some native property owners who have lots with houses on them that are generally in poor condition, in locations of high value for tourism and business. These natives refuse to sell their land but face the problem of the high valuation and the big amounts they owe the Intendancy in property taxes. It is foreseen that if they are unable to pay they will be taken to court and compelled to sell at low prices or have their property auctioned off. This could cause great social problems.

c) Cultural affairs

   (1) Education

   (a) The educational level

   Education in San Andres and Providence, from the time of English and Spanish colonization, has evolved around the churches.

   It can be said that, as regards primary and secondary

education, no problem exists, since the supply of classroom space coincides with the demand. Thus, there is practically no illiteracy in San Andres and Providence.

To get a university education, the young high school graduate must go to the interior of the country or in many cases to foreign countries.

(b) Educational institutions

On the heels of the signing of the new Concordat between the National Government and the Hoy See, the Catholic Church which, by disposition of the National Executive was charged with directing and inspecting teaching in the mission territories, transferred this responsibility to the Government. As part of the transition formula it was agreed that the Church would continue running those centers that it and the authorities agreed on.

[page 8]

For the case of San Andres, the National Government and the Apostolic Prefect signed Agreement No. 03 whereby the educational centers were placed under the following conditions of administrative dependence:

1 Secondary education

a National educational centers

- La Escuela Industrial

b Intendential Educational Centers

- Colegio Bolivariano (day, secondary sec.)

- Colegio Bolivariano (night)

- Colegio Junin (Providence)

c Catholic educational centers under contract with the National Government

- Colegio Sagrada Familia

d Non-Catholic educational centers, supported by the

Intendancy:

- Colegio Modelo Adventista (Secondary section)

- Colegio Bautista de la Loma (Secondary section)

e Private educational centers, getting aid from the Intendancy:

- Colegio de Capacitación Comercial

- Colegio de Secretariado Bilingüe

- Academia Comercial

- Escuela Comunal de la Loma

- Escuela de La Unión

- Liceo Infantil de Sarie Bay

Every year an increasing number of students graduate from high school, ranging from 17 in 1967 (the first graduating class) to 132 in 1975. As has been already stated, the high school graduate hardly has access to university studies.

(c) The Student and Teacher Population

The attached table, taken from "Diagnosis of the Socioeconomic situation of San Andrés," a document issued by the Planning Office of the Intendancy in 1976, shows the growth of the student and teacher population between 1965 and 1976.

(d) The Regional Educational Fund

The Regional Educational Fund (FER) began to operate at the beginning of 1977, with some problems during the initial months. Its directive Board is made up of the Intendant, the Secretary of Treasury, the Secretary of Education and, in representation of the National Government, Mr. Felix Palacio.

(e) Educational Problems

The main educational problem lies in the difficulty in gaining access to university education or intermediate technical careers once high school studies are completed. Some proposals for solving this problem include the possibility of creating a school of Ocean Sciences or Marine Engineering. Linkage with the interior of the country could be facilitated through military service for high school graduates, admission to the Military Schools for Officers or to the National Police Officer School.

[page 12]

It is also foreseeable, that if the Regional Educational Fund is run wholly by islanders, through it an important push might be given to the cultivation of "Patois," to the teaching of the English language in detriment of Spanish, and to the spreading of Protestantism, hindering in this way the complete integration of the Archipelago into Colombian nationality.

(2) The Cultural variable

(a) Language

The English language and Spanish are spoken in the Archipelago although currently practically all persons understand and speak Spanish.

Among natives there are three kinds of English: the first is "Patois" or broken English. It is the general means of communication and is understood and spoke by everyone. Among the low or uneducated class, in is spoken with a pronounced African accent.

The second kind is English which might be called "Spanglish," which is an English with words in Spanish, generally used among young people and children.

Finally, British English is spoken by upper class and educated natives.

In summary, the older inhabitants, even when they understand Spanish, tend to reject it and speak English correctly. Among young and middle-aged persons Spanish has gained much ground in recent years.

Teaching in Spanish is compulsory, English veing a subject which is studied in schools, especially as regards reading, writing and grammar.

Language has kept the natives and the popular immigrant class of people apart. These two sectors of the community drift farther apart every day closed in language circles; they never communicate because they do not understand each other, and they do not understand each other because they do not speak the same language.

[page 13]

(b) Religion

Because of their Puritan and African origin, the people are very religious with a tendency to superstition. Protestants as well as Catholics have built churches in all sections of the islands, in numbers given by the following information:

  6 Catholic churches in operation and under construction.

  8 Baptist churches

  2 Christian Mission

  3 Seventh Day Adventist

  1 Jehovah's Witness

It is estimated that 50% of the population profess the Catholic religion and the remaining 50% the Protestant. Among Arabs there are Christians and Moslems.

The highly religious Puritans built their churches while they organized their settlements, so for a long-time only Protestantism existed. The second religious source is the African, a magical and religious concept based on a belief in good and evil spirits, in supernatural powers, in the worship of living beings, in the forces and phenomena of nature and in superior beings personified in said phenomena.

The Protestant hegemony was maintained until the arrival of the Catholic Mission sponsored by the Government, more than 50 years ago.

At present the people profess different beliefs, mutually respecting one another and cooperating in different ways.

(c) Some customs

The concept of family is very important to the islander and occupies a preferential position in his conversation, together with subjects having to do with relationships between sex and marriage. This is observed in the long descriptions of relatives that two

[page 14]

people have in common and which is explained in detail and heartily to third parties who up to then did not know about the relationship. Islanders talk about themselves as if they were one big family, which to an extent is true given the complex network of relationships that unite them.

Immigrants of the poorer classes generally arrive alone to the island, but because of communication difficulties with the natives, they bring their relatives the first chance they get.

Native music in the islands is a variation of themes found mainly in Jamaica, Trinidad and Panama and consists of Euro-American as well as Afro-Caribbean elements, characterized by the use of American songs with Latin-American beat and accompaniment. Music from the Colombian Atlantic Coast has wide acceptance.

Amusements are mostly of European and African origin. They are practiced by religious and secular groups and consist of theatrical plays taken from literature or written for the occasion, recitals and solos or group singing. Another type of amusement are picnics or parties during the daytime, especially on holidays, organized by youth groups or churches, with dancing and food for all.

Natives cultivate friendship very much. They frequently meet to chat and play dominoes, to tell stories, riddles, jokes, proverbs and make very original toasts that reflect the religious spirit of the people. Each one has a word of counsel, a moral, a warning, almost all being of typically African origin, narrated in Patois.

A new phenomenon among young islander men has popped up due to the appearance of foreign girls, mostly American, who have a certain weakness for blacks and pass the time going with them and making love to them. Genetically predisposed to eroticism, they sit back and wait for the waves of Gringa hippies to "trap" them as if it were the most natural thing in the world.

[page 15]

(d) Occupations

As a group, natives devote themselves especially to farming, to fishing and to the bureaucracy. Because of the islander's idiosyncracy, which leads him to think only in the present since God will provide for the future, he is considered to be an undependable worker, which is why he is being displaced by Continental manpower.

The immigrant sector fills the jobs in stores, restaurants and hotels working as errand boys, writers, clerks, doormen, receptionists, bellhops, room attendants, etc., as well as in the construction area. With the latter occupation there is the problem that once a building is finished, the workers are unemployed while waiting for a new opportunity.

(e) Public Health

The San Andres Health Service, which has the job of providing sanitary aid to the native, resident and tourist population, is offering an efficient service to the community, so much so that all of its available resources are not used.

The health service in San Andres and Providence is organized as follows:

(1) Institutional services

(a) Outpatient and hospitalization

- Obstetrics
- Surgery
- Internal medicine
- Pediatrics

(b) Hospital

- Santander Hospital in San Andres, with 48 beds
- Providence Hospital, with 8 beds
- Emergency, diagnostic, general and administrative services

[page 16]

(c) Peripheral Consultation

- The Hill Health Center

- The San Luis Health Center

- Bottom House Health Center (Providence)

- Barrio Obrero Health Post

- Lazy Hill Health Center (Providence)

- Cajamal Outpatient Clinic

- Public Works Department Clinic

(d) Community Health

-Health operating licenses

-Sanitary certificates

-Home inspections

- Community education

- Control of dogs, cats and other domestic animals

- Control of public business places

- Port sanitation (animals, plants)

- Pest and rat control

(e) Epidemiology and Preventive Medicine

- Human port sanitation

- Epidemic watch

- Vaccination

- Chronic and Contagious diseases

- Research

(2) Resources

(a) Economic

For operations in 1976 23,000,000
For new projects
(building new hospital 9,500,000

It is observed that the availability of resources per inhabitant is an average of $800, constituting one of the highest in Colombia

[page 17]

(b) Human

In San Andrés

Specialists	3
Physicians	9
Sanitary engineer	1
Bacteriologists	4
Registered nurses	5
Nurses	40
Nurse aides	8
Physiotherapists	1
Odontologists	2
Nutritionists	1
Social worker	1
Auxiliary personnel	98

In Providence

Physicians	2
Bacteriologists	2
Registered nurses	1
Nurses	4
Nurse aides	3
Odontologists	1
Administrative personnel, general services, etc.	9

(3) Coverage

The Regional Health Service covers 85% of the population through the outpatient services offered at its hospitals and health centers. It is estimated that the remaining 15% are covered by private doctors and social security institutions.

The government should provide that area with the services of the Institute of Social Security.

As to hospitalization, it is offered to the entire community through the two Government hospitals in San Andres and Providence. At present a new hospital is being built in San Andres with a 150-bed capacity, so this most important service will be covered for many years.

f) Political affairs

In party politics there is an undefined number of groups and movements. Each boss or aspirant to the Intendential

[page 18]

Council or Chamber of Representatives has his own fief and the struggle, notwithstanding the narrow electoral framework in which it is waged, although not violent is at least bitter. Especially in the Liberal Party, the number of political groups are identified by the bosses heading them: Rosales Hooker, Reno Rankin, Ben Levi Pechtbal, Alvaro Archbold, Gerardo Williams and others.

Politics is carried on with a sense of agressiveness, activists confront one another in violent quarrels and the bosses do their best no to meet their opponents.

During the recent visit of Dr. Julio César Turbay A. to the islands it was observed that each boss wanted to participate without cooperating with the others, displaying disorder and lack of coordination to such an extent that it was not possible to realize the manifestation planned at the airport for his arrival.

2) Effects of the social situation and the problem

It is a fact that in San Andres and Providence social unity does not exist but three social groups which have been unable to integrate live within a small place, and this has begun to create confrontations. To this is added at vacation periods the influx of large numbers of tourists from the interior of the country and from Central America, who in the majority of cases do not go lured by the idea of resting but by the hope of earning some money taking advantage of the customs regulations existing there.

The "native" feels displaced, the Costeño feels that he is in a strange land while the investors, Colombians and foreigners, regard themselves as owners of the island. The existence of different languages, especially "Patois," facilitates the holding of meetings where these subjects can be discussed without being easily detected. However, the presence of the "Costeño" group which is beginning to settle in the island and considerably increase the "Continental" population, is a factor of much importance for the incorporation of the Archipelago into Colombian nationality. Another favorable factor for this incorporation is the pacific spirit of the "native" group. The keen interest

[page 19]

which the National Government has shown for this cornier of the fatherland, and the support which has been given in all aspects, is a positive factor towards the elimination of the problem.

c. The economic aspect

a) Background

Following the era of the cedar forests that the Dutch and Jamaicans exploited, the island of San Andres was, during English colonization, an island devoted to the cultivation of tobacco. During Spanish domination it became a cotton island. Finally, as a consequence of growing slave emancipation it became an island of coconut palms. A change which should not be attributed to the supposed indolence of the inhabitants of the tropics, but to the interests of the United States which, for a long time, monopolized the coconut commerce and industry. In 1873 coconut exportation to the United States exceeded two million nuts; ten years later this number rose to four million and the prices kept going up until Jamaica and Panama entered the competition with 33 and 19 million, respectively. Droughts, especially the 1938 one, hurricanes and the diseases that attacked the plantations reduced production and as a consequence the occupation of natives. Many were obliged to travel to Central America, especially to Panama and Nicaragua, and to the interior of the country in search of work. Others embarked on different vessels as seamen.

In 1953 the Central Government decided to create the Free Port of San Andres and Providence. The ease of importing foreign merchandise facilitated change. The immigration of nationals from the interior and foreigners to establish business and hotel activities began and, through the development of important infrastructure projects, and era of great expansion.

[page 20]

In 1964 several measures were adopted to restrict contraband, the business activity of San Andres and the introduction of merchandise to the interior of the country being regulated, and this checked the rapid development that resulted.

b) The current situation

Tourism constitutes the basic economic activity. To cater to it hotels and business have been amply developed. This is the reason why, according to statistics supplied by the Planning Office of the Intendancy, nearly 50% of the available labor force is employed in services, the tertiary sector, about 15% in industry and commerce, the secondary sector, and only 4.4% in farming and fishing, the primary sector.

Law 1 of 1972 decreed a 10% tax on goods imported to San Andres and another 15% to transport them to the interior of the country. Adding to this the high cost or fares and the illegal commerce from several frontier areas with the interior of the country, a trip for purely business purposes is not justified. The businessmen complain that they are at the brink of failure. However, business as well as the general activity of the island seems very prosperous. The 10% importation tax is being collected upon receipt of the merchandise. Collection of the 15% tax to take it to the interior of the country is done at the airport, but this is the cause of much confusion. In reality, neither the maximum amount of goods allowed, nor the payment of tax are complied with because of the outrageous under-invoicing that takes place.

Industrial activity is minimal. In the year 1954, on the initiative of the National Government, a coconut oil factory was established in San Andres with the object of promoting cooperatives among the inhabitants and at the same time of offering the natives and opportunity for economic betterment. Many islanders bought shares and began to build up the industry, but the firm's management ran into difficulties that ruined its cooperative system, leading the new factory to failure. In face of the decline in management and production, the Institute of Industrial Development took over the factory, buying 99.99% of the shares.

[page 21]

Despite this change, the factory has not increased its productive output for lack of raw materials.

Coconut production goes down every day and its local price keeps going up, while that of the Continent is dropping. At present the factory only does copra processing to extract oil.

Islanders from both San Andres and Providence have been, for the most part, dependent on a subsistence economy based on non-technical fishing and farming. Up to a short time ago Providence was an important producer of citrus fruits which were sent to San Andres and Cartagena, but disease and pests destroyed the plantations. From the farming standpoint, the alarming loss of fresh water due mainly to the stripping of the forests and vegetation must be taken into account. This endangers the little farming and cattle raising that still exists there.

2) Effects of the economic situation on the problem

Concentration of most of the economic power in the hands of national foreign business and hotel people have made the "natives" feel even more isolated, and this can constitute another source of separatist ideas. The permanent settlement of the group of investors is a factor of utmost importance for the maintenance of sovereignty particularly since Law 1 of 1972 provides for limitations on propertied owned by foreigners.

The fact that notwithstanding the limitations imposed by law, tourist activity has not declined is a sing that Colombians from the interior now travel to San Andres less for making money and more for relaxation.

At the present time there are insistent rumors on the existence of oil deposits in the general area of Providence, which in case they are true, would change the problem radically.

[page 22]

Another factor to bear in mind is that the excellent location of the Archipelago in the middle of the Caribbean Sea, with access to the Antilles, Central and North America, Colombia and Venezuela, with important infrastructure elements and having achieved a high degree of development, could attract the attention of powerful supranational interests (banks, casinos, international mafias, etc.) that might be interested in setting up a secure and well-located base of operations offering taz advantages, and encourage and support any independence movement.

[page 23]

3. THE SEPARATIST PROBLEM

a. Background

1) In the Bogota daily newspaper "El Espectador" of 26th of May 1947 there appeared an article entitled "ANOTHER 20TH OF JUYLY IN SAN ANDRES," in which the antipatriotic attitude of the Intendant was featured. The incident hat to do with a speech delivered in English on the preceding 24th of February by Intendant Carlos Federico Lever, in which he spoke of the need of leading a movement similar to the one begun in the capital city on July 20th, 1810. The article also stated that the Intendant has unleashed real persecution against Colombians from the interior residing in there.

Mr. Lever justified his attitude saying he was referring to a local affair against the growing influence of Spanish priests residing there.

The incident, though it was not serious, shows that even then there was confrontation between "natives" and people from the interior, as well as religious problems due to the spread of Catholicism and the Spanish language by the Capuchin Order.

2) An exact date for the creation of a separatist movement cannot be given really, but it is known that due to the signing of the Missions Agreement, in January of 1553, a great deal of tension developed between Catholic and Protestant groups because of the power to direct and supervise education that the Agreement granted to the Apostolic Prefecture. According to the Prefecture, it was only a matter of complying with the official program regulations and the teaching of Spanish. It is believed that the tension created could have fed separatist aspirations held by some and could have encouraged the distancing between the "native" group and the continental group.

3) In her study "The other face of the tourist paradise" the sociologist Dilia Robinson states that due to the violence

unleashed in the interior of the country in the forties, the Government kept San Andres and Providence forgotten, so much so that the San Andreans, desperate because of the difficult moment their economy and people were going through, decided to join another country.

[page 24]

Faced with this situation, the Central Government decided to occupy itself with San Andres and this is why on the 14th of November 1953, the President personally visited the island and announced the creation of the free port.

4) Towards the end of 1967 and during the year 1968 the separatist idea was secretly promoted as was the creation of a mini state. At private meetings a plebiscite was made which according to some people, got together around 10,000 members.

5) In 1969 Marcos Archbold Britton, an islander residing in New York and supported by several natives, presented to the United Nations a list of accusations against Colombia and a memorial in which he promoted the creation of a mini-state with the name "Old Providence Island" or, if this were not possible, the annexation of the Archipelago to the United States.

6) An event worthy of mention was the unofficial visit made to the Island of San Andres by the United Nations High Commissioner for Refugees in the year 1970. When his representative in Colombia was asked about this, re replied that the High Commissioner's visit was of purely personal nature and that he was on vacation. However, the fact that it took place after the documents mentioned above were received by the UN, makes it suspicious.

7) During the Conference of Foreign Ministers held in Bogota in November of 1973, Mr. Dudley Thompson, the Jamaican Foreign Minister, on the eve of his departure made to a Bogota journalist the following statements which were published in Cromos magazine on November 26th 1973:

> Yes, I think that San Andres should be independent. Colombians speak Spanish, they are white or mestizo, they are Catholic and descend from Spaniards. The Saint Andrean, on the other hand, speaks English, is black, Protestant and descends from Englishmen or Antilleans. In what way does a native of San Andres look like a Colombian continental?

In no way. The fact that San Andres belongs to Colombia means that there is an entire people, living on several islands, under the domination of another people with a different language, different customs, religion, race and origins. These are factors that make a nationality.

[page 25]

Come to think of it, is there any reason to believe that the St. Andrean is part of the Colombian nationality? Every people has the right to choose the moment it wishes to be free.

8) In January 1974 our diplomatic legation in Jamaica sent a confidential memorandum in which they made the following points:

1) The current Government of Jamaica, presided by Prime Minister Michael Manley, seeks to place Jamaica in a position of leadership of all former British possessions.

2) The shaping of a Caribbean Commonwealth Federation is foreseen, to include all islands whose people are English-speaking, Protestant and black.

3) This plan would encompass the Archipelago of San Andres and Providence, which meets the above ethnic conditions.

4) The strategy used by Jamaica to carry out this action would consist of encouraging, by all possible means, the flourishing in the Archipelago of San Andres and Providence of a movement, one of autonomous nature, based on the juridical principle of self-determination of peoples.

9) Toward the end of 1974 the Armed Forces had information that certain English-speaking individuals, apparently of Jamaican or American nationality, frequently held clandestine meetings at the Hill section with natives of the region, during which they gave lectures and speeches on separatist and independence topics. According to the same reports, each year the visitors were the same persons, carrying out their proselytizing activities three months at a time.

10) Dr. Abel Carbonell, Ambassador to the United Nations General Assembly, makes clear the following statements he made to the daily paper "El Espectador," published on January 27, 1977:

I am under the impression that in San Andres Island there are persons with special interests who have made contacts with the Government of Jamaica to get help in getting the case of San Andres and Providence Islands on the next agenda of the United Nations General Assembly, as territories supposedly colonized

[page 26]

by foreign powers. The origin of this separatist movement has as its inspirational source the proselytizing activities carried out by foreign churchmen (American Protestants), abusing the hospitality and protection granted them by Colombian laws and authorities.

11) The position of Nicaragua

Notwithstanding the clarity of Colombia's historic possession of the Archipelago, Nicaragua has repeatedly tried to disclaim Colombia's sovereignty over said area.

On March 24th, 1928 the Barcenas-Esguerra Treaty was signed, under the terms of which Colombia ceded the Corn Islands and the Mosquito coast to Nicaragua, which in turn recognized Colombian sovereignty over the Archipelago of San Andres and Providence. The treaty was approved by the Government of Nicaragua with the understanding that the Archipelago of San Andres does not extend beyond the 82° meridian west of Greenwich.

In 1969 Nicaragua granted concessions to some American oil companies to explore the undersea continental shelf located inside the area of the Archipelago, east of the 82° meridian.

In November 1976, the Nicaraguan Chamber of Deputies approved a motion to review the treaty of Colombia with respect to the cays of Roncador, Serrana and Quitasueño. "Once the treaty is challenged all conflicts will end since the cays, located on the Nicaraguan Continental shelf at considerable distance from the Colombian coast, are Nicaragua's," said Deputy Arnulfo Rivas Solórzano.

During January and February 1977, an undersea exploration team contracted by Nicaragua was operating at 14°43'51" N and 81°39'50" W, that is, east of the 82°W meridian, in other words, in Colombian waters.

Likewise, the constant presence of Nicaraguan fishing vessels around the cays in Colombian waters is a known fact.

[page 27]

b. The current situation

1) The Betty Bee sinks

a) On Sunday, December 1st, 1976, the vessel "Betty Bee," which ferried cargo and passengers between the islands, ran into mechanical problems, began to drift and later sank. There were about 62 people aboard, of which 30 were over the limit, and 42 perished, giving rise to great consternation in the islands. The disaster is still being investigated by the proper authorities.

b) Because of this regrettable occurrence, persons interested in a separatist policy carried out a propaganda campaign against the Central Government, declaring that the tragedy was due mainly to Colombian neglect and carelessness with regard to the territory. On December 23rd an "open letter" was mailed from Providence to the Colombian people, censuring the National Government and the local authorities for not giving immediate aid to the victims and, in general, for the abandonment of the region.

c) Another article appeared on the same subject entitled:

"Disheartened islanders ask President for help."

In it the "inhuman" treatment given to islanders was emphasized.

In another passage the following is stated:

> International recognition is needed for a free mini nation in the West Central Caribbean Sea, and if the United Nations has authority to grant it we shall request it.
>
> Down with the idea of being Colombians.
> People, it is the time to declare our independence, let this colony separate and be free from Colombia.

[page 28]

Why not clamor for our independence once and for all?

The people of the United Nations are our hope, let us seek their help and attain separation from Colombia.

Liberty is the theme, let us be free once and for all. Let us call on our neighbors from the north and center for help. They feel our sufferings more that our own Government.

2) Publications

On the heels of the same tragedy, the national press made a series of publications on separatist ideas that may be summarized thus:

16-Feb-77 – Cromos Magazine, Issue No. 3083

"Separatists infiltrate the Intendential Government"

This issue led to a confrontation between the Intendant and the Apostolic Prefect, for in it the above statement was attributed to Monsignor Ferraniz. The Intendant sued the Prefect in Criminal Court but the Prefect denied making the statement.

23-Feb-77 – Cromos Magazine, Issue No. 3084
"No, we are not separatists."

2-Mar-77 – Cromos Magazine, Issue No. 3085
"A blow for separatism."

23-Mar-77 – El Tiempo daily newspaper, first page
"Separatist movement surfaces in San Andres."

24-Mar-77 – Radar Magazine
"San Andres will be annexed to the United States.

3) Official visits

On behalf of the President of the Republic the minister of Labor visited the islands on February 2nd with a committee made up of Dr. Eduard Gaitan Duran, National Director of SENA, Dr. Juan

Ramírez, National Superintendent of Cooperatives, Dr. José Fernández Isaza, Director of Intendancies and Commissariats, Brigadier General Alberto Maldonado M., National Director of Civil Defense and other senior representatives of the National Government.

The Committee members had talks with the different sectors of the community on the problems of the Archipelago and already steps have been initiated to solve them.

The President of the Republic visited San Andres on April 15 of the present year and in a public speech severely attacked separatist ideas.

c. Organization of the movement

In a publication in the weekly paper "El Caracol" dated October 25, 1975, Dr. Mauricio McNish Pusey, about whom there are suspicions that he once belonged to separatist groups, after making clear that he is not a separatist and insisting that nationality is the sum of language, religion, race and territory, states:

> Although many people laugh at separatism, three of its committees got 10,000 signatures in four nights of work to send to the United Nations. Those were more that the total number of votes for us politicians in the name of the glorious national parties.

Farther along, he continues:

> The weakness (of separatist groups) may be summarized in two shortcomings. Separatists are divided into pro-English, pro-Americans, and neutrals. This plays into the hands o their opponents to weaken and divide them.

> The second one is even more serious. Neo-imperialism is no longer interested in possessing dominated territory, but in exploiting it economically. That's why the United States "returned" the cays of Quitasueño and Roncador to Colombia, but retained the right to fishing, which is what counts.

[page 30]

d. Action fronts

The various separatist manifestations revolve around the postulates of racial, linguistic and religious unity.

The "natives" have preferred to remain isolated, without mixing with other ethnic groups. This fact has been counterproductive, however, since due to so much mixing among relatives, a certain degeneration of the native race has resulted, but tends to diminish. The presence of an important black group from the interior of the country can effectuate the breaking up of the unity which they have tried to maintain. In Providence at an earlier time there was even greater mixing with whites, but their isolation makes their racial group even more closed.

In regard to language, both "Patois" and English have undergone a significant backward slide. There are reports regarding the presence and interest of the Summer Language Institute for the purpose of studying and promoting "Patois," with the indications that they want to make Providence into a Caribbean center for the spreading of "Patois." The radio and television stations in San Andres, as well as the newspapers, have had an important role in spreading Spanish, but there is a noticeable isolation in this regard in Providence where, though the local papers arrive on time, the same cannot be said of the national newspapers, signals from the San Andres stations are difficult to pick up and there is no television. While in San Andres the whole island practically understands and speaks Spanish, in Providence this is not the case.

In regard to religion, Protestantism has been kept up, despite great advances by the Catholic Church; however, at present there is no religious confrontation. Since the creation of the free port and following the convergence of "natives" with different beliefs, the numbers are growing of those who, even though they may be members of different churches, are highly indifferent to religion.

e. Possible supports

   1) It is believed that due to reasons of international politics, neither the United States nor Great Britain openly support a separatist movement.

   2) Jamaica, eager for a role among Caribbean countries, could offer veiled support through the use of secret agents in the islands, and give them political support in the United Nations.

[page 31]

3) Nicaragua has been announcing at every opportunity its sovereignty over the area despite the existence of the Barcenas-Esguerra Treaty. Its position as a country with a Pacific Ocean coastline places it in an unfavorable condition to support any action in San Andres. Nicaragua has an economic interest in the area due mainly to the fishing resources near the cays. Acts of penetration through fishing are being directed from Corn Islands. Another important factor is the possibility of oil in the area of Quitasueño. Already, there has been an incident caused by the presence of an exploration platform 35 miles northeast of Quitasueño working for the Nicaraguan Government. This platform remained active from January 15th to March 28th, when it was withdrawn.

4) Cuba could be interested in encouraging a separatist movement with the aim of setting up another base for spreading its ideas in the Caribbean region. However, the natives' way of thinking and the Latin American policy conducted by Cuba of late, make such support unlikely.

5) Another source of help for a separatist movement could be the large international interests which see in San Andres an ideal location for setting up a "tax haven."
If a mini state is created in this area which grants all manner of "laundering" facilities to international banks, tourist centers, casinos, drug traffickers, etc., these latter in turn, could support and even promote, an independence movement in exchange for such facilities.

f. Conclusions

The previous analysis leads to the conclusion that there exists a separatist movement in San Andres and Providence, which, though it may not be organized nor guided by well-funded or unanimous principles, poses a threat which must be eliminated at its root

And such a movement becomes even more dangerous when it is used to pressure the Central Government whenever a problem arises or a demand is made, without consideration of the great effort made by the country to give the Archipelago all the attention it deserves.

[page 32]

4. POSSIBLE SOLUTIONS

a. The internal front

The main function of the internal front is to seek the sociopolitical and territorial integration of the entire nation.

In the case of San Andres and Providence a certain degree of integration has been achieved from the juridical, political and even economic standpoint, but not from the ethnic, cultural nor social standpoint. Therefore, the incorporation of the Archipelago into Colombian nationality has not yet been achieved since this implies the gradual elimination of the "diversity," for the constitution of a homogeneous body.

To achieve the desired incorporation the following aspects must be taken into account:

1) Unity of governmental action

   a) Government plans and programs

   The National Government must indicate clearly the objective it seeks in San Andres in accordance with its current potential power. This objective could well be to make San Andres into a point of support for projecting Colombia into Central America and the Caribbean.

   Once the objective is precisely defined, all power fronts and their representatives in the islands must work to achieve it.

   b) Harmonious development of the power fronts

   It is a fact that in San Andres there has been a lopsided development of the economic front, which has not been in harmony with the other fronts. It is not a matter of curbing economic development, but of according aspects of internal integration of the islands, their image abroad, their technical and scientific development and their armed force.

   c) To seek the support of the whole community for the achievement of the objective sought.
   [page 33]

Three groups exist for which coordination has so far not

been possible. Generally, leadership in the Archipelago has been in the hands of those wielding economic power and lately, by "native" representatives, which have been unable to work together. The largest group, the "Costeños" is almost ignored and have no representative even though they play an important part in the total integration of the Archipelago into Colombian nationality. This group should get full Government support in order to obtain definite settlement in the island.

Of utmost importance is the role of the representatives of the Central Government in that area, who should constitute themselves as neutral arbitrators, to coordinate and integrate the three groups without creating additional tensions.

2) Training of the leaders

It seems that the current island leaders have acted only with a selfish vision, for they have only sought their own benefit, whether it be of an economic or a personal nature. So, while some only seek the tourist development of the islands to achieve greater economic advancement, others have gone so far as to encourage the confrontation of the "islanders" with other groups who only seek political power.

It seems that many of the best persons of the island live in the interior of the country or abroad, since they did not find favorable conditions for living there. It would be convenient to try to find jobs for them and link them again to the development of Government programs.

Support for the new generations graduating from secondary schools plays an important role in the future of the islands.

3) If granted, integration has been achieved from the juridical, political and even economic standpoint, it is maintained only be means of airlines which permanently tie the islands to the interior of the country. To achieve definitive territorial integration, it is necessary to increase unity by means of permanent maritime services with the Continent and by means of the development, study, and exploitation of the natural resources.

[page 34]

4) Cultural integration

The ideal would be to achieve definite incorporation, gradually eliminating the diversity of social groups. Since this is a slow process, in the short run the integration that has so far not been achieved should be sought, within the existing situation. Following are some aspects that should be taken into account:

a) Patriotism

As to educators, it is important to impress on them the need for spiritual training in a "Colombianist" sense, and make sure it is carried out, for this is born and developed essentially during childhood and youth.

The radio and television stations can cooperate effectively, as well as the Armed Forces representatives garrisoned there.

The performance of Central Government representatives is of utmost importance in developing this sentiment since they, in the final analysis, are the physical representatives of our nationality.

b) National morale

This depends essentially on the degree of patriotic fervor that can be worked up. At the present time there is no social unity and little patriotic fervor, and this is why there is so much confrontation between social groups. It is necessary that the members of each group understand that the only way they can solve problems and overcome difficulties is through unity.

c) The religious aspect

At the present time there is mutual respect and harmony among the different churches represented in the islands. But there is a lessening of pious practices, a normal consequence of tourist development. The appearance of casinos, of liberated, pleasure-seeking young women, of "hippies" of all kinds, and all manner of legal and illicit amusements have a bearing on this phenomenon.

[page 35]

Support for the spreading of Christian morality by the

Government is of utmost importance, provided it does not lead to frictions that can be a setback to the cultural integration that is sought.

Administration of the Regional Educational Fund (FER) by island Protestants could hinder this integration, so it is important that the National Government name a Catholic as its representative, preferably the Apostolic Prefect. Every support should be given to the Colombian religious orders represented in the islands, in the various schools and hospitals.

d) Work

Jobs must be developed not only to cater for the growing tourist industry but also for traditional industries such as farming and fishing. This implies providing technical training of workers to fill the need for skilled labor. The SENA has already begun such a program. And the ICA has started studies to find solutions for the agricultural problems of the region.

e) Health and social security

Services in these areas are very good and will become even better with the setting up of the local office of the ICSS and the construction of the new Santander Hospital in San Andres.

b. The external front

The function of the external front is to create and broaden an international political breathing room.

The principal threats that could rise against Colombian sovereignty in this area come from Nicaragua and Jamaica. To counteract them the following steps must be taken:

[page 36]

1) Foreign policy

a) With respect to the Nicaraguan position that the 82°W meridian is not the boundary between two countries but only implies the extension of the San Andres and Providence Archipelago, Colombia should firmly confirm that it is the boundary contained in and guaranteed by the Barcenas-Esguerra Treaty, and take steps to make Nicaragua realize its mistake in juridical judgement. Wide publication should be given to the content of the Barcenas-Esguerra Treaty in the interior of the country as well as in San Andres and Providence.

b) As to the designs of Jamaica it must be clearly pointed out that any kind of problems arising in the Archipelago are of an internal nature and the country will by no means allow them to be dealt with in international forums.

c) Actions must be carried out to get the United States Senate to ratify the Vasquez-Saccio Treaty of 28th September 1972, which has already been approved by the Colombian Congress through Law 052 of 1973.

2) Diplomatic representations

Bearing in mind the objective of projecting Colombia into Central America and the Caribbean through San Andres, and simultaneously neutralizing the possible influence of some of these countries on the internal problems that may arise there, it becomes necessary to reorganize our diplomatic and consular positions in said area so as to, on the one hand, have them placed where they can supply timely and accurate information on the evolution of the problem and on the other hand, intensify the presence and influence of Colombia in the region.

3)

A study of the creation of a free zone in San Andres, commercial interchanges with the different countries of the region and its projection more as an exporting than as an importing center will solidify Colombian presence in the Caribbean.

[page 37]

4) Cultural projection

Instead of making San Andres and Providence into a Center for Spreading "Patois" ways must be found to turn them into a Center for Spreading Colombian Culture.

a) A study must be made of the possibility of creating a school of Ocean Sciences or Marine Engineering to which not only Colombians but students from Central America and the Caribbean area may have access.

b) The development of Colombian communication media operating out of the islands is of utmost importance. It is convenient to study the technical possibilities whereby the radio stations can have sufficient power to be picked up in a large part of the Caribbean and Central America. Their transmission must be done in Spanish and under no circumstances authorized in English.

c) The transmission of some live television programs from the capital of the Republic will result in great influence, no matter the cost this means for the country. If it were technically possible, treaties might even be made with some Central American countries so they could be picked up there, and this would increase Colombian influence in that zone.

d) It is indispensable to spend whatever is needed in order that Colombian television get into Providence even if its operation is not profitable.

c. The economic front

It is evident that the economic aspect has had great advances in San Andres and Providence thanks to advantages of all kinds afforded by the Central Government. However, its growth has not accorded with growth in other areas. The following suggestions are made to better project the business aspect and through it foment the development of other fronts.

[page 38]

1) Education for development

It is important that the economic front determine the educational needs and training of skilled workers it requires for its expansion and the best ways to use them.

Technical training must be geared toward meeting the requirements of the islands' growing tourist industry, to avoid having to import skilled workers.

Likewise, for farming, livestock raising and fishing. The SENA has begun to train skilled workers to meet these needs, but efforts must be closely coordinated with the needs of the economic development of the Archipelago.

2) Rational exploitation of the resources and raw materials

The development of San Andres has been centered on the tourist industry, forgetting other fronts such as fishing and farming, which were once the base of the islands' economy especially in Providence but which at the present time are moving fast on the way down. The Administrative Department of Intendancies and Commissariats has signed important contracts with the ICA, in order to revive these programs.

3) Use of the economically active population

This depends basically on the training this population may have received. Since San Andres has special problems, different from those in other zones, the training the community needs to solve them must be special and not tied to standards for the rest of the country.

d. The technical and scientific front

The technical and scientific front is destined to become the spearhead of advancement in all areas of activity, since none of them can escape its influence.

In San Andres and Providence there is practically no problem with respect to primary and secondary education.

[page 39]

It is of utmost importance to found schools or institutions of intermediate careers as true centers for the spreading of Colombian culture, as well as covering certain scientific needs of that region such as hotel and tourist management, marine sciences, oceanography and such.

e. The military front

This is the front of national power responsible for the physical security of the territory. To better fulfill its function the following suggestions are made:

1) Internal security

The forces that are currently on the island are sufficient to maintain public order, however it is indispensable to increase their number in Providence since it only has a reduced number of policemen.

The mayor of Providence has offered to donate part of a lot to have Navy personnel quartered there. This opportunity to have a permanent small force there should not be lost.

Likewise, in Providence there should be some representations of the DAS for the purpose of controlling the foreigners who for whatever reason travel there.

While it is true that there are no major public order problems in San Andres and Providence, it is necessary to bear in mind that the services that currently exist on the islands have been unable to detect the members or instigators of the separatist movement, or whether the Summer Language Institute is present in the region, this points to the need for providing better means to the forces stationed there.

[page 40]

2) External security

The presence of the Military Forces should be increased for the purpose of guaranteeing national sovereignty. It is considered indispensable to assign airborne elements for patrolling and controlling not only the airspace but also the territorial sea, plus some kind of naval means that make reaction possible when our rights are violated, to carry out patrols in the area and to relieve the personnel assigned to the cays.

A greater number of troops, air and naval means would not only ensure sovereignty before foreigners but would also serve to deter any separatist movement that might be attempted.

3) Contribution to development and social integration

The influence of troops for fomenting patriotism and in all aspects that enhance national pride is of utmost importance, as is the admission of young islander men to the Military Schools of Officers and National Police.

The presence of planes and naval vessels is a security factor in cases of emergency.

[page 41]

5. RECOMMENDATIONS

The recommendations outlined in the foregoing to the national power fronts constitute an integrated solution to the problems which at the present time are faced by the Archipelago and which have given rise to the blossoming of separatist manifestations.

In case the recommendations are accepted, each of the Fronts must elaborate detailed studies to integrate a general action plan that will counteract any separatist movement that, with the support of foreign interests, might gather force in the future.

[page 42]

BIBLIOGRAPHY

PUBLICATIONS

1. Dilia Robinson Davis: "The other face of the tourist paradise." A graduating monograph presented, as partial requirement to obtain a college degree in sociology, to the Social Catholic University of La Salle. Bogota, 1974.

2. Planning Office of the Special Intendancy of San Andres and Providence: "Diagnosis of the Socio-economic Situation of San Andres." A study made between September 1975 and February 1976.

3. Manuel Castelar Benlloch, Capuchin: "San Andres and Providence." Bogotá, 1976.

4. General Procurator of Colombian Mission Territories: "Mission territories." Bogota, September 1973.

NEWSPAPER ARTICLES

1. El Espectador, May 26th, 1947. "Another 20th of July in San Andres?"

2. Cromos, 26th November, 1973.

3. El Caracol, issue No. 156 of October 25, 1975. "Separatism and Reality." Article written by Dr. Mauricio Mcnish Pusey.

4. La República, December 2, 1975: "The border situation with

Nicaragua. A minute of silence... what for?" Article by Rear Admiral Oscar Herrera Rebolledo.

5. Revista de Misiones, July and August, 1976. "The Capuchins in San Andres and Providence."

6. El Espectador, January 27, 1977: "Campaign in the U.S. and Jamaica to separate San Andres." Statements by Dr. Abel Francisco Carbonell.

7. Cromos, issue 3083 of February 16th, 1977: "Separatists infiltrated in the Intendential Government." Report by Fabio Roca Vidales.

[page 43]

8. Cromos, issue 3084 of February 23rd, 1977: "We are not separatists!" News report by Fabio Roca Vidales.

9. Cromos, issue 3085 of March 2, 1977: "A blow to separatism." News report by Fabio Roca Vidales.

10. El Tiempo, 23rd March 1977: "In San Andres: A separatist movement surfaces." News report by Fernando Barrero.

11. Radar, issue of March 24th, 1977: "San Andres will be annexed to the United States." News report by Wilson Rey.

12. El Tiempo, April 18, 1977: "San Andres and Providence: A complete Archipelago..." Article by Darío Restrepo V.

DOCUMENTS

Documents from the archives of Department 2 of the General Headquarters of the Military Forces.

[END OF SECRET DOCUMENT]

SELECTED BIBLIOGRAPHY

Canales, Cristóbal (1976). *50 años de misión cumplida*. No additional data.

Collette, C.F. (1837). *The Literary Gazette and Journal of Belles Lettres, Arts, &c.* London: W.A. Scripps.

Díez Bermúdez, Lina María (2014). *La Vieja Providencia y Santa Catalina: visiones de unas islas en el Caribe / Old Providence and Saint Catlina: Visions of some Islands in the Caribbean*. Medellín, Colombia: Lina Díez Editora.

Dittmann, Marcia (2013). "English in the Colombian Archipelago of San Andrés," in Tometro Hopkins and John McKenny, eds. *World Englishes* (Vol. II). London: Bloomsbury Academic Publisher.

Duarte French, Jaime (1988). *Los tres luises del Caribe ¿Corsarios o libertadores?* Bogotá: El Áncora Editores.

Exquemelin, Alexandre Olivier (1967). *The Buccaneers of America*. New York: Dover.

López Michelsen, Alfonso (1999). "S.O.S. por San Andrés y Providencia", El Heraldo. Barranquilla.

Mitchel, Dulph W. (1973). "Why We the Raizal (Earliest Surviving Inhabitants) of The Archipelago of Saint Andrew, Old Providence and Saint Catherine Are Not Colombians! (And need to struggle for our independence)", *Cromos*. Bogotá.

Newton, Arthur Percival (1985). *Providencia: las actividades colonizadoras de los puritanos ingleses*. Bogotá: Banco de la República.

Parsons, James J. (1964). *San Andrés y Providencia. Una historia geográfica de las islas colombianas del mar Caribe occidental*. Bogotá: Banco de la República.

Petersen, Walwin G. (2002). *The Province of Providence*. San Andrés: Christian University of San Andrés, Colombia.

Robinson, Dilia (1974). "The other face of the tourist paradise." Unpublished. Text presented as partial requirement for the degree in sociology. Bogotá: Universidad La Salle.

Robinson, J.C. (1996). *The Genealogical History of Providencia Island*. San Bernardino, California: Borgo Press.

Sons of the Soil (S.O.S.) Movement, *Secret Plan for San Andres and Old Providence*. Typewritten manuscript. San Andrés, Colombia.

Turnage, Loren (1977). *Island Heritage. A Baptist View of the History of San Andrés and Providencia.* Cali: The Historical Commission of the Colombia Baptist Mission.

Wilson, Peter J. (1973). *Crab Antics. A Caribbean Case Study of the Conflict Between Reputation and Respectability.* Prospect Heights, Illinois: Waveland Press.

www.ingramcontent.com/pod-product-compliance
Lightning Source LLC
Chambersburg PA
CBHW071404300426
44114CB00016B/2174